The Fictional World of BHARATI MUKHERJEE

The Fictional World of BHARATI MUKHERJEE

Vandana Singh

Prestige

an international publishing house

Published by
Prestige Books
New Delhi 110 008
email: prestigebooks@gmail.com
website: asiabookclub.com

Associate Office
60/29-45 Parramatta Road,
Concord, NSW 2137
Australia

ISBN: 81-7851-055-3

Printed at Chaman Offset Press, New Delhi 110 002

Contents

Abbreviations

Darkness	*D*
Days and Nights in Calcutta	*DNC*
Desirable Daughters	*DD*
Holder of the World, The	*HW*
Jasmine	*J*
Leave It to Me	*LM*
Middleman	*M*
Tiger's Daughter, The	*TD*
Tree Bride, The	*TB*
Wife	*W*

Preface

The journey, which began as a research scholar, slowly transformed into a journey of self-realization. Though tedious and slow, the progress took me unawares and the novels, which at first glance looked obscure, slowly unfolded themselves. Reading through the novels was my own evolution as a reader. As I went through each and every novel, every time it offered a different perception from the previous one. Evolving along with characters proved to be a journey unto my own realms of mind as a reader.

The paucity of material caused initial slackening in my research, but as I went through the novels again and began my work, slowly everything changed. The first work, which I read was *Jasmine* and then *The Middleman and Other Stories*. Understanding the narrative, language and style was difficult. Browsing through material on computer about the life of people in America and perceptions of the New World helped me comprehend the novels. With each novel, characters unfolded and once I could interpret my own views of life, I could see their point of view, and it was an easy venture.

The chapters of this book deal mainly with the novels of Bharati Mukherjee, the short stories, and the journal written in collaboration with her husband. The collection of short stories has been succinctly amalgated into the book, keeping in proximity with the novels.

The first chapter deals with the psyche of Bharati Mukherjee, which is the basis of each of her novels. The second chapter deals with a myriad of characters in the novels of Bharati Mukherjee who pursue their journey of discovering their inner being and carve a future in the New World. The third chapter deals with the experience of exiles, expatriates and immigrants, who are still caught up in the midst of two cultures. The fourth chapter reflects on the dilemma as well as the fluidity of characters, which brings about an apocalypse, changing their life forever. The fifth chapter focuses on the ingenious style of Bharati Mukherjee, her perceptions of life which mould her characters, yet seem to exist in their individuality. The sixth chapter deals with cultural difference of the First World and the Third World countries, the mutual transformation of the merging culture of the 'colonizer' and the 'colonized.

I cannot close my prefatory remarks without expressing gratitude to all those who helped me in the preparation of the present volume. I express my gratitude to late Professor S.D. Singh who offered his valuable support, encouragement and supervision in the preparation of the present project. I am thankful to all the members of my family who have been patiently bearing with me, guiding me morally and intellectually. I am especially thankful to my second sister and brother-in-law who mailed me latest critical material on Bharati Mukherjee and my eldest sister and her daughter for helping with primary material for the book. I will also like to put on record the invaluable help extended by my cousin who read the chapters of this book. I am thankful to my parents, especially my mother, who kept coaxing me to finish my work. I am grateful to my youngest niece who helped with the typing of the initial chapters. I also extend my thanks to staff of Sahitya Akademi and American Library in Delhi who helped me to procure my material initially. I am grateful to Prestige Books for the exacting and quality editorial work and for bringing out the book so elegantly, conforming to international standards of production. Finally, with the blessings of the Almighty, I feel content that I am able to complete my journey.

VANDANA SINGH

Chapter 1

Introduction: The Psyche behind the Novels

Bharati Mukherjee was born on 27 July 1940 in Calcutta to Bengali Brahmins—members of the highest caste among Bengali Hindus—Sudhir Mukherjee and Bina Mukherjee. Her father, Sudhir Lal Mukherjee, was a chemist who had studied and done advance research in Germany and the United Kingdom. Her mother, though not very educated, ensured that all their three daughters received the best of education. As a consequence, Bharati Mukherjee and her two sisters attained postgraduate degrees.

In Calcutta, Bharati Mukherjee grew up in a middle-class joint family at Rash Behari Avenue. The dominant influence on Mukherjee's early years was her father, which becomes evident in her first novel, *The Tiger's Daughter*. As Bharati Mukherjee remembers him in an interview given to *Canadian Fiction Magazine*, he was "an extraordinary man . . . very much the benevolent patriarch" who "wanted the best for his daughters. And to him the best meant intellectually fulfilling lives."[1]

In 1947, after being duped by his Jewish partner, Sudhir Lal Mukherjee left for London to do his research, taking along his family—wife and daughters—with him. Bharati Mukherjee therefore spent a part of her childhood in London and in Basel, Switzerland, where her father did some scientific research.

In 1951, Sudhir Mukherjee returned to Calcutta to take up an active role in business. On return, instead of returning back to his joint family house, Sudhir Mukherjee settled his family in a mansion in the factory compound, complete with swimming pool, a lake, armed guards, and an entourage of servants. For Bharati Mukherjee this move on her father's part was like a release from a "terrifying communal bonding."[2]

These were the golden years of Bharati Mukherjee's childhood, made possible by her father's success as a businessman as well as a scientist. The family lived within the walled compound which meant that the daughters were becoming "increasingly alienated from the middle-class Calcutta of their early childhood."[3]

Sudhir Lal Mukherjee moved to Baroda to start afresh after the quarrel with his partner and then again to Chembur, Bombay, in 1967. By this time his daughters were married; they all had love marriages. Sudhir Mukherjee seemed to have shaped Bharati Mukherjee's decision to be a writer, not only by imbuing her with his belief 'in the power of the word' (1987 interview 39) but also by taking the initiative in sending her off to the Writers' Workshop at the University of Iowa."[4]

Bharati Mukherjee reveals the very essence of the Indian Hindu culture when she says:

> In traditional Hindu families like ours, men provided and women were provided for, my father was a patriarch and I a pliant daughter, the neighborhood I'd grown up in was homogeneously Hindu Bengali-speaking, and middle class, I didn't expect myself to ever disobey or disappoint my father by setting my own goals and taking charge of my future.
>
> Until the age of 8, I lived in a house crowded with 40-50 relatives. My identity was viscerally connected with ancestral soil and genealogy. I was, who I was, because I was Dr. Sudhir Lal Mukherjee's daughter because I was a Hindu Brahmin, because I was Bengali-speaking and because my *desh*—the Bengali word for homeland—was an East village called Faridpur.[5]

A rebellious tone is evident when she points out that she has no recognition by herself but because she is her father's daughter. To realize this at the age of 8, signifies a girl of grit, which later on made her what she is today.

It seems that Bharati Mukherjee developed a sense of isolation within herself at this early juncture of life. It is not very easy to assert one's independence at an early age of 8. So she found an alternative by drawing herself within to discover her own identity. Says she,

> There was absolutely no sense of privacy, every room felt crowded. In fact in the traditional Bengali Hindu family of my kind to want privacy was to be selfish. That was why I was so entranced by the idea of Iceland having little population and lots of space. . . . So in a sense what I did was in order to make privacy for myself make a little emotional

> physical space for myself, I had to read. I had to drop inside books as a way of escaping crowds. As a result I became a very bookish child, I read and read and read all day. And I learnt to read and write and go into first grade school, in fact, when I was three years old. So that it's a very accelerated "education literacy."[6]

An era when education of women was not given so much of importance, Bharati Mukherjee managed to give herself a very early start. She went for serious reading. She read writers like Tolstoy and Dostoyevsky at an early age. The little girl with an incisive focussed mind could comprehend her future career as a writer at the age of 10: "I know from when I was very young long before I was ten, that I was going to be a writer."[7]

A recluse at the age of 3, decisive about career at the age of 10, predicts her rebellious nature, which later on goads her to marry Clark Blaise even though she knows that her father would oppose the alliance. Though "rebellious" would be a very strong term but she has a mind of her own. She is astute, an open-minded person who can transform herself to suit her needs.

Bharati Mukherjee discovered her identity rather very early in life. She carefully found a pastime for herself, which not only gave respite from the chaos around her, but a future which held lots of openings for her. Her parents encouraged her, her mother especially seems to be a stimuli to an early start in life: "Bina Mukherjee played a major role in her daughters' upbringing. On many occasions for instance, it was her determination to see her daughters independent and safe from the humiliation often suffered by middle class women in traditional Hindu marriages that led her to "make sure they're well educated so no one can make them suffer."[8]

Bharati Mukherjee at an early stage of life came to encounter the various facets of life of Indian culture where a bride commits suicide due to dowry demands (an aunt of Bharati Mukherjee committed suicide). Atrocities inflicted on women moulded her bent of mind: "To be a woman, I had learned early enough, was to be powerless victim whose only escape was through self-inflicted wounds." (*DNC* 229)

Besides joint family system of living with 30-40 odd relatives did not make life easy:

> I was not happy in that joint family; perhaps some of my mother's frustration seeped down to me. People say that I look very much like her, a collector of resentments and insults, and I am stubbornly unforgiving. I suspect that in those early years, it was more important to me to retain my position as my father's favourite daughter (he has written a poem about me titled "Treasure of the Hearts") than it was to imitate, in proper fashion, the personality of my mother. But I am sure that from her I learned to feel relief when we could close the door of our bedroom and shut off the forty odd relatives. (*DNC* 180)

The family squabbles made her turn inwards into herself, making her a loner.

> Sometimes there were invasions by cousins or younger uncles. Once my mother, sisters and I returned from our customary afternoon visit to Southern Avenue to find that my eldest sister's British-made painting book and paint box, which she had won as a school prize, had been vandalized. Another time, the lock of the wooden cabinet in which my mother kept her jewellery and small cash savings had been forced open, and some money was missing. I was taught to think of these episodes as an assault on our desire to maintain slight separateness within the context of the joint family, rather than expressions of mischief by relatives. (*DNC* 180-81)

Further she says, "within the small perimeters of that room, it became clear to me that if I wished to remain sane I should not permit myself to squander my affections on too many people or possessions. With overpopulation of that sort, possessions and relationships could at best be fragile." (*DNC* 181)

The sabbatical year in India with her husband in 1973 made her realize the after-effects of such holding back of emotion, the intense repercussion resulting in her becoming a neurotic child. "But when I entered those flats, took my Italian platform sandals off near the entrance, answered ritual wisecracks about my skinniness, my adult composure was bruised by the memory of myself as a neurasthenic child given to reading in dark corners and to nursing sick headaches." (*DNC* 221)

In Indian culture and Hindu family, and especially in a joint family, everyone is concerned about the other person. Everyone tends to butt-in, in the affairs of others and the name given to it is 'concern' and 'love':

> So when Clark and I, at my uncle's request, visited the room where I had spent the first eight years of my life, I saw superimposed on that uncluttered and recently painted bedroom wall the image of a wavy-haired, narrow-shouldered child crouching under the barred window, her skin powdery with green paint. But even as a child in that sun-striped room I had moved from the Central to the metaphoric in my pursuit of privacy. Survival from too much love. That was what privacy meant to me. But in the middle-class India, to escape love is practically impossible; however disastrous, however murderous, it is still love. (*DNC* 222)

While going through the novel *Wife*, a question always recurs: if some personal experience was involved while narrating the character of Dimple Dasgupta, a girl from middle class, Bengali Brahmin family whose idea of marriage is of 'freedom. It always occurred, why a middle-class girl? A girl from any class faces the same situation with little variation in some cases in the Indian orthodox society. A society where girl foetus is killed, Dimple skips her way to freedom by aborting her child. Bharati Mukherjee has chosen a protagonist from middle class who is ambitious but is also neurotic. The aim in her life is to get married to a man who will give her freedom. But still her ideals are "Sita" and "Savitri." To an extent, the neurotic part reflects Bharati Mukherjee's own childhood, when she tried to exclude herself from hordes of relatives:

> I even as a small child in a large joint family had learned that frugality of feeling was my best defence against assault. I loved my headaches, later, with a Bengali's typical love of adumbration, I added to that a love of vomiting, of slipping long delicate finger over the rough grained tongue and down the silky, fleshy walls of throat and gullet until I was rewarded by an arc of fluid which I watched splatter against the rusty grid of the old-fashioned bathroom drain. Headaches meant that I would be made to lie down with a cold rag over my forehead and eyes, while my mother would try to snatch as many minutes as she would from her cooking for the enormous family tribe and knead the pain out my forehead. (*DNC* 222-23)

Reference to relatives as an "enormous family tribe" reveals the resentment she felt at being neglected, because her mother was generally busy with performing the household chores. Her father's decision to leave Calcutta and settle down in London relieved her from her agony. Bharati Mukherjee felt happier because now they had the happiest time of their life. After three years, they were back in Calcutta but this time they decided to stay away from Ballygunge and the joint family. During this period, Bharati Mukherjee became bilingual and bi-cultural: "It was a time of forgetting Bengali and acquiring English until I reached an absolute equilibrium." (*DNC* 102)

Back in Calcutta, insistence on the part of Bina Mukherjee got them admitted into a Convent school instead of traditional Bengali school. "Like the feminists that my mother was, who didn't know the word feminist but who managed to give me, at great physical expense, she really had to put her body on the line in order to get me into English medium schools, guarantee me the best education so that I would not end up, she said as chattel, to a traditional Bengali husband."[9]

But as English became her medium, she was totally cut off from her mother-tongue, though she never felt guilty about it. The mental block, which was manifested during her early stay in big family, was released through contact with outer world. English language and life-style proved cathartic and gave the balance in life. This catharsis is denied to her character, Dimple Dasgupta, and results in death and murder. She observes that when a language is sacrificed, the person is uprooted: "That gradual erosion of the vernacular also contained an erosion of ideas I had taken for granted. The sense that I had had of myself in Ballygunge, of being somehow superior to my cousins, was less destructive than this new sense of being a minority on account of my colour. I felt I was a shadow person because I was not white." (*DNC* 182)

This same feeling is recurrent while she is in Canada. Racialism in London made her more passive than she was in Ballygunge: "I began to regard facility in English as my chief weapon for bending my own personality and for making friends among the British." (*DNC* 182)

Adaptation and transformation became her two weapons very early in life. Passivity in outside world makes her more rebellious, when after marriage she has to settle in Canada and face the problems of racialism and multiculturalism. Her attitude to adaptation helps her to make the decision to reside in U.S.A. as an immigrant than to struggle to be accepted as an expatriate writer in Canada.

Life in Calcutta in the middle of 1959, living in the compound of the pharmaceutical factory (set up by her father and his Jewish partner), was a phase in their family which her parents referred to as 'the good days.' Bharati Mukherjee considered the compound walls to be the boundaries of her own kingdom, and two sisters and herself as the princesses, who were escorted back and forth from school to home, attending the celebrations at factories, distributing sweets to the factory workers. The grounds of the Victorian house were metamorphosed into a beautiful garden, complete with pool and imported rarities: "I saw the conversion as a triumph of the new order over the old, and felt no remorse. Nothing would return me to the drabness and tedium of Ballygunge." (*DNC* 183)

The sabbatical year in Calcutta makes her realize that she is more of a misfit in the old world and though she is unable to reconcile with her new world, still it is the world which she prefers. "There was surely nothing ignoble in our desire to better our condition. In a city that threatens to overwhelm the individual who is passive, there was nothing immoral in self-protection. But we had refused to merge with the city." (*DNC* 185)

The city was infested with Naxalite agitation, workers beaten up, and hell raising riots, recurrent on a permanent basis. The Victorian mansion inside the factory compound with sprawling garden and field cut her off from the world, which was dark and frightening. So was the mansion in which her friends stayed, cut off from the world of hunger and filth. A feeling of colonialism prevailed even after the British left, because the bungalow and mansions were the heritage of the British who had built them in order to alienate the outside world: "Out there beyond our walled vision is reality that disgusts and confounds the intellect, and a populace that is too illiterate, too hungry, too brutish, to be gently manipulated." (*DNC* 187)

Her published work consists of seven novels, *The Tiger's Daughter*, *Wife*, *Jasmine*, *The Holder of the World*, *Leave it to Me*, *Desirable Daughters* and *The Tree Bride* and two works of nonfiction, *Days and Nights in Calcutta* and *The Sorrow and the Terror* and two collections of short stories *Darkness* and *The Middleman and the Other Stories*, the latter winning her the 1988 National Book Critics Circle Award.

In her works, Bharati Mukherjee creates a vivid, complex world about the disruption and transformation, that arises in the face of an intermingling of cultures: the terrain which she has so brilliantly made her own in her acclaimed novels and culture, the trials and tribulations and traumas afflict immigrants trying to establish their identities in the new world and adverse conditions, have been deftly handled in her writings.

The Times Literary Supplement critics held that Bharati Mukherjee's elegant first novel, *The Tiger's Daughter* is skilfully wrought with lively dialogues and full, descriptive passages. Bharati Mukherjee's writing largely reflects her personal experiences.

In *The Tiger's Daughter*, the author creates a heroine who, like herself, returns to India after several years in the West to discover a country quite unlike the one she remembered. Memories of a genteel Brahmin lifestyle are usurped by impressions of poverty, hungry children and political unrest. In other words, "Tara's westernization has opened her eyes to the gulf between two worlds that still makes India the despair of those who govern it."[10]

The second novel, *Wife*, is the story of a young Indian woman Dimple Dasgupta, who attempts to reconcile the Bengali ideal of the perfect passive wife, with the demands of real life. Dimple is married off to Amit Basu, an ambitious engineer, about to immigrate to the United States. Dimple finds the adjustments to marriage more difficult than she had expected. The move to New York leaves her in a state of shock and despair. There, she "watches television, sleeps, studies *Better Homes and Gardens*, and timorously meets people."[11] She keeps contemplating ways to commit suicide. In fact this alien environment and Dimple's inherent instability are two combined forces which prompt her to contemplate suicide or murder. She develops insomnia and eventually stabs her husband to death: "Underneath the passivity lives rage which the heroine is hardly conscious of until it fully extends itself from fantasy to reality."[12]

Consequently, the existent deteriorating pathetic conditions of Calcutta were totally excluded from their lives, which was limited to the Company's walled compound, and the walled compounds of Loreto Convent School run by Irish nuns who regarded the "walled-off school compound in Calcutta as a corner (forever green and tropical) of England."[13]

Bharati Mukherjee was not only far removed from the Calcutta life but was also being cut off from the Bengali culture. The nuns were stimuli in devaluation of the belief in her own culture and Hinduism: "But I realize now that what the school in India, the very English postcolonial school in India forced me to devalue my own Indian or Bengali literature, language, ways of thinking."[14]

In the English convent, Bharati Mukherjee and other students were taught to look down upon their own culture and rever English literature miming British tradition of logic, satire, irony and realism. In India, educating their daughters in Convent, with girls from elite class, was an ambitious move on the part of Bharati Mukherjee's parents (generally it was a status symbol to have children study in English schools). In spite of her English education, Bharati Mukherjee had to face racialism which made her realize the damages of colonialism: "It was only when I came to Iowa, to the writers' workshop, that I realized the damage of colonialism. I wasn't aware of it growing up in independent India where I was part of the mainstream—but coming here and being part of a minority, and then realizing what I had been robbed of in a way."[15]

The seeds of uprooting were sown early in her high school, later on she leaves for America for further studies. She decides to marry during a lunch break and decides to settle as an immigrant in United States. After graduating from Loreto Convent School, she completed her graduation (with honours) in English from University of Calcutta in 1959. She did her postgraduation in English and Ancient Indian Culture from the University of Baroda. The education in Baroda which involved study of ancient culture and the rich heritage of Hindu origin, reinstated her beliefs in Hinduism, and the values inculcated into her by her traditional devout Hindu parents. The interbalancing of traditional and modern ideas inculcated in her by her parents gave birth to a person who became independent and self-confident to seek a career as a writer and an academic in a far-off land.

Even before she was in her teens, Mukherjee wrote a novel of 60-80 pages about English children when she was in England. She wrote short stories for the magazine *Palm Leaves* in Loreto Convent School, which contained fictionalized episodes from European history.

By the end of the college, she had made the decision to be a writer which was endorsed by her father. Fate played a major role when a UCLA drama professor was invited to their house for dinner. He was in India with few students on a "project India" and suggested that Bharati Mukherjee be sent to Professor Paul Engel in Iowa, and later on, the wife of a visiting Fulbright Professor gave her a recommendation letter. This lady helped Bharati Mukherjee to bag a scholarship with PEO Group, eventually landing her in Iowa's Writers' Workshop in September 1961. In 1963, she earned her MFA from the University of Iowa. She was admitted to doctoral programme in English and Comparative literature which she completed in 1969.

Her father expected Bharati Mukherjee to return back home after two years of her stay abroad, but in the meantime, Bharati Mukherjee met Clark Blaise, who was a Canadian North-American citizen, fell in love, and after a short courtship married him. She informed her parents about the marriage, and Sudhir Mukherjee easily adapted to the idea of his daughter marrying a complete stranger, and that also, a foreigner. Clark Blaise considered himself a Canadian writer and both of them started living in Canada in 1966. Though her husband was accepted and received accolades as a writer, Bharati Mukherjee had to face the problem of racialism: "And then when we went to live in Canada in1966, as soon as was legally possible we took out Canadian Citizenship. And then after fourteen years, in 1980, because I found that as a dark-skinned Canadian, as a non-European immigrant to Canada, life was really impossible."

Earlier, a problem faced in a school of England had led to her decision to go to United States of America. The feeling of colonialism was there in both England and Canada. In England, she realized the negative attitude generated towards an individual, who was not fair enough to mingle into the English crowd.

Marriage to Clark Blaise had an impact on her life and career as an academic and as an author. As she herself says, her marriage is "an intensely literary marriage."[17] Mutual adjustments and compatibility helped both of them to have a healthy married life, with two sons. When Clark Blaise needed to find his roots in Canada, Bharati Mukherjee moved to Canada in 1966 to teach at McGill at his insistence though reluctantly. Later on, Clark Blaise agreed to leave Montreal in 1980 because Bharati Mukherjee could not reconcile with the racial attitude of Canada, and they both settled as immigrants in America. The traumatic upheavals drove Bharati Mukherjee to revolt against the system initially but, later on, she decided to live in a congenial environment as an immigrant in U.S.A. Her brief sabbatical journey to India further proved a step towards being an immigrant in U.S.A. Her visit to India proved, that the notions, which everyone—expatriates and immigrants—has about one's motherland prove to be wrong. It is a fact that everything changes with time. But the people, who leave behind their motherland, try to maintain the same attitude towards the old world.

The visit to Calcutta made Bharati Mukherjee realize that India had changed a lot. The colonial attitude still existed among the upper class people but now, the exploited and downtrodden had reached their tether's end, and started revolutions, which had changed the whole scenario. Staying with relatives and attending marriages was nostalgic, but the changed situation forced Bharati Mukherjee to realize the nuances of the two cultures. The freedom of West did not exist in Indian metropolis. The behaviour of aristocratic parents (who like Indian parents loved her to the extent of smothering her) was enough reason for her to decide her future as an immigrant. The aristocratic behaviour, which charmed little Bharati Mukherjee early in life, did not hold the same attraction: "Of course I had other reasons for going to India. I was going because I had discovered that while changing citizenship is easy, swapping cultures is not." (*DNC*, 169)

> On the other hand, Clark Blaise is more inclined and impressed in fact, charmed by the exotic Indian culture and people. Commerce, community, marriage, family; on the nights when I was feeling not Marxist but somehow Hegelian, I would have dropped five rupees—a good week's wages—into those hands, or others. And I would think they were the same thing, somehow—commerce, community, marriage, family—all part of the Indian's identity, part of the world image that antedated my own. (*DNC*, 156)

Clark Blaise's ideas have been of great inspiration for Bharati Mukherjee, as she has pointed out in her interviews. He has been a great support, a willing audience and critic of her works. At times his advice has been crucial for her work. For example, when writing her first novel she could not make up her mind about inserting an episode where her heroine is seduced by a less-than-agreeable character because of her fears that people would conclude that "something similar happened to her."[18]

Together the couple has created two full-length works entitled *Days and Nights in Calcutta* and *The Sorrow and the Terror*. The first part of *Days and Nights in Calcutta* is by Clark Blaise and the second part is by Bharati Mukherjee. When introduced, India seemed a poor country to Blaise, but slowly, reconciliation brought about a change in attitude, and Clark Blaise is more sympathetic to Indians than Bharati Mukherjee herself. Bharati Mukherjee's self-imposed exile created havoc with her life in Canada and a feeling of uprootedness seeped in, after the realization that India of yesteryears had changed beyond recognition. She felt more comfortable in America where life was easy:

> It is, of course America that I love where history occurs with the dramatic swiftness and interest of half-hour television shows. America is a sheer luxury, being touched more by the presentation of tragedy than by tragedy itself. History can be dealt with in thirty second episodes; I need to suffer its drabness and continuum. (*DNC*, 168)

Coming to India was her husband's idea, because Bharati Mukherjee joked that going to India would be a death wish for him. So it was just the children who visited India in summers. Her belief that she knew the rules in India proved wrong because her notions were presumptuous. Not only India but her autocratic father who was idol of little Bharati seemed to be overbearing and their attitude of protection more of a "crushing parental love." (*DNC*, 283)

The nostalgic trip to India made her realize that she was more of an immigrant, than an exile, because she was more comfortable abroad than India. The constant hunger-strikes, violent labour disputes made life pathetic. The helplessness led to irascibility, which she encountered all around her. The low-class, middle class and high class faced the same anger towards the situation in the country:

> Do ghosts exist, or don't they? That debate is dull and meaningless; the interesting point is that in India different perceptions of reality converse without embarrassing anyone. My year in India had showed me that I did not need to discard Western education in order to retrieve the dim shape of my Indian one. It might have been less painful if I could have exchanged one locked trunk of ethics for another, but I had to admit

> that by the end of the year in India I no longer liked India in the unreal and exaggerated ways I had in Montreal. (*DNC*, 284)

The mirage tended to disappear on the hard rocky earth of reality. The childhood memories were crushed and an irritable, mature Bharati Mukherjee refused to become a split personality. The decision to stay abroad bore no guilt on her conscience. India instantly became another Asian country rather than homeland: "As I prepare to leave Bombay for the slow flight westward, I realized that for me there would be no more easy consolation through India." (*DNC*, 285)

Bharati Mukherjee emphasizes that her confidence and modern education generated enough strength and ability to adapt to any situation in the country but she seems more of an escapist, who leaves a vital part of her inheritance as soon as she encounters the ugly facet of that part, which she thought and visualized as beautiful and secure. The instant perdition seems more cynical on her part and a will, which is very strong. In a way, this belief in cutting off from a situation, which is beyond control, helps her to adapt to the new environment: "It was hard to give up my faintly Chekhovian image of India. But if that was about to disappear, could I not invent a more exciting—perhaps a more psychologically accurate—a more precisely metaphoric India: many more Indias?"[20]

The struggle to make a place for herself in adverse conditions makes her a defeatist from one point of view because she always takes an easy way out. Chucking off her native country and her husband's native country seems to get inter-balanced and finally, both decide to settle in America as immigrants. This statement might be presumptuous and prognostic but this defeatist attitude is clearly reflected in the characters of Dimple Basu in *Wife* and Tara Banerjee in *The Tiger's Daughter*. Dimple's case has been presented in its extreme, where she is neurotic. Bharati Mukherjee tends to change herself due to her western education, but a tradition-bound wife, Dimple does not change for the fear of displeasing other people. The corroding characteristics in Dimple's nature reflect the childhood of Bharati Mukherjee. Early exposure to western education helped her to broaden her attitude whereas Dimple Dasgupta's sudden exposure to western culture imbalances her already-split personality.

Changing countries eventually made Bharati Mukherjee resilient and more tolerant and adaptable to all kinds of situations. Adjustment and withdrawal symptoms were already ingrained in her from childhood. The self-protective sense, developed early, helped her to switch countries. The transition from self-inflicted exile as an expatriate to self-preservative settlement as an immigrant is evident in her novel *Jasmine* where the protagonist prefers change instead of warmth and safe cocoon of family protection and love.

Mukherjee's attitude towards exile, expatriation and immigration has changed over the years. Although she now has a full and joyous sense of herself as "an immigrant, living in a continent of immigrants," she had at first felt like an exile, or at best an expatriate. As an exile, Mukherjee felt drawn to the country she had left behind and compelled from time to time to evaluate the nature of her ties to her "home." As an expatriate in Canada, she considered herself superior to immigrants, people who appeared to her as "lost souls, put upon and pathetic," while expatriates "knew all too well who and what they were, and what foul fate had befallen them."[21]

The soul-searching questions began after the sabbatical year in India. The need to stay in Canada was basically due to the urge to live in the new world. The old world seemed far off and dead. Though facing racism and multiculturalism in Canada again forced her to change and set herself anew in North America. The melting pot approach to immigration in America was appealingly welcome. She therefore moved to the United States, willing herself to think like the immigrants to whom she had once felt superior. She was going to be, she decided like the countless immigrants before her who had "the will to bond . . . themselves to a new community against the ever present fear of failure and betrayal."[22]

Accepting and adjusting to new situation with aplomb seems to be a regular feature of her life. Jasmine's decision to leave her country to fulfill her husband's dream, uptaking all kinds of dangers and challenges seems to reflect a facet of the author's life.

There are several phases in Mukherjee's life: the first phase of early childhood in a joint family till the age of 8; the second and the happiest phase was her life in England; the third was return to India where she led a protective and sheltered life in her father's factory compound. A new venture is on uptaking when she leaves for U.S.A. to pursue her academic career.

The uprootedness in her life began early. Changing countries became a regular feature of her life. Unsettled life and insecurity brought bitterness which did not last long because of co-operation of her husband and their decision to shift to North America as immigrants:

> Mukherjee's life in North America can thus be divided into three phases. At first she lived the life of an exile in Canada, thinking of herself as an Indian, even as she raised a family and pursued a career in Canada. In the course of her year-long stay in India, however, she discovered that India has become "just another Asian country." Mukherjee then felt ready to commit herself to Canada and embrace the life of an Indian expatriate in that country. But as soon as she perceived that Canada would not accept her as one of its own, she resolved to move to the United States. In the third period of her life in North America, Mukherjee can be seen in a celebratory mood, upholding the life of an immigrant in the United States.[23]

Her works can also be divided into three phases corresponding to the three phases of her life in North America. *The Tiger's Daughter* and essays of *Days and Nights in Calcutta* are of the first phase when Bharati Mukherjee considered herself in exile and felt oneness with India. The second phase works are most of the stories of *Darkness*, the essay "An Invisible Woman" and *The Sorrow and the Terror* (a work written in collaboration with her husband). This is the phase when Bharati Mukherjee had shaken off the ties with India. The works of second phase project the life of Indian expatriates in Canada. The third phase includes works like *The Middleman and Other Stories*, *Jasmine* and her essays which reflect the life of immigrants. The work reflects her happy mood, the attitude of transformation and adaptation to new terrains.

In *The Holder of the World*, she shows off her Indian heritage by incorporating it into her fiction to make a place for herself in the world of American fiction. The book is a transit from Indian to American. The fact is more emphasized in *Leave it to Me* where she has emphatically pointed out the fact that she is an American citizen. The protagonist in *Leave it to Me* searches for her roots, leading a carefree life, fulfilling American Dream. The transformation of Bharati Mukherjee seems to be complete, the confusion of Indian and American culture in *Wife* swiftly changes into a confident protagonist of *Leave it to Me* who believes in "Karma." The Indian beliefs still come through strongly but the blending is crystal clear and emphasized.

The decision to cut off from the state of exile from native land decidedly proved to be a turning point in her life. Reconciliation with present inevitably comes through strongly in her two novels, *The Holder of the World* and *Leave it to Me*. Self-satisfaction made her concentrate on the problems of expatriates in North America.

The aggressive attitude towards immigrants in Canada made her revolt against the system; the sustenance power took a back seat after 14 years in Canada. The resilient hardness is more markedly prominent in the characters of Jasmine in *Jasmine*, Debby Di Martino in *Leave it to Me* and Hannah in *The Holder of the World*. The desire to change and adapt to foreign elements runs in the veins of these characters: "As far as Mukherjee was concerned, 'multiculturalism' was essentially an excuse for not allowing other cultures to merge with the dominant culture and to keep new immigrants like her outside mainstream Canada."[24]

Life in America was easier going in spite of usual mugging, robbing, cheating and attacking. Compared to discrimination in Canada, this seemed to be welcome because she was not facing marginalisation or the abusive treatment in New York. She became a part of the "melting pot": "In her opinion, American society at least allowed a new immigrant like her to slug it out, while Canadian society degraded South Asians even though it permitted them to be citizens."[25]

In 1988, Bharati Mukherjee, already having written two novels and a collection of short stories, wrote a controversial and thought-provoking essay titled "Immigrant Writing: Give Us Your Maximalist." Published in the *New York Times Book Review*, it focussed on the American fiction and its policies of immigration. With this piece, Bharati Mukherjee not only established herself as a decisive voice in the US multiculturalist debate, but also "consolidated her position as one of the best known South Asian American writer."[26]

The questions argued by Bharati Mukherjee revolve around the position of the new Americans from non-traditional immigrant countries. Being a multiculturalist country for a very long time, the literary imperialism still does not adequately reflect on the existence of its multicultural society. The question which is asked by her in the essay is, "But where in fiction do you read of it? Who in other words, speaks for us, the new Americans from non-traditional immigrant countries? Which is another way of saying, in this altered America, who speaks for you?"[27]

Bharati Mukherjee in her essay has distinctly categorized the two types of American literary circulation, as "minimalism" and "maximalism," the former concentrating on fictions revolving around subjects like mid-life crises, childlessness, divorce and prevalent hazards in the society like drugs and AIDS. Maximalist fictions evince the experiences of the immigrants, their emotional upheavals characterized by change. Immigrants who have shelved their past lives, culture and language, rummaging through new realms, live through centuries of history in a single life-time. Going through a rumbustious emotional upheaval—village born, tradition bound, educated and colonized individuals—still ruminative about past securities, forms a basis, an inception of myriad themes, for the novels of Bharati Mukherjee. Instead of being a burden she celebrates the immigrant experience. She claims herself to be labelled as an American writer and her writings mirror the social and historical reality of United States of America's demography and experiences. The sub-labelling of her work as ethnic fiction by the American fiction world is like disinheriting her as a citizen of America.

The two essays, "American Dreamer," published in 1997 in *Mother Jones* and "Two Ways to Belong in America," published in *New York Times*, 1996, are contentious pieces on policy of immigration and citizenship in America.

The two non-fiction articles as well as other such papers are Bharati Mukherjee's effort to define the experiences of immigrants in America. "Two Ways to Belong in America" reflects the disparate attitude towards citizenship in America. Bharati Mukherjee's sister Mira insists on returning to India, choosing a life of expatriation whereas Bharati Mukherjee accepts her status as an immigrant in America to free herself from the bondings of past. America is a place where she has carved a niche for herself as a writer. The article depicts the mentality of two separate individuals, who co-incidentally are conceptualizing two different attitudes towards citizenship in America.

> Like well-raised sisters, we never said what was really on our minds, but we probably pitied one another. She, for lack of structure in my life, the erasure of Indianness, the absence of an unvarying daily chore. I, for the narrowness of her perspective, her uninvolvement with the mythic depths or the superficial pop culture of this society. But, now, with the scapegoating of "aliens" (documented or illegal) on the increase, and the targeting of long term legal immigrants like Mira for new scrutiny and new self-consciousness, she and I find ourselves unable to maintain the same polite discretion. We were always unacknowledged adversaries, and we are now, more than ever, sisters.[28]

"American Dreamer" has more of personal ruminative musings upon Bharati Mukherjee's life and her transitions, her marriage to Clark Blaise and her moving to Canada, the turbulent years spent there and her sabbatical year in India, which changed her decision to become an immigrant, which proved a pivotal moment in her life, innervating her evolution as an individual and as an author. Her continuous self-assertion regarding her own status as an immigrant, her viewing it from America's point of view, of what America faces in its multicultural diversities, somehow proves her undoubted allegiance to her new homeland.

> Questions such as who is an American and what is American culture are being posed with belligerence and answered with violence. . . . But in this decade of continual, large-scale diasporas, it is imperative that we come to some agreement about who 'we' are, and what our goals are for the nation, now that our community includes people of many races, ethnicities, languages, and religions. The debate about American culture and American identity has to date been monopolized largely by Eurocentrists and ethnocentrists whose rhetoric has been flamboyantly divisive, pitting a phantom 'us' against a demonized 'them?' [29]

Bharati Mukherjee vehemently denounces the terms 'melting pot' and 'cultural mosaic' in terms of immigrants infiltrating and changing America. She prefers to discard the notion of centre versus periphery and favours the paradigm of 'us' versus 'them' mentality, "one that will think of American culture and nationhood as a constantly re-forming, transmogrifying 'we,' that is, a labile and plural communal identity."[30]

The label of 'Asian American' writer is also vociferously rejected by Bharati Mukherjee simply for the fact that it is a replica of "hierarchical model of ethnic relations."[31]

A question that recurs through her novels is infliction of hyphenated existence on the non-white American: "Rejecting hyphenation is my refusal to categorize the cultural landscape into a centre and its peripheries; it is to demand that the American nation deliver the promises if its dream and its Constitution to all its citizens equally."[32]

The dual experience of immigration provides a myriad subject for Bharati Mukherjee to dwell on in her novels. Identity undulated between 'we' and the 'other' provides her with a set of identities, which are fluid in their rootedness, or identities still dwindling between dilemmas of uprootedness, an arena of variegated lives, she can venture into in her fiction, that is not a manifestation of her own life. Bharati Mukherjee's preoccupation with seeing ourselves, as others see us, has been discussed in reviews and interviews. As far as the aspect of dualism or doubleness is concerned, it is bought forth in her choice of titles of her novels where she has often used words and phrases to manifest the thematic pattern of her novels. *Leave it to Me* (is also the name of the agency she works in) can be read, in two ways and the meaning changes. *Leave it to Me* manifests the intertwined theme of legacy and agency. In *Wife*, Dimple, the female protagonist, has been named ironically, as Dimple is described as 'slight surface depression' by the author, symbolic of physical beauty in Indian traditional set up, but the characteristic flaw in Dimple.

The mentality of 'us' vs. 'them' has its own hazards which Bharati Mukherjee points out in her essay "American Dreamer":

> We must be alert to the dangers of an "us" vs. "them" mentality. In California, this mentality is manifesting itself as increased violence between minorities, ethnic communities. The attack on Korean-American merchants in South Central Los Angeles in the wake of the Rodney King beating trial is only one recent example of the tragic side effects of this mentality. On the national level, the politicization of ethnic identities has encouraged the scapegoating of legal immigrants, who are blamed for economic and social problems brought about by flawed domestic and foreign policies.[33]

An analytic viewing of Bharati Mukherjee's characters reveals her own experiences of Canada, in *The Tiger's Daughter*, *Days and*

Nights in Calcutta (depicts her confusion at being treated as an outsider in her own country, an exotic foreigner). The stories in *Darkness* reveal her frustration and anger at the multiracial and multicultural policies of Canada and her inclination towards immigration to America. Three of the stories are set in Canada and focus on the threats and tensions gripping the South Asian characters as they strive to immerse themselves into the new world. The rest of the stories are beset with problems faced by immigrants in America, 'the melting pot' culture and find that melting is not so very easy. To do so, one has to let go the inhibitions of past culture.

The two books that Bharati Mukherjee co-authored with her husband, one of them *The Sorrow and the Terror*, and the story "The Management of Grief" from *The Middleman and Other Stories*, and the stories of *Darkness* throw light on her preoccupation with Indians experiencing multiracial discrimination in Canada, which could be undoubtedly traced back to the Canadian immigration policy. The stories which are about the Indian immigrants in America are tinged with doubt at the success of their assimilation in the American culture. The multifarious activities of her characters remind the readers of her own experiences.

> In the United states, however, I see myself in those same outcasts; I see myself in an article on a Trinidad-Indian hooker; I see myself in the successful executive who sides Hindi film music in his tape deck as he drives into Manhattan; I see myself in the shady accountant who's trying to marry off his loose-living daughter; in professors, domestics, high school students, illegal busboys in ethnic restaurants. It's possible with sharp ears and the right equipment to hear America singing even in the seams of the dominant culture. In fact, it may be the best listening post for the next generation of Whitman. For me, it is a movement away from the aloofness of expatriation, to the exuberance of immigration.[34]

A notable recurrent feature of Bharati Mukherjee's novels is that they depict the new-immigrant women who are forced to mutate, transforming themselves to become self-emancipated, self-confident members of the American society. Exceptions are there, but the male protagonists are the only ones, who tend to dwindle between the two cultures, and in spite of their patriarchal superiority, in comparison to the female protagonist seem dwarfed and demeaned.

In the four novels of Bharati Mukherjee, *Wife*, *Jasmine*, *The Holder of the World* and *Leave it to Me*, the women metamorphose in the wake of a physical move from India to new culture. *Wife* and *Jasmine* move from India to America, to be forced by violent acts, to self-mutate. In *The Holder of the World*, Hannah Easton travels from the puritan society of Massachusetts to South India, where she self-mutates into becoming an Indian concubine. In the novel *Leave it to Me*, the central character Debbie Di Martino undergoes a voluntary transformation in quest of her Indian origins, tracking down her physical and psychological roots. With each transformation, a new name is associated with the characters, somehow sinister in essence, marking the re-birth of each character. Wife/ Sita/ Dimple in the novel *Wife*; Jyoti/ Jasmine/ Jane/ Jase in *Jasmine*, Hannah Easton Fitch Legge/ 'Salem Bibi'/ 'Precious as Pearl' in *The Holder of the World* and Faustine/ Debbie/ Devi in *Leave it to Me*. The transmutation is sometimes forced and sometimes voluntary. By intertwining the philosophies of 'Hinduism' and 'Buddhism' into the structure of the novels, Bharati Mukherjee has clearly emphasized the fact that every death marks a new life. The oral teachings and narration of Hindu mythological stories make their way insidiously into the plots of each novel. The juxtaposing of traditional Hindu culture with the New American culture gives a new flamboyant outlook to each of her novels.

The novel *Wife* depicts the plight of the female protagonist. Torn between being the ideal wife like 'Sita' and the need for self-expression dooms her to her fate. Freedom in marriage becomes a bondage to a life of servility and the chaos of thoughts proves fatal for her. Her predicament as an immigrant wife in North America worsens her condition as she is unable to root herself in the new environment. Unable to voice her self-suppressed feelings, she fumes with a fury which finds an outlet through butchering her husband.

Dimple's faith in freedom through marriage leads to her envisioning her husband. Her idol being 'Sita,' she wants to be an obedient, soft-spoken wife and fantasizes of sacrificing herself for the sake of her husband. But marriage to Amit Basu turns out to be a nightmarish experience, because instead of freedom she is rebuked by her husband for forgetting her duties. The expectations of in-laws, of not being able to decorate her own bedroom, bring her out of her reveries and fantasies.

The situation worsens as Dimple becomes pregnant and simultaneously, Amit Basu's immigration to America is confirmed. In order to free herself from the burden of carrying a baby, symbol of old traditions, Dimple finds out ways to aborting the foetus. Her pregnancy seems forced on her and the traditional ties seem to stifle her. As Simone de Beauvoir writes:

> It is sheer hypocrisy to hold that a union based on convenience has much chance of inducing love; it is pure absurdity to maintain that two married persons bound by ties of practical, social, and moral interest, will provide with sex satisfaction as long as they live. But the proponents of the marriage of reason have no difficulty in showing that the love match, also, is not especially likely to assure the happiness of the couple.[35]

The situation in Canada and the United States further disheartens her as she slowly shrivels up inside, with nothing to do, remorse sets in. Now that they are in America she is shocked to find that actually Amit wants her to be like Sita. Ludicrously Amit suggests her to be American but not too much American. Lack of self-confidence makes her flounder in the new social set up. Conscious about not being able to possess the fluency of English language, the situation becomes exacting for her. Amit Basu is of no help, as he is busy in establishing himself in the New World. He is unable to fathom the disintegrating situation of his wife. Back in India, impersonating her frustrated self in a dead rat, she finds satisfaction in beating it to death. The rat seemed pregnant to her and she revels at herself. It is like killing a part of her self. Replicating the scene, Dimple butchers her husband, finally finding an outlet, to her freedom.

> When an Asian man comes to America he comes for economic transformation, and he brings a wife who winds up being psychologically changed. This is one of the tragedies you see being played out in all the New Jersey shopping malls these days. The Indian women walking around in the malls with nothing to do all day, while the men are out busily making money. The men have a sense of accomplishment. They have no idea of staying here. The idea is saving money and going. But they don't realize the women have been transformed.[36]

Seduced by the American consumerism, she is forced into awakening to her surroundings and is introduced to the social openness of the American society by an Indian wife, who is totally Americanised, who presents America to Dimple with her short tops, which show the midriff, and who smokes. Through Ina Mullick, who moves in and out of the Indian social circle and beyond it, Dimple is initiated into her feminist awakening. Finally her self-confidence makes her have an affair with Milt Glasser but as she takes a step forward in transforming her old traditional values, it makes her step back. The transformation is forced upon her and she is seen rejoicing, which somehow feels·lugubrious. Her assumption is that she would go scot-free, and one tends to question: "Where"?

Tara in *The Tiger's Daughter* travels back to India to discover her self-identity which is a fledgling attempt of a child who runs back to the father for reassurance of security. Unsure and embittered with her being treated as a minority in America, she is nostalgic about her peaceful existence in India. Coming to India, unexpectedly she faces the situations which are a replica of the one she has run away from. Contrasted with the chaos in the outside world, she finds the security of her father's house soothing. Awakening of spirituality gives her a self-confidence that coaxes her into letting down her guards, and leave herself open for lechers like Tuntunwala to creep insidiously, into her life. Taken unawares, she is violated by Tuntunwala which leads her to catapult into self-realization and self-confidence which sees her through the rest of her stay in India with a calm, benumbed state of mind.

The cataclysmic incident consequently forces Tara into realizing her potential as an expatriate in New York. Joyonto Roy Chowdhary, an old self-realized man, who awaits an apocalypse, and tends to think in phrases, voice fragments from T.S. Eliot's 'Gerontion' and much earlier in the novel, when he sees Tara, he remembers lines from Rupert Brooke's poem "The Soldier." Tara, who is unable to comprehend the old man, understands his and her own vision about the existing situation, towards the end of the novel.

> So madness was as simple as that, a wild man in loincloth reading palms and an old man in sandals reciting Rupert Brooke. Now her faith in Joyonto Roy Chowdhary was slowly breaking. She had hoped he

> could guide her through the new Calcutta, but his face seemed sinister as he pushed in through the open windows of the rover.[37]

The novel begins and ends at the same place, outside Catelli Continental, significantly symbolizing the meeting juncture of Old and New Calcutta. The riot outside is a blemish, which does not disturb the warm, luxurious interiors of the hotel. The entrance might be shabby and the walls are patterned with rust and mould yet the interiors pose for a place, where the elite crowd comes and spends time, having espresso or tea, ignoring the chaos outside. The hotel is symbolic of Calcutta itself.

> The Catelli Continental Hotel on Chowringhee Avenue, Calcutta, is the novel of the universe. Gray and imposing, with many bay windows and fake turrets, the hotel occupies half a block, then spills untidily into an intersection. There are no spacious grounds or circular driveways, only a small square courtyard and dry fountain. The entrance is small, almost shabby, marked by a sun-bleached awning and two-patted hibiscus shrubs. The walls and woodwork are patterned with mold and rust around vertical drains. The sidewalks along the hotel front are painted with obscenities and political slogans that have been partially erased. (*TD*, 3)

At this point of time, Tara wonders how her husband David Cartwright would react to Calcutta. She cannot imagine him as a foreign tourist in Calcutta. Her friend Pronob seems to her as flabby compared to the energetic, ferocious and aggressive Tuntunwala. He somehow presents a replication of her father.

In *Days and Nights in Calcutta*, a collection of journals, worked on separately by husband and wife, with mutual understanding to keep it separate to be later compared, discover ironically both their works had lots of similarity. Clark Blaise's journey to India proved a quest into understanding his wife. "My quest was nothing less than the retrieval of a buried self, the understanding of my marriage." (*DNC*, 84) Bharati Mukherjee's journey to India was more like giving into the nostalgic comforts of hometown. "I knew the rules in India (I hoped I still remembered them)." (*DNC*, 168)

Bharati Mukherjee's writing in the *Days and Nights in Calcutta* is based mostly on the lives of her women friends of the upper middle class who had married well and were involved in charity work, helping the society. Still not recovered from her traumatized existence in Canada, the affluent society of friends and bureaucrats seems to grate on her sensitized self. Her decision to not stay in India is more of her own evolution to venture into the world of America as an immigrant. Her sabbatical year in India seems to be a fateful event, deciding her future.

In *Days and Nights in Calcutta*, Bharati Mukherjee has taken up the women who belong to upper and upper-middle class in the city and yet face the gender bias in Calcutta. In fact, Bharati Mukherjee is shocked at the conditions of women in modern India being a replica of one which she had accidentally listened to as a child about a relative who had been tortured for dowry and had been driven to insanity. Listening to the stories and experiences of the affluent women and finding it disgusting, Bharati Mukherjee slowly realizes that her own fate would have been similar if she had decided to stay back. Though her parents are loving by nature, they are given in to their own whims. Past experiences in a joint family have made Bina Mukherjee paranoid about locking things, to the extent, that Clark Blaise gets irritated, when their son's new toy is locked in an almirah.

> I was leading two lives that year, set against each other, they suggested a painless but mocking harmony. In Ballygunge I was the dutiful relative who paid Sunday morning visits to the family, ate rice and curried delicacies with her fingers, and sat on the edge of a bed gossiping with aunts or listening to the Bournvita quiz on All India Radio. But in downtown Calcutta, especially on Park Street or Chowringhee, I was the Indian memsahib with a white escort to be lewdly stared at, or to be whispered "good day" to by elevator-boy-pimps. These lives—my lives—were separate, contiguous; they impinged but did not collide. In Calcutta, I could not help thinking, hundreds of thousands saw themselves leading craftily welded lives. I was one of many. I saw my Calcutta as transparencies the banality of quotidian encounters reduced or enhanced by photographer's tricks. (*DNC*, 239)

Though Bharati Mukherjee's novel displays an array of Hindu philosophies, the motif of self-revelation through suffering is downplayed. The only character who embodies this characteristic is Tara in *The Tiger's Daughter*. The traumatic experience is not conveyed to her friends and the parents are bewildered at their daughter's decision to return to her husband. The sufferings of her mother at the hands of in-laws and other members of the family seem to be entrenched on adult Bharati Mukherjee's mind and the suppressed anger finds its way into the seams of her novels. As Bharati Mukherjee herself points out that as a sensitive individual she hardly forgets any wrong done to her. As a 'neurasthenic' child, given to headaches and vomiting, all incidents more or less fabricated, in order to gain attention of her parents, somehow, validates Dimple's behaviour in *Wife*.

The Middleman and Other Stories marks the exuberance of belonging, and having conquered the New World. The stories in this collection flaunt a conglomeration of variegated characters hailing from different countries who find their way to the New World. The collection gives new meaning to gaining access to the land of dreams. The access gained by importing prostitutes labelled as 'mail-order,' symbolic of embracing the imperialistic world is done with aplomb. A father embraces his daughter denouncing the ideologies of West, or a Muslim wife enticing a white man and with mutual consent they sleep together to enjoy the socially sanctioned sexual relationship in America. The role-reversal of the husband acting indignant, the wife of James Beamish taking her husband's affairs in her stride, somehow deflate the spirits of Nafeesa, who is trying to be Americanized lying down nonchalantly in James's bed. But her sensibilities get ruffled when she is not able to provoke any reaction from James's wife. The very feminist American attitude that Nafeesa poses backfires and Nafeesa enjoins her experience to the one in Lucknow, where a young girl is beaten for falling in love with a boy of different caste. The guilt, which expected rebuking from the white wife, would have been a symbol of acceptance into the cultural and moral code of America.

> That half-hour wait for the cab, as Kate related tales of the grandson to her distracted husband was the most painful. It came closest to what Husseina must have felt. At least her father, the Nawab-Sahib, had beaten her. (*D*, 33)

Alfie Judah in 'The Middleman' is saved from being killed or rather he is used to camouflage the terrorist ongoings, by a nymphomaniac, Maria, or be it Jasmine a girl from Trinidad, renouncing her past vehemently and, is unaware of being used by her American employer. A myriad of characters exemplifies the canvas of this collection.

The most poignant story of this collection is 'The Management of Grief' where Shaila Bhave and many others face the destiny of losing their loved ones due to the calculating Sikh terrorists of Canadian origin. The story is a depiction of individuals having their own ways of handling their grief. Though the insensitiveness of the Canadian Government is evinced with belligerent attitude, yet the citizens are shown paying condolences to the deceased and offering flowers to the Indians who have lost their relatives.

> Dr. Ranganathan whips the pockets of his suit jacket inside out. Squashed roses, in darkening shades of pink, float on the water. He tore the roses off creepers in somebody's garden. He didn't ask anyone if he could pluck the roses, but now there's been an article about it in the local papers. When you see an Indian person, it says, please give him or her flowers.[38]

Jasmine forms the focal point of transformation and evolving of Bharati Mukherjee's protagonists. The transformation of Jasmine in the New World, marked with her being raped by Half-Face, and Jasmine avenging herself, depicts in a way her avenging the innocent death of her husband, by killing Half-Face. The term 'Death incarnate' occurs in Jasmine's mind as she stands over the dead body of her rapist. In *Jasmine*, we find the second generation Indians who revolt against the traditional rules in their patriarchal families. An individual who has escaped fate of death from the time of birth, Jasmine goes against the norms of the family to educate herself with the help of Masterji in the village. With the help, or indirect consent of the elders (her family being a large one), Jasmine marries a boy of her choice. The brothers help her to meet Prakash and they resort to marrying in court. Unfortunate death of Prakash subdues her for a short period before she gears up to find a way to go to Florida. Arranged by her brothers and with the help of Professor Vadhera, she reaches America. Avenging herself seems to appease her anger, she walks forward to find her future in the New World where she transforms with each incarnation. Forging through, Jasmine herself is not aware of the reactions, the havoc, that is created by her actions. Till the end, Jasmine is like a child, playing hide and seek with the prognostic predictions of the astrologer.

The bond that she shares with Du, seems to be the only emotional attachment which is in a way treasured by Jasmine, be it due to their origins or be it due to strangeness, but the relationship reflects the one which she had with Prakash. Jasmine's hesitation in encroaching Du's world of technology is a replica of Prakash's involvement in computer technology, having the same flair for technical equipment.

This bond is figured almost as a conspiracy in the text at one point as Jane observes 'secrets roll like barbed wire between us.' And it is Du's ultimate fate in the text that also, somewhat paradoxically, provides the denouement of Jane's own story. Near the end of the narrative, Du announces his intention to move to Los Angeles to live with his Vietnamese sister, whom he has tracked down through Vietnamese acquaintances, and who runs a taco stall, and will, he says, care for him. Jane's reaction to this is significant; her shock at the prospect of losing her adopted son is overshadowed by her realization of Du's successful amalgamation of his Vietnamese and American selves.[39]

Bharati Mukherjee in her novel *The Holder of the World* blends the historical period of colonial New England and the cultural and trade contract between South Asia and America via the East India Company in the 17th century. The historical contact between South Asia and America is tracked down through the contemporaneous perspective of the narrator and a 20th century American asset hunter, Beigh Masters, whose purpose is to find the spectacular diamond which is called the "Emperor's Tear," for a client. During her quest she chances upon the paintings of Salem Bibi and gets deeply absorbed in the life of the woman who had travelled through continents to end up being the white bibi of Raja Jadav Singh. The Hindu Raja somehow brings forth her self-realization and at last she exists congenially with her 'past' and 'present' and 'future'—her mother, herself, and her daughter.

In 'A Four Hundred Year Old Woman,' Mukherjee said of *The Holder of the World* that it would be 'a major work, historical in nature, that nevertheless incorporates a much earlier version . . . [of] the making of New Americans. Although in this assertion Mukherjee seems to locate her work within her ongoing multicultural project despite its status as a historical novel, in fact we should regard *The*

Holder of the World as an important component in her oeuvre, precisely because of 'its historical sweep, which offers an alternative history of colonial New England, One inflected and influenced by contact with Asia. . . . And which comes to disrupt and question the very categories of 'immigrant,' 'native' and expatriate,' long before America became the multicultural nation it is today."[40]

Leave it to Me is a novel which symbolises the rooting of the author into the American culture. In a way, she celebrates her American status, with livening up the novel, with the social and economic realities of the society, but again, the blending of Indian origins of the female protagonist emphatically points out the equipoised personality. The new novel exhibits the cross cultural metamorphosis of the female protagonist, Devi. Bharati Mukherjee's novel revolves around Devi, who is the adopted daughter of Italian-Americans, but as she grows, the uniqueness of her physical attributes ostensibly innervate doubts into her mind about her birth origins. The quest is to find her lost identity, to understand her psyche and to find her bio-parents. Her journey is of an American to search for her Asian roots. Devi is not searching for a new identity, but her journey somehow indicates the journey inside to find one's own identity in this universe. Having the spiritual tinge to her quest, Debbie reincarnates herself as Devi. Like the Hindu Goddess, Devi slaughters the demons in her universe and paves a bloody path to reach her goal.

> Destiny works itself out in bizarre loops. I made the 911 call. Domestic dispute, I told the dispatcher. Let them find out how bloody. I heard the urgent police sirens. I waited a long while for the waist chains, handcuffs, leg shackles, and just when I prayed for my misery to be over, the waves rocked wild and heaved last chance free of its moorings.[41]

The narration of the novel is split narrative, which somehow makes the readers look inside and outside simultaneously—the impression on mind is empathic. The journey is more of retrospection than progression. The language of Devi is more arrogant than her action. The outspoken protagonist is filled with anger which she vents on her unsuspecting victims like Frankie Fong and Stark Swann. The serial killer who is Devi's Bio-Dad, is like a colonized individual, more of a psychopath who murders with a sense of enjoyment. His traits are juxtaposed to the violence of American society. Bharati Mukherjee's evolution as an author is manifested in the themes that she has chosen to focus on. Her journey from the cloistered environs of upper middle class Bengali in Calcutta to the cosmopolitan world of North America is epochal. The multifarious themes are unravelled with delicacy, the tightly woven structure makes an impact on the reader's mind. Be it depiction of the deep-rooted racism in Canada, or the semblance of white characters in *The Middleman and Other Stories*, the turmoils of Tara with memories of genteel past clashing with the realities of poverty and strike-infested Calcutta, be it the world of colonial Massachusetts melting the Aurangzeb-era India, be it the confused world of fantasies in which Dimple dwells, or Jasmine foraging through her past memories and the present to carve a future for herself or be it Devi, the living fury, Frankenstein, all the characters are enjoined into Bharati Mukherjee's self-created constellation, a galaxy of individuals, who are the centre of their own universe, individuals, with their own realities and destiny to deal with and emerge triumphant. Feminism (but not the conventional extremist feminism) in the characters of Bharati Mukherjee is equipoised to make them vibrant and flamboyant. Each one of the characters is an individual. The power inside each one of them which is dormant at some point is forced out to make its presence felt. The very aspect of femininity, the vulnerability turns into pulsating self-empowerment, which helps them to move forward in their life. The passive existence of each character undergoes a dramatic change. The attitude of servility, to look upto men with reverence, might be evident in the traditional Indian patriarchal set-up, but the protagonists in each novel, by the act of violence, self-mutate and transform to live as they wish, in the New World. The image of 'Shakti' is used ingenuously to project the power within and it has been highlighted in each of Bharati Mukherjee's works. Her mother being an inspiration for her, Bharati Mukherjee believes that her writing can have an impact on the readers:

> I use my mother who in her very, very quiet way in a hostile crowded household in Calcutta made sure no matter what the physical cost to her body that we three sisters got the best education. That's the kind of feminism, quiet but full of action, that I've adopted as my motto. What I want to do is change the world, make people alert to the good and the bad and if at all possible, provoke them to see everyday life in a fresh

> way and then make it happen through social action, political action in real life after they've finished my novel.[42]

The influence of her mother, a strong-willed lady who is not subjugated to the atrocities of society, is etched on Bharati Mukherjee's mind. The strength that she gained as a child, the nurturing qualities of her mother (that is evident in the character of Jasmine) fashioned Bharati Mukherjee's overall personality. The resilience power inherited from her parents enables to take a stand in life, her unwavering stance, which sees her through all the experience in Canada and North America helps her in her ingenious delineation of characters in her works:

> When I'm writing I'm not conscious of anything other than getting in the skin and into the skill of my character but when I'm finished with a draft and look at it to realise that very often it's about mother-daughter relations and about the formation of a very strong woman. And that strength may sometimes express itself in negative and violent ways but I still think of all my characters as women who've asserted themselves according to their own improvised moral code even if they murder or hurt other men who've hurt them earlier, the hurt that they inflict comes out of their own very precise sense of Right and Wrong.[43]

NOTES

1. Fakhrul Alam, *Bharati Mukherjee: Criticism and Interpretation* (Twayne's United States Author's Series, 1996), p. 1.
2. Bharati Mukherjee and Clark Blaise, *Days and Nights in Calcutta* (New York: Penguin, 1986), p. 181.
3. Fakhrul Alam, p. 2.
4. *Ibid.*, p. 2.
5. "American Dreamer," *Mojowire*, p. 1 http://www.mojones.coml motherjones/JF9/mukherjee.html.
6. Bharati Mukherjee, an Interview with Runar Vignisson, Diasporas, *Span*, Nos. 34-35 (1993), p. 1.
7. *Ibid.*, p. 1.
8. Fakhrul Alam, p. 3.
9. Bharati Mukherjee: An Interview with Runar Vignisson, p. 8.
10. Willa Swanson, Antiock Review, barnes and noble, p. 2. http://shop.barnesandnoble.com/booksearch/butorcombiography.
11. *Ibid.*, p. 2.

12. *Ibid.*, p. 2.
13. Fakhrul Alam, p. 4.
14. Bharati Mukherjee, An Interview with Runar Vignisson, p. 2.
15. *Ibid.*, pp. 2-3.
16. *Ibid.*, p. 4.
17. Fakhrul Alam, p. 6.
18. *Ibid.*, p. 7.
19. *Ibid.*
20. *Ibid.*, p. 285
21. *Ibid.*, p. 9.
22. *Ibid.*, p. 10.
23. *Ibid.*, p. 10.
24. *Ibid.*, p. 35.
25. *Ibid.*, pp. 35-36.
26. Helena Grice, 'Who Speaks for us?' Bharati Mukherjee's Fiction and the Politics of Immigration, http://www.sagepub.co.uk/journal s/details/issue/sample/a03170.pdf, p. 83.
27. *Ibid.*, p. 83.
28. Bharati Mukherjee, "Two Ways to Belong to America," p. 1-2 http://*www*.ncl.ac.uk/~n5311095/main1.html.
29. Helena Grice, p. 85.
30. *Loc. cit.*
31. *Loc. cit.*
32. *Loc. cit.*
33. *Mojowire*, pp. 3-4.
34. Bharati Mukherjee, *Darkness*, p. 3.
35. Simone De Beauvoir, *The Second Sex*, p. 445.
36. Fakhrul Alam, p. 41.
37. Bharati Mukherjee, *The Tiger's Daughter*, p. 82.
38. Bharati Mukherjee, *The Middleman and Other Stories*, p. 186.
39. Helena Grice, p. 91.
40. *Ibid.*, pp. 92-93.
41. Bharati Mukherjee, *Leave it to Me*, p. 239.
42. 'Being a Woman Writer,' p. 1. Her Story/ BBC World Service http: //www.bbc.co.uk./worldservice/arts/features/womenwriters/mukherjeework.shtm
43. 'Key Influences and Themes,' p. 1. *Ibid.*

Chapter II

Portrayal of Characters in the Novels of Bharati Mukherjee

The female protagonists seem to spread all over the canvas, a life size projection in the novels of Bharati Mukherjee. The male counterparts hardly seem to get to inch into the scene. The strength in the female leads, the feministic attitude, especially in *Jasmine*, *Holder of the World* and *Leave it to Me*, leaves the reader bemused. It feels as if the female characters are an extended zealous form of Bharati Mukherjee herself.

The struggle that she faced in Canada is also faced by her heroines. It is a fact that a person has to struggle to adapt and assimilate in a new environment, and those who succeed are people who change rapidly according to the circumstances and feel comfortable. The Canadian experience left Bharati Mukherjee embittered, which is evident in her earlier works like *Jasmine*, *Darkness* and *The Middleman and Other Stories*. At a conference of the South Asian Students Alliance (SASA), citing a personal experience, she said: "The Indian High Commission in Ottawa refused to renew my passport after I married an American." She says that the action was irrational since men with Indian Passports did not face the same action.[1]

The element of Feminism does not come through harshly but her characters do have a tinge of feministic attitude in them, which makes them resilient and adaptable. As Chaman Nahal points out in his paper "Feminism in Indian English Fiction": "I define feminism as a mode of existence in which the woman is free of the dependence syndrome."[2] But the exceptions are there, like Dimple Dasgupta in *Wife* who keeps dwindling between the dependence syndrome and independence.

Bharati Mukherjee has tried to assemble all types of temperaments in her work where she has worked out the mental and physical interaction of female mind. The complexities of a human feeling have been projected through her characters.

The projection of female characters is so vivid that the rest of the characters, especially the male counterparts, are subordinated. The basic instinct of male mind, especially that which is imbibed in Indian males—the feeling of superiority, is very much evident in her novels. Amit Basu in *Wife* gets angry with Dimple because she has not prepared the drink, which he takes immediately after entering his house.

> When Amit came back from the office and found her in bed with letters to the editor, he seemed angry.
>
> "Where's my fresh lime and water?"
>
> "I forgot to make it. I'm sorry: I was busy reading."
>
> "But you know I like fresh lime and water when I come back. You know this little thing means a lot to me." (*W*, 28)

A subjugated Dimple makes him happy later on, and boosts his male pride.

> "Who said I want fresh lime?" He said roguishly. "You lock the door, Dimple, and I promise you some very interesting things." (*W*, 29)

Debbie Di Martino is poles apart from Dimple Dasgupta. Debby, the protagonist in *Leave it to Me* seems to be assimilated American form of Bharati Mukherjee. Debbie, though named Devi by her friend, feels comfortable with herself and knows how to conduct herself in the world. Her parentage can give her a setback but that becomes a feature which enhances her strong will. She is not like Dimple bemoaning her conditions, though the basic difference is that Dimple Dasgupta is an immigrant and has to adapt herself to a new environment but Debbie is brought up in America. Debbie finds her inner peace after taking revenge on her lover and marches forward nonchalantly, finding a new identity in the process.

> Inner peace. That's what I gained that smoky summer night as a wide, gracious porch smoldered and Frankie wept. Nirvana is finding the tiger balls within you. (*LITM*, 53)

Debbie is more like Jasmine in the novel *Jasmine*. Jasmine acclimatizes in the new country and environment. Adaptation, in spite of all hurdles, is the crux around which her identity evolves. She defies the astrologer's predicament of widowhood by not marrying her benefactor in the U.S.A. though she had to face the murder of her husband Prakash in terrorist-infested Punjab.

> Adventure, risk, transformation; the frontier is pushing indoors through uncaulked windows. Watch me re-position the stars, I whisper to the astrologer who floats cross-legged above my kitchen-stove. (*J*, 240)

Debby says, "I had to learn all that Hindu, Jain, Buddhist shit at the U. of T." (*LITM*, 71)

The role is reversed in *The Holder of the World*. The female protagonist is made to adjust in pre-colonial society and she fights to adapt herself into a society which is different from her homeland. Though her home country is also war-torn, the conditions are more or less primitive.

Basically the protagonists of Bharati Mukherjee's novels are mixed elements of feminine incarnations of Hindu idols like Sita and Kali, with a tinge of imbalance which tends to tip over the brim, if not handled with extra care. Not a single character can be defined traditionally because each has a "dimensional facet" to its personality. Each character represents different characteristics of feminism. But the basic set of rules is that one has to step out of the rigid confines of conventional rules and adapt to the new environment. Femininity is enhanced if one retains the tradition, giving way to modernity. The imbalance in personality takes place if one rigidly refuses to walk with changing times while still retaining one's values and tradition. The problem that faces immigrants is the basic need to hold on to their tradition and culture, and in the process they forget to adapt to the new culture, thus resulting in split personalities, who are unable to handle themselves in the new environment. Professor Vadhera in *Jasmine* is one such character who follows his laid-out rules and tries to keep his family in control, his code of survival as an Indian in the United States. His wife keeps following the laid-out rules and they live in a fictional world sans reality. It gives rise to another problem. Either they keep holding onto their dreams and be unsatisfied and feel guilty or like Professor Vadhera involve themselves in a profession, which is totally out of proportions. He sells human hair but his status as a Professor is intact. To survive in the United States, he has taken up a profession, which he considers below his dignity.

His profession is not known to his parents because they have another code of morality, which cannot be overlooked by Professor.

In another case, the immigrants start involving themselves into the new culture by forgetting their imbibed values and like suckers they try to assimilate by compromising with new culture. They make all sorts of compromises to adapt and in the process they again feel out of place, harassed and guilty.

The tussle in the mind to maintain the imbibed principle, yet feel a craving to live a free life where there is no tension makes Dimple Dasgupta in *Wife* live on the edge. The reconciling process for her is a difficult one because she always wants what she does not have. She keeps on craving for something else.

A natural process of acculturation and assimilation is evident in an Indian marriage where the girl has to adapt to the new home, compromise and adorn herself with a new identity. In one case, the girl might retain her original identity by refusing to compromise and thus generate unfavourable conditions. In other cases, it might happen that the girl is subdued.

In both the above cases, there are two respective extreme cases of aggression and subjugation, which might result in extremities. The feudal upbringing of the girl child is conventional in Indian families and can subdue all the qualities except how to make a husband happy by cooking good food and wait on him. The natural instinct of a girl child makes her immune to the basic nature, i.e. freedom of her own self. The existing feudal mentality in the husband does not help much. A bride who retains her own identity as well as generates goodwill in her new home might be an ideal feminist.

This feudal mentality in both the genders is battered very badly in the American atmosphere where the lady is exposed to the freedom of the self and becomes aware of her feminine vices and virtues. The male partner receives another shock to their feudal mentality. It is hard for them to adjust to the fact and try to control the exposure to an alien atmosphere, which would imbalance the stated, laid out rules.

> "That is a good sign," Amit said, smilingly. "You're becoming American, but not too American, I hope. I don't want you to be like Mrs. Mullick and wear pants in the house!" He left the table to get a cold can of beer. He came back with the beer and a wine glass for Dimple, and

> poured her an inch of foam from his can. "Just this once," he begged. "It's a celebration, I mean, we have to celebrate my job and your Americanization, so go on, take a sip of beer." (*W*, 112)

A perfect balance between tradition and modernity is put through the character of Jasmine in *Jasmine*, who retains her values while she keeps changing identity like a chameleon and keeps pace with the American life. Her driving force is to prove the astrologer's prediction of widowhood and unhappiness false. This makes her adaptation or acculturation easier. Every time she changes her identity she is reborn and rejuvenates in her rebirth. She refuses to stagnate, and live a life of sacrifice but not be happy in it. She leaves Bud to be with Taylor in the end because of this virtue of falsifying the astrologer's predictions and the belief that nothing lasts in America: "In America, nothing lasts. I can say that now and it doesn't shock me, but I think it was the hardest lesson of all for me to learn." (*J*, 181)

The basic thing working behind this detachment is the doctrine of the *Gita* which says that nothing lasts forever. Everything comes to an end except the inner being or "Atman." It keeps on living and takes new forms to be reborn again and again. Jasmine proves the fact correct that those people survive who are resilient i.e. "survival of the fittest."

Adaptation of Bharati Mukherjee's characters undergoes continual process of transition. The transmigration covers and exemplifies a very vast periphery which is not just national but transnational. Transition is evident virtually in each of her characters which is her own self portrayed in her characters, bringing out twists and turns, mishaps and pains, the intricacies woven delicately to paint the right effect, to make her readers feel the pain which the immigrants go through, even inspire her readers to change their attitudinal problems and hesitations and sympathize with each one of the characters who struggle to create a new identity, a new home for themselves in a foreign atmosphere. Her protagonists rejuvenate in the new open atmosphere; their exhilaration is something which is infectious. The choice of being your own-self prevails over all the struggles and hurdles of life and gives a new hope. Women tend to feel guilty and this guilt is there in some of the characters like Dimple in *Wife*; the protagonists of later novels like *Jasmine*, *Holder of the World* and *Leave it to Me* seem to be a platform from where Bharati Mukherjee asserts her happiness in being an emancipated immigrant in the United States of America.

Debbie Di Martino is supposed to represent the American ethics of individualistic attitude, of taking and giving only that much which is wished by oneself. The gory details of murder and torching the house of her lover seem to be a part and parcel of life. Dangerous timing and lack of moralistic attitude features highly in Debbie's character. But still she craves to find her parents. She is not satisfied with her adopted parents. Bharati Mukherjee's realization of finding roots in America instigates her to model her protagonists on extreme feministic attitude where Debbie avenges her enemies like Goddess Kali and fights for her rights, achieves and pursues what she believes in: "What I did was torch Frankie's precious home on Saratoga Springs, Flippant Frankie was right: there are only two categories of people, those with wants, and those with needs." (*LITM*, 36)

Jasmine in *Jasmine* is a character who defies the predicament of an astrologer and lives a life of her own choice, the way she wants to. She is another example of feminity who does not annihilate her ideas and culture to live a new life; she adapts to new life with ease while retaining her old culture. Balance between the two makes her a whole person. The Indian culture, which taught her "to give," makes her live a life with disabled Bud and have his child by artificial insemination. Her adaptable mind which allows going through the artificial insemination might be revolting to an Indian mind. Hannah in *The Holder of the World* carves a niche for herself by curing people, adapts herself to a new culture and lives a life with jubilation instead of breaking down under pressure.

Dimple Dasgupta, the protagonist in *Wife*, symbolizes the basic mentality of Indian culture, which imbibes a basic fact in every girl's mind, that she has to be protected all her life, firstly by her father, then her husband and later on by children. The attitude of putting the girl under the pressure of conventional ideas that one gains freedom after marriage, warps the basic freedom of mind for Dimple. Though she is projected as an imbalanced personality right from the beginning, her attitude of freedom is warped. In America the adaptation becomes difficult and she loses her mental balance. The tug of war, to be traditional and yet have the freedom to be an individual, leads her to become imbalanced. As one critic puts it:

> Indian woman's experiences, as Mukherjee perceives them, seem to adhere to the ambiguous nature of Hinduism. She invents the term "Hindu Imagination" to describe the form she uses to shape her work and combines it with her argument for the reconstruction of the women's self. She uses the term to mean the collectivity of Hindu woman's consciousness which is ingrained within the mythical tradition that has contributed to constructing her values.[3]

Bharati Mukherjee's characters have been modulated, time to time, through her own personal experiences. The protagonists of earlier novels exhibit a conflict in character. Characters are not able to adjust in the new environment. They are like babies reborn in a new culture, not able to forget the past and apprehensive of the future, they forget to live the present. The adjustments take a valid turn either way. They assimilate or turn out to be split personalities.

Bharati Mukherjee's writing largely reflects her personal experience in crossing cultural boundaries. In novels such as *Jasmine*, *The Tiger's Daughter* and *The Holder of the World*, as well as in her award-winning short stories, Indian-born Mukherjee "adds to the authority of her [multicultural] background an acute sense of the violence and chaos, however restrained, which can lie beneath the surface of society, old or new, or of a person," explains Ann Mandel in *The Dictionary of Literary Biography*. Mandel adds: "A request for recognition—the desire to be 'visible' . . . to be recognized as person rather than as ethnic stereotype characterizes much of Mukherjee's writing, her characters sometimes cry out to be seen for who they really are; and sometimes weak or tired, they surrender to taking in the identity of the 'type' that others see them to be."[4]

A question that always arises is: why does Bharati Mukherjee take up the case of heroines who get easily ruffled by the circumstances and take to violent acts, and tend to become so violent as to kill their husband? This frustration seems to have its seeds in the author herself as she has mentioned it in her work, *Days and Nights in Calcutta*. The frustration comes out loud and clear at her own helplessness in understanding the old society she had left and the eccentricities of the new world which did not embrace her.

> And sometimes in the flickering darkness and heat of our guest room during power cuts, propelled by the same misplaced bitterness, I quarrelled with Clark, accusing him of having forced expatriation on me.

> Could he live out his life in Calcutta where he would have to learn a new language, a new way of making friends, where he could not expect his readers to understand too well intents of his fiction? (*DNC*, II, 221)

Human relationships are fragile in those continents, whether Europe or America. In India, the human relations are stable to a large extent. The stability of these relationships in India is due to the traditional virtues of our culture. In the United States of America and Canada and the Western countries, civilizational matters tend to develop, more on rational, scientific and materialistic lines.

Daughter of Mr. Bhowmick in 'A Father' in *Darkness* is the perfect example of symbolically dysfunctional Indian values in her character. Her continuous sniggering stance against the Indian values and traditions mocks the values generated. Though her father Mr. Bhowmick is unable to consider his daughter as feminine, still he is magnanimously adapted to his daughter's multifarious activities, but revolts against her decision to have a child through artificial insemination. The warped ideas of feminity do not let him accept his self-sufficient daughter. He knows that his daughter will help him if he is in need and in spite of her learning to dance and sing she is not perfect in his eyes. "Babli was not the child he would have chosen as his only heir." (*D*, 63)

The individualistic characteristics get imbibed in the children of second and third generation who are settled in the United States of America. As a result, the values of family as an institution have tended to become loose whereas in India, the family institution is still very strong. Though with globalization the attitudes have permeated into Indian lives too and they are breaking age-old traditions to give way to new thoughts and ideologies. The freedom which Dimple seeks, simply asserts the fact that she has been stifled by the various norms and values which chained her down.

> The waiter walked between tables, restless, grim, carrying nothing, she wished he would go away. He had no right to make her feel guilty. Milt was a nice person, impulsive and frank. Besides, he was Marsha Mookerji's brother, guardian spirit of the plants. Amit could not object to her having a pizza with him. (*W*, 195)

In such a situation when a human being, particularly a female, when transplanted to other countries especially to other western or European nations, gets bewildered, when faced by the free society and violent (to a certain extent) atmosphere of the United States of America, struggles to survive and to maintain a balanced attitude, one tends to have broken identities. When the expectations, which arise due to false notions, are shattered, they leave a person like Dimple in a void. She is unable to handle the violence shown on television; she is unable to decipher the fact from truth aired on media. Watching television and reading magazines seems to be the only way to penetrate the strange atmosphere and assimilate in the New World.

> It might have been on television: it was getting harder and harder to distinguish between what she had seen on TV and what she had imagined. She thought of the television set as her only friend; it was so undemanding so it gave and gave and asked nothing of her in return. (*W*, 157)

To completely get her into the mainstream of the American society, she has an extra-marital affair with Milt, who seems to be a gentleman and who understands her fragility of mind. She is in two minds—she wants to be like her ideal Sita and still is not able to take the responsibility. She craves to come out of the bondage, to be free completely but cannot handle the situation. She moves back and forth between being the ideal, and craving the freedom of Western society. The psychedelic condition leads to violence where she kills her husband. It is the only way she feels Americanized, and her way of asserting her independence by the act of violence:

> She thought how horrible to have to spend a whole lifetime watching him spill sugar on counters, how many pounds of wasted sugar that would add up to in thirty years or forty years; but she never thought of such things, never thought how hard it was for her to keep quiet and smile though she was falling apart like a very old toy that had been played with, sometimes roughly, by children who claimed to love her. (*W*, 212)

Her tired mind is belligerent and she is delirious, while, still very conscious, working with precision and attacking Amit.

But a doubt always crops up: Is Dimple supposed to be a role model for middle class girls? It is more appropriate to say that Dimple Dasgupta is not able to take a stand and balance her personality. If she had a balanced persona, she would have easily adjusted in the new atmosphere, would have been able to pinpoint the hazards of the new society, inculcated the positive points and left the things which she felt were not appropriate.

When we zero in on to the three characters of Bharati Mukherjee, namely, Jasmine in *Jasmine*, Hannah Eastern in *Holder of the World* and Debby Di Martino in *Leave it to Me*, we see a similarity and one comes to the conclusion that one has to compromise with one's own inheritance of virtues to assimilate into the New World. Though this is a very basic fact that a person who visits anyone he/she has to absorb first in order to adapt. That is to say that even when a married girl leaves her house to be in her new household she has to change herself, still retaining the good qualities which she imbibed earlier. All the three characters live a life which is beyond the norms and values of Indian lifestyle or, for that matter, denounced even by the American high class society. They are more balanced than Dimple Dasgupta, who is from a conservative background.

Dimple is always on the periphery of balance of mind and trips on to the other side of sanity. She is doomed to kill her husband. Her overactive imagination creates havoc with her senses.

> Premonitions should be accompanied by courage and caution; they are cruel in a person whose instincts have been worn down by overuse. Dimple felt helpless and old. She wished Ina had stayed though she was always miserable when Ina stayed. Ina would have known how to cope with disaster. And with the fear of disaster. But Ina could not have consoled her. That was the hateful thing about Ina; she promised happiness, independence, love, but no consolation. (*W*, 156)

Tara in *The Tiger's Daughter* seems to be more balanced due to her education in England, though her ideal in life is her father and she always feels safe and secure with him. While in India, she starts to forget the details of her husband, being in a distant land she loses her sanity under pressure though time to time she reaches out to seek help from outside, eventuating her decision to return.

Whereas Dimple forges her way into a new culture and wants desperately to get rid of her native identity, Tara Banerjee travels back to her home country and city to trace her own inherited identity. The new culture, in which she was sent at the age of 15, seems to be a little traumatic in the beginning and she seems to lose contact with reality.

> Surrounded by this army of relatives who professed to love her, and by vendors ringing bills, beggars pulling at sleeves, children coughing on tracks, Tara felt completely alone. Only the Bengal Tiger, body half turned away from her while he shouted instructions seemed to her real. (*TD*, 28)

Dimple commits murder when she aborts her child. It's like an act of freedom and she does not regret it, to the extent that she justifies it as a hurdle from old world. Early pregnancy in her case seems to enchain her freedom. Marriage to her is a road to freedom, an intermediary, through which she can have a new life, a new beginning. "It's not like murder," Dimple said one afternoon in June, "I could never commit murder." (*W*, 42)

Dimple is ambitious and cannot let anyone in her way of achieving a life of her dreams in America. It seems a step to free life. One can easily compare this act to the act of murder which Lady Macbeth plans in order to fulfill her ambition of seeing her husband as the king and herself as a strong, rich lady. She instigates her husband to kill. Consequently, the murder drives her to insanity and she feels her hands having spots of blood on them. She keeps rubbing them together to wash away the spots but fails to do so. She becomes an insomniac and sleepwalks, talking to herself.

> Out, damned spot! Out, I say! One, two; why then 'tis time to do't. Hell is murky. Fie, my lord, fie! A soldier, and afraid? What need we fear who knows it, when none call our power to account? Yet who would have thought the old man to have had so much blood in him?[5]

She is unable to handle the guilt and in the end dies. To be in Lady Macbeth's position is not what Bharati Mukherjee has in mind. Dimple is driven to the brink by her own ambition and is caught in the web of being a dutiful wife, yet wanting the free life of America. The result could have been different. If Dimple were in India, she would have committed suicide, or would be driven to insanity like Lady Macbeth in Shakespeare's *Macbeth*. But for all her efforts to assimilate America drains her off and in her frustration to equipoise her mind and soul, she commits the murder. Her only way to freedom is by killing whereas for Jasmine, in *Jasmine*, killing becomes a necessity to maintain sanity. She avenges her rapist, reconciles and moves forward because the driving force behind Jasmine is to commit self-immolation in America where her husband wanted to go. The intention is very different because Jasmine loves her husband enough to commit "Sati." Prakash moulded her, and released the chains for her to have a life, which was different from that which she had in her parents' house. The confidence given to her by her husband helps her to lead a balanced life because she has faced the basic realities of life.

Dimple is not aware of the realities because throughout the novel she lives in a world of dream. She has her own world of fantasy. She fantasizes a world away from her own reality. Her husband is more in her fantasies than reality and she has to painstakingly make an effort to not to visualize him as other than what he is, in order to restore her sanity.

> She watched Amit intently so that she could remember how he ate, how his fingers—he had hairs on two joints of each finger—curled around the fried rice and made firm little balls, how his chin worked up and down quickly and his mouth made little noises, how he spat out the lemon peel and chicken bones. She wanted to remember him exactly as he was—not as a face on TV or in an ad but as a very solid person. (*W*, 166-67)

Devi is an orphan, discarded by her parents, and leads a very different life, but the fact is that she is human and she craves to know her identity, yet she is a rule unto herself.

Hannah Easton in *The Holder of the World*, compared to Dimple, is a whole character who has a balanced disposition. She faces the situation of being discarded by parents, marries a conman, and goes to India to escape the puritan American life of Massachusetts, to be the mistress of a king in India, to finally return home as a more mature and understanding personality. She can now fathom her own culture in a broader perspective. Her love for Raja gives her the courage and audacity to go to Aurangzeb's tent to plead Raja's case and her self-empowerment is like the Goddess who can endure any pain to restore her lover.

> The night that Hannah was consigned to the zenana, the women's rooms, as a wife but no more than a wife, she had a vision. The life inside her compelled it; she would offer her life, if necessary, to end the war. Only a person outside the pale of the two civilizations could do it.

> Only a woman, a pregnant woman, a pregnant white woman, had the confidence or audacity to try it. (*HW*, 259)

Each character of Bharati Mukherjee displays innate qualities of humanity, "duality in personality" being a prime target to be analyzed on the basis of Hindu doctrines which seems to be ingratiated into the seams of each plot. This is a factor which is visible in reality and each human has it in his character.

Ann Mandel says that characters of Bharati Mukherjee sometimes cry out to be seen and judged as they are and other times it might be that they take on the identities which are approved by others. Her characters, like those of the later novels, change and take on life headlong. Concept of dualism is an ideology extracted from the Vedas and the *Bhagvad Gita* where each person is bound to have a duality in his personality—one which is meant for one's own self, and the other, which can be categorically analysed as behavioural attitude. "The duality of the material world is felt in terms of heat and cold, or misery and happiness."[6]

Dualism is a factor which exists in each and every mortal being and is evident in each character of Bharati Mukherjee, be it Dimple, Jasmine, Hannah Easton or Devi. As a writer, Mukherjee has claimed a special legacy for herself. She calls it the colonial writers' "legacy" of "duality," the "learned" ability "to be two things simultaneously; to be the dispossessed as well as the dispossessor."[7]

Here one can cite the example of Hamlet—the protagonist of Shakespeare's play *Hamlet, Prince of Denmark* whose indecisive attitude and prejudice lead him to his downfall like Dimple Dasgupta in *Wife*.

> To be, or not to be—that is the question;
> Whether 'tis nobler in the mind to suffer
> The slings and arrows of outrageous fortune,
> Or to take arms against a sea of troubles,
> And by opposing end them?[8]

The later characters of Bharati Mukherjee are more determined and strong-headed, characters like Devi, Jasmine, Hannah Easton, who are way off from characters like Dimple Dasgupta and Tara who exist in psychedelic conditions. Devi hurtles forward destroying each impediment out of her way, perplexed and hesitant in the beginning but sure and determined later on, to achieve her goal of finding her biological parents. Nothing can stop this inbuilt hurricane. Her belief is that when one does not inherit anything the whole universe is hers for asking. Her belief in herself leads her to transformations and adjustments at various stages in her journey, and each hurdle builds up a new force with which she continues to fight her way to victory. Though she seems a hard nut to crack, there are moments when we come across a Devi with sensibilities which are ruffled and lead to slaying of demons. Devi, with her individualistic attitude towards life, can be seen defending a corpse from being degraded and her own self-respect taking a priority when she avenges her boyfriend's insensitivity.

The inhuman behaviour on the part of the male counterparts comes across with clarity, that men can destroy without their sensibility being involved and this is a fact which one comes across again and again in Bharati Mukherjee's characters. People like Loco Larry, who is a victim of Vietnam war, can get avenged. Frankie, to establish himself as an immigrant in America, can go to any extent and can be insensitive and use anyone to achieve his dream. He never really meant to get married to Devi. Contrary to this, the liberated sensibilities of Americanism are bought out with aplomb in the character of Ham. Knowingly, or unknowingly, he is dating Devi as well as Devi's bio-mom. One finds the situation hilarious from the American point of view, and it is pathetic when it is seen from the Indian immigrant's point of view, people still holding on to their cultural traditions and views.

The female characters not only have to fight to get rooted but they have to face the gender difference, the cultural differences and the choices are theirs to make. Jasmine would have easily reverted to her decision to commit suicide, and after rape she had more reasons to do so because for a village girl for whom "adoption" and "widow remarriage" are something alien, instead she chooses to survive, as she realizes that she is in this world to do something and she cannot leave with unfinished business, emphasizing the philosophies of "Holy Gita."

The father in "A Father" tries to be an epitome of virtues and tries to adapt himself to the ways of his wife and Americanised daughter. He is unable to come to terms with the fact that his daughter is having a child through artificial insemination. The idea is so revolting to him that he hits her, emphasizing the fact that the only solution to a problem in American life is violence, or to kill himself in Indian style. While he magnanimously allows his daughter and wife to dominate him into docility, the eruption of his feelings results in hitting his own child. The right to win, to assert apparently leads to a conflict of mind and finally, the belief in his own ideas and the Indian mental set up overcomes his struggle to be American, and he ends up beating his daughter. This "existence in dualism," of wanting to be something and still not wholly committed to it, leads him to the same consequence as Dimple in *Wife*.

> There was no question of going back where he'd come from. He hated Ranchi. Ranchi was no place for dreamers. All through his teenage years, Mr. Bhowmick had dreamed of success abroad. What form that success would take he had left vague. Success had meant to him escape from the constant plotting and bitterness that wore out India's middle class. (*W*, 65)

Still Mr. Bhowmick is unable to embrace American lifestyle completely. The submerging of emotions takes a toll. Having child through artificial insemination is quite accepted in India though the Indian beliefs or rather policy of dualism cannot let him accept it. What he accepts outside his home is unacceptable and abhorred by him when he is faced by it.

The Oxford dictionary's meaning of "Duality" is a theory recognizing two independent principles (mind and matter) idealism and materialism; good and evil in the universe; two personalities in Christ.

Precisely, this is what is happening with each character and for that matter it is true about mortals, but for Jasmine, whose sole ambition to self-immolate takes her to America where she slays her rapist, adjusts with all types of situations and conditions, yet keeping her mind focused on living life on her own terms. There is a vast difference between the girl who lives in a village and the woman she transforms into. The defiance in her is evident right from the beginning when she smells the stench of a dead dog and the mark on her forehead is like the third eye.

The "third eye" signifies the opening of mind, of knowledge as in Hinduism. Her marriage to Prakash leads to her transformation from a coarse village girl Jyoti into Jasmine:

> *Pygmalion* wasn't a play I'd seen or read then, but I realize how much of Professor Higgins there was in my husband. He wanted to break down the Jyoti I'd been in Hasanpur and make me a new kind of city woman. To break off the past, he gave me a new name: Jasmine. He said, "you are small and sweet and heady, my Jasmine you'll quicken the whole world with your perfume." (*J*, 77)

Jasmine seems to forage through her destiny and she is guided towards new horizons and she embraces each opportunity thrown her way and each event is celebratory for her. She has no hassle in staying with Bud who is an invalid. She is pregnant with Bud's child and yet she leaves with Taylor to find new happiness. She does not stagnate for one moment because traditional beliefs do not bind her. She revolts against leading a life of a widow in her village. Instead she chooses to go to America which is a journey into flow of life. Jasmine changes identities and flows with it. The cravings for the unknown make her reach out and grab.

> Jyoti would have saved, but Jyoti was now a Sati-goddess; she had burned herself in a trash-can funeral pyre behind a boarded up motel in Florida. Jasmine lived for the future, for Vijh and wife. Jasmine went to movies and lived for today. In my closet hung satin blouses with vampish necklines, in my dresser lingerie I was too shy to wear in a room I shared with Duff. (*J*, 176)

Comparatively the same transformations seem inadequate in the case of Dimple Dasgupta in *Wife*. Her assertion of freedom takes a different voyage altogether. Her life transforms too, and there are different phases of her change and the inculcated ideologies of being an ideal wife misfires. Dimple craves for freedom but remains enchained to her ideologies. She keeps craving for what she does not have and it proves to be self-immolation in itself. Her attitude does not let her forego the consequences of her actions. Her attempt at freedom leads her to Milt but her guilt of her action makes her decide not to further it. The comparison of her husband with her imaginary ideals doesn't let her advance her relationship with Amit, whereas Jasmine stays and nurtures Bud Ripplemeyer satisfying his demands, being a lover and a wife, and a mother to Du. She is pregnant with Bud's child through artificial insemination and is comfortable with her situation. Naturally her instinct to survive in any situation makes life celebratory for her.

> Bud has changed my life. I am grateful. I am carrying his child. I want to tell him that when I was a girl in Hasnapur, only playboys in Bombay movies wore bathrobes, dark glasses, whisky, cigarettes: these were shorthand for glamour that we Hasnapuris were meant not to have. I have triumphed. But how can I explain such small odd triumphs to Bud? (*J*, 231)

Mr. Bhowmick's ideologies seem antipathetic to Jasmine's, and he retaliates in hitting his daughter with a rolling pin. "Rolling Pin" seems very significant because generally women are associated with a rolling pin and there is a role reversal where the father is unable to adjust to the idea of his daughter having a child through artificial insemination whereas the mother protests against the father hitting his daughter. The mother is more of modern ideas but yet her old culture is omnipresent even if she denies the very existence of an unnatural baby. 'Like animals' his wife said. For the first time he heard horror in her voice." (*J*, 73)

Evidently, Jasmine in *Jasmine*, Devi in *Leave it to Me* and Hannah Easton in *The Holder of the World* have the initial hesitation but no qualms as such, in flowing with life, changing and transforming as life demands. This itself brings a new perspective on Bharati Mukherjee's own change of thoughts and ideologies, her decision to be an immigrant and be a part of the majority instead of being constantly branded as the "other."

Dimple goes through the assimilation times over, when she gets married, when she skips through her pregnancy, her extra-marital affair with Milt Glasser, the last attempt being the most convenient path into Americanization but for her moral set up, she is unable to go through fully into being herself. She wants to find her own identity but is conscious about behavioural conduct. Even before she could settle in her marriage, accept and understand Amit, she is thrown into a totally alien culture where she craves for Amit's understanding but is faced with male chauvinism. Though she craves for and tries to enfold everything into her being with eagerness, she bounces back everything into abyss of age-old habits and goes overboard.

> She felt that Amit was waiting for just the right answer, that it was up to her to uphold Bengali womanhood, marriage and male pride. The right answer, 'I do not need stimulants to feel happy in my husband's presence . . . my obligation is to my husband,' seemed to dance before her eyes as though it were printed on a card. (*W*, 78)

Basically, the protagonists of Bharati Mukherjee's novels are a mixed bundle of Hindu feminism. Influences of incarnations of "Sita" and "Kali" come through forcefully into their beings, still there is always a human tinge of imbalance, which tends to tip-over the brim if not handled with extra care. Not a single character can be defined on a traditional pattern of set rules because each one has been given a multi-dimensional facet to their personality and therefore to judge their predicaments is difficult and the reader seems to be in a lackadaisical situation. Each character seems to be an epitome of feminism but to put them on the pedestal of feminine idols is a mistake on our part as readers, because one tends to encounter human follies in each character immediately.

Bharati Mukherjee claims that her three novels *Jasmine*, *The Holder of the World* and *Leave it to Me* are a trilogy. As she says, "The protagonist of each novel—Jyoti/Jasmine, Hannah/ Salem Bibi, and Debby/Devi—is a strong woman who longs for a world that's more just and more generous than the one she inherited at birth. These women are also bold enough, or maybe foolhardy enough, to act out their dreams. They are idealists and romantics; and because of this they are also restless. But each woman responds in her unique way to dreams for a better life."[9]

The "lackadaisical" immediately conjures up in mind the "philosophy of duality" which is constantly being projected through the characters of Bharati Mukherjee. The very basic principle of life is to constantly adjust and adapt to lead a satisfactory life but human mind is full of dualities which lead to conflict of heart and mind, imagination and reality, and the fluidity of life, if hindered due to one's own thought process, leads to limbo. Stagnation is bound to follow creating a vacuum which may not be so easy to breach if there is lack of will power to maintain balance. To avoid this, one has to constantly adapt to new and have a carefree life. One does not need to let go off one's own thoughts and belief, but one can always make concessions for changes in life, which is the easiest way to happy life. The philosophy of life is all about moving forward, instead of clinging to some frame of mind which has been moulded to set patterns. If we go into details, a few characters in *Darkness* and Dimple Dasgupta in *Wife* seem to be an epitome of this situation.

Dimple Dasgupta is unable to handle her sensuality. When faced with the situation of expressing her emotions, Amit being of Indian male mental set-up is not able to understand her whereas she is comfortable, and yet not comfortable, with Milt Glasser.

> But Milt entered so swiftly, twisting his long elastic body and bending over her head (over the unpleasant curls of the crown), kissing her on the right cheek and saying "Hi Dimple" so softly, that she couldn't say a word.
>
> "After that, the evening fell apart for Dimple." (*W*, 122)

It does not end at this but the soul which is dissatisfied with Amit's Indian male behaviour conjures up a different feeling for Dimple and her pent-up emotions held in control, wish to ponder on the kiss in her kitchen.

> She liked kitchens, considered the ideal places for confidence. She could have spent the entire evening surrounded by canned soups, cereal boxes, glass jars of rice and pulses—the pillars of security—thinking of Milt's kisses. A kiss was never a happy event. (*W*, 123)

The discontentment is obvious and so is the mental set up of Dimple's mind. Though she has options but enchained in her thoughts and restrictions of Indian household she finds solace in kitchen, her security being cereal boxes and jars of rice, yet she wants to break free within the security of her traditional bondings imagining details about a peck on the cheek by a stranger.

The simple sentence that "a kiss was never a happy event" brings forth the conjugal happiness that she does not have with Amit. Her frustrations are evident and she in spite of herself, wishes a repeat performance by Milt. "At the door, when she saw Milt Glasser getting ready to leave and monkeying around with Ina Mullick, Dimple wondered if he were about to give her a good night kiss." (*W*, 127)

The burden of compromising with situation of lack of marital bliss is again evident in Hannah Easton's married life with Gabriel Legge in *The Holder of the World*. Gabriel is involved in his own adventures and his tales lure Hannah to travel to India but like Dimple, Hannah's senses are not sated. She has her fantasies which exist in her dreams. "She kept a journal of events, protection against a jealous husband's ferocity. Though her embroidery and much later through her stealthily penned MEMOIRS, she revealed to herself her deepest secrets. She was without Gabriel's company for weeks at a time while he toured." (*HW*, 128)

Though there is a difference: Hannah Easton in *The Holder of the World* has the courage to disown her husband when she becomes aware of his infidelity with his black bibi. The knowledge about her husband transforms her life. "We might call the explosion, the attendant shame and the arrogant visit of the bibi a very loud wake-up call, a sign to Hannah that tolerance and patience and even a pragmatic trade-off between luxury and uncertainty were no longer bearable." (*HW*, 198)

Contrary to this, to transform and assert herself Dimple has to literally butcher her husband with a kitchen knife to death. The knife again is a weapon from her kitchen which is her place of "freedom."

Jasmine's life is transformed with the murder of her husband and Devi's life takes a new turn when she finds about her parents not being her biological parents. Quest for self leads to transformations with a difference in each of the characters of Bharati Mukherjee.

Transformation is omnipresent in *The Middleman and Other Stories*, as characters from different Asian countries celebrate their Americanism, especially the second generation who are totally into the American society and have gained freedom on their own terms, particularly Panna in "A Wife's Story" and Maya Sanyal in "The Tenant." Maya is a naturalized American and leads a life which is promiscuous by Indian standards but yet she is jubilant and free. Panna is free from the bounds of Indian in-laws and enjoys her freedom. She is magnanimous to her husband but refuses to return with her husband to India and lose whatever she has in America, "freedom" being the foremost.

The basic exercise behind the transformations is to cross the periphery of being minority in America, instead of melting into the culture to become one with America. Adaptation to new, instead of clinging to the past leads each character to live a life according to their own beliefs. Some pass through very easily whereas few characters especially in *Darkness* (another collection of short stories) are hung up with the strings left behind and like Dimple in *Wife*, life is abnormal for them where they want to cut off the umbilical cord but are not able to sever the threads swiftly.

Nafeesa Hafez in "The Lady from Lucknow" tries to be an American but falters when snubbed by the wife of her lover. "She sat on my side of the bed. She stared at me. If that stare had made me feel secretive and loathsome, I might not have wept later." (*D*, 33)

The different shades in characters of *Darkness* depict the pain of people trying to assimilate into the mainstream, where each character has a different experience to relate, whereas the characters of *The Middleman and Other Stories* are full of individuals who are already there or are trying to achieve their dreams.

Assimilation is not very easy. The feeling of isolation is apparent for being in a new world and a new culture, but so is the isolation inside each one of the characters. People around in the real world are also isolated because each one is searching for something which can make them a whole.

Each one of Bharati Mukherjee's characters seems to be precariously balanced on a tight-rope in case they fall. In order to balance between the beliefs of old culture, which seems binding in the new environment, and the New World which offers new horizons to these enchained souls, they take new course with each character. Dimple in *Wife* is unable to handle the pressure whereas Jasmine juggles through each new avenue with flourish. It seems easy for Jasmine but Jasmine has nothing to lose. She enters the new world as Goddess Kali who had avenged the onslaught on her. Dimple aborts her child in order to gain freedom in the New world yet does not have the grit to find a foothold for herself because she is always insecure and dependent on Amit Basu to offer freedom on the platter of marriage. Naturally the husband becomes an adversary when he is not as per her fantasies.

Reality is something which is missing in Dimple's life. Contrary to this, Hannah's mind is fragile too, due to the fact that her mother leaves with her Nipmuc Indian lover and Hannah marries a man who is too involved in his own self, yet she is firmly rooted and finds a way to have a life which transforms and satisfies her. "And having seen India, and America, Hannah knew she could never be content in England." (*HW*, 156)

Various coincidences weave a path for Hannah Easton—her husband supposedly being drowned in the cyclone (though his death is not revealed), his infidelities and new alliance with Bhagmati and her community empower Hannah Easton to have an affair with Indian culture and Indian Rajput king. Her passions are realized and she transforms. Fakhrul Alam says:

> Hannah Easton has, in effect, entered the world of romance, and true to the logic of romance, she now is going to have the grand affair of her life with the raja. No doubt Rebecca Easton's plunge into the arms of her Nipmuc Indian lover had made her similarly heady and disdainful of restraint and reason, for Hannah now abandons herself to the India King.[10]

It's not that Hannah does not have her reservations. Being a victim of fate and machinations makes her reticent in making a swift decision about Raja yet she seems to be attracted to him. Her elaborate description about the physical beauty of Raja makes one interpret that she falls in love with the Raja at the first sight. The wantonness of senses is unusual for Hannah who is used to the abstinence that she maintained with her husband. But meeting the Raja, her sensuality gives vent to her feelings in her full-fledged participation in her affair with Raja. She is like Jasmine in her later stage of life while her earlier dwindling can be compared to that of Dimple in *Wife*. "For what it's worth, the Lady pushed the Lion of Devgad down on the carpet alive with lion hunters grasping griffins with amber manes. The Lion trembled under her touch at first, and then, as though he too was under a spell, submitted to her slow deliberate caresses." (*HW*, 229)

The seductress in Hannah Easton is like a volcano which finds its way into her mind, body and soul and her quest for self-realization is realized with the Raja. She is not enchained to the duality of mind and heart but both are one and the same and the decision is in favour of her saviour, the Raja.

> Before this longing, she had conceived of emptiness as absence, detectable only by the circumference within which it was contained. Now the void became a pleasureful pain, subsuming all the old Salem virtues, such as duty and compassion. She wanted the Raja and touch nothing else, she would sacrifice anything for his touch and the love they made. (*HW*, 229)

Jasmine has no inhibitions in making love to Bud Ripplemeyer though her intention is to give pleasure to Bud and she is the dominant partner. "When we first met and began making love in my rented room and in the motel rooms of neighbouring towns, he was active and inventive, very sure of himself, he loved games. Now I must do all the playing, provide the surprises. I don't mind." (*J*, 36)

This is Jyoti of Hasnapur who survived her mother's sniping, who refused to lead a life like a cattle in her village, and who has been predicted to be a widow. The transformation is colossal in its magnitude. "I survived the sniping. My grandmother may have named me Jyoti, Light, but in surviving I was already Jane, a fighter and adapter." (*J*, 40)

Devi in *Leave it to Me* has no qualms in having a relationship with a man who is also involved with her bio-mom. "Okay, I heard myself say, I wanted to say, Hey, you're a widow! Daddy's dead, no fear he'll pop up and ruin your life. We know what men who've shared that same woman are like, but what are women who've shared the same man like?" (*LITM*, 152)

Throughout the novel *Wife*, the protagonist Dimple tries to jettison out of her old life and old beliefs to merge into the New World but she is fickle-minded. Every time she dwindles back to her original stance because the basic notion, ideas, the basic grounding seem to go haywire on the new turf. Her conflict to be like Sita, still trying to slay her fears like 'Kali' and step out into the new world goes awry. "Sita" is her childhood idol. Indeed, every girl-child is groomed to be virtuous and patient like Sita who is an epitome of patience and sacrifice. Dimple ends up in a quagmire of mixed emotions. She is frustrated and never satisfied with the life she has because she always craves for something of which she is afraid simultaneously. The major crux of the problem is that she is not as good a juggler of emotion between new and old as Jasmine or Hannah or for that matter Devi, born and brought up in a traditional conservative

Hindi Bengali family does not allow her to give in to the freedom of senses she craves. She is unable to mutate her weakness into strength as Jasmine does. She is unable to cross the "Lakshman-rekha" though she tries to step out of it, she again finds solace behind the line. Here she fears her husband's disapproval and what rumours would be generated in Calcutta.

Once she thought she almost had him in a Dewar's profile:

> Amit Kumar Basu
> Home: New York City (or should she cancel that and put Calcutta)
> Age: Twenty Nine
> Profession: Mechanical Engineer
> Hobbies: Cricket, also rearing parrots.
> Last Accomplishment: Decision to emigrate.
> Quote: Husbands should not permit their wives to wear pants. A healthy society and mutual respect are based on the clear distinction between the appearances and the functions of the sexes. (*W*, 160)

The cynical attitude in Dimple for her husband is evident as she becomes aware of the fact that instead of gaining freedom, marriage is an institution which bonds a wife to function around the peripheries, the centre being the husband. The demolishing of her dreams and the effort to break free weakens Dimple to the extent that she starts hallucinating and conjures up variety of fantasies which is pathetic, yet a reality encountered by every female.

Hannah Easton is faced with the jealousies of her husband. Her virtue is questioned every time Gabriel returns from his voyages. Her efforts are to save her marriage. Like a dutiful wife she crochets and does her needlework or socializes with the wives of the British officers. She does not prefer to meet chief factor or any male officer in the absence of Gabriel Legge. "She remained within the protective magic circle she had drawn for herself." (*HW*, 179)

The line drawn in Hannah's case is self-imposed whereas for Dimple it is something imposed by her husband. It is like a master who is controlling Dimple and he lets loose the strings a little bit, for his own ego which makes him magnanimous towards his wife from time to time and the ironic fact is that his magnanimity extends only in the presence of social groups. "Dimple did not drink any of the Liebfraumilch. If Amit had not been there she thought she might have permitted herself a sip or two. But Amit would always be there beside her in his shiny conscience and common sense." (*W*, 126)

This attitude evinces the Indian male hegemonic mentality pertaining to the basic instinct to rule. This mentality broadens a little bit in their American counterparts where Taylor in *Jasmine* is benevolent enough to accept pregnant Jasmine. Though the relationship is open, one cannot impose on the rights of the other.

Adverse conditions faced by the female characters in the novels of Bharati Mukherjee are faced, with clarity in case of Hannah Easton, with ferocity by Devi and resilience to survive by Jasmine. Likewise the characters in her short stories have varied experiences and they face the condition and mutation, for some emerge triumphant, whereas others due to preconceived notion end up in a bizarre situation. Someone like Dimple ends up in a bloody quagmire. Naturally, Hannah Easton wonders about "Sita" in *The Holder of the World*, her mental condition while in her imprisonment, while being burnt in a fire and still being outcasted during pregnancy. The female emancipation must have been felt by the Queen while being banished from the kingdom and being asked to prove her chastity again and again.

The transgression is more emphatic as the female characters in *The Holder of the World* cross the border of "self" by giving in to their sexuality and again there is a role-reversal where Hannah surrenders to Raja Jadav Singh, becoming his white bibi, whereas Bhagmati still cherishes the memories of Henry Hedges. Naturally, Hannah Easton is full of wonder; the immensity of self-empowered "Sita" perplexes her sensibilities.

Accepting her fate is what makes Jasmine a survivor. Hannah accepts her fate though she is aghast at first. She is unable to reconcile with the fact that she is still washed up in India while trying to escape,

> "This is no country for Christians!" she cried. This was not the place she wished to be entombed. But where could she run to? She saw the folly of a governess's job in Cambridge. There would surely be no welcome there for a pirate's widow, and no place in old Salem for an Indian lover's daughter. (*HW*, 215)

Perturbed at her audacity to have had sexual relation with Milt Glasser, Dimple retrieves whatever is left of her conscience and takes solace behind the walls of her so-called virtues. The guilt of prevarication does not let her sleep with Milt. Though the continuous pestering on the part of Amit makes her revolt, she wanted to shock him into reaction every time but she gets more stressed than her husband.

> Dimple wondered if this was a good time to tell him that she had seduced Milt Glasser and that if it had not been for the project assessor—there was always an assessor lurking in the dead ends of her life—she might have been sleeping with Milt on a regular basis, like some of the wives on soap operas, and leading an exciting double life and nearing a bad end. (*W*, 211)

The frame of mind, with which she marries Amit, is to gain freedom through marriage. She spreads out her wings but soon finds that it is all a hoax. Her expectations are shattered. She does not have a fulfilling married life. She has no self-expression and self-suppression is continuously hoarding away all the energy in Dimple. The struggle to get right calculation in life is something which bewilders another character of Bharati Mukherjee, that is, Tara of *The Tiger's Daughter* who is unable to become independent. She is unable to shed away her childhood insecurities and her wall of protection is her father, Bengal Tiger. Education seems to be a primary factor which gives a sense of self-dependency but if we go through all the characters we come to the conclusion that it is determination that makes one independent. If education is a necessity then the characters like Dimple Dasgupta in *Wife* and Tara Cartwright in *The Tiger's Daughter* are better educated than Jasmine, Hannah Easton and Devi. If we look closely at the social strata of these characters, Tara and Dimple come from high middle class society but a conservative one where a girl child is protected till the time she is married whereas the society to which Jasmine belongs is strict village society where a girl child is considered a curse. Devi is brought up by foster-parents whereas Hannah Easton's mother leaves with her lover to have a life which she wants. The rigours gone through by Devi, Jasmine and Hannah Easton are a result of the fact that they have lost whatever they perceived to protect and they no longer have anything to lose. There are no strings of attachment so they go and embrace what life has to offer. Naturally Devi claims that when one has not been given anything then everything belongs to her.

The self-efficiency which comes from within oneself is lacking in Dimple and Tara. They blame the rest of the world for changing but they do not realize that the flaw of character emanates from their very own being. Amit becomes a target because he is the subjugating stimuli whereas Tara gets bewildered and cannot judge the slimy politician and is raped.

The decision to sleep with Milt or Tara being raped by a slimy politician is in a way projection of their momentary flow towards the unknown. Milt is exotic for Dimple, the craving for freedom though is a longing from a very early time but yet to let loose is a difficult decision. It seems that Dimple wants the endorsement of her husband whereas the over-protectiveness of Tara's life does not make her better judge of a situation or an impending danger in the company of Tuntunwala. To assert her independence, which is expected of her, being married to a foreigner, seems to make her falter like a baby who is learning to walk. It seems that Tara belongs to a century where ladies are cosseted and waited upon and it is literally her background in Calcutta, in a parental home, she is coveted like a princess. Dimple is a victim of fantasies and refuses to be realistic.

> She considered herself a master of situations in which passions are discreetly restrained. Ina, Dimple knew, would either have led the man to the deep, brown sofa or shoved him out in the hall when he showed her the decal. That was the trouble with people like Leni and Ina who believed in frankness, happiness and freedom; they lacked tolerance, and they abhorred discussions about the weather. (*W*, 161)

The craving to be like Ina Mullick is evident profusely when she talks about self-restraint. Her upbringing might and do make her reticent yet the craving to be free from chains of morality is primeval. To taste the new is something which outcasted Adam and Eve from Garden of Eden because Satan is lurking around the corner and takes over the moment one's guards are down and in case of Dimple to gain freedom is a perpetual habit which develops into psychological blockage. Both Tara and Dimple are given to moments of terror. Their imagination plays havoc on their senses and they see trouble where there is none. Caught in the web of their own making, they do not step out of the stupendous dreams. The situation is vitiated by the simple facts surrounding them, Amit in case of Dimple in *Wife* and the father in case of Tara in *The Tiger's Daughter*. This same vicious circle of traditions and beliefs is discarded by Jasmine so that she can lead a life of her own choice.

> In a bizarre sort of way, Jasmine is released from her traditional identity as a de-sexed widow soon after she arrives in America, for in being raped by Half-Face, murdering him, and walking out of the scene of the crime in full possession of herself, she has already transgressed all the norms she would have expected to live by.[11]

Characters of Bharati Mukherjee are constantly fighting in order to exist in a world of "Otherness." This "otherness" cannot be limited to New Culture but the constant fight is within their own identity. It is constantly the question of self/other, that is to say, the mutation outside triggers a chain reaction within the soul of each character and they are busy fathoming each given situation. The question is to find oneself or give way to the "Other" to capture and control. In case of Dimple, it is a constant fight within—the bonded and enchained Dimple who wants freedom and Amit acts as stimuli, which exacerbates the whole phenomenal problem. The spirit within is unable to give voice to her thoughts.

The fight to control "self" to refrain and restrain the natural instincts of sensuality, dreams and expectations from marriage, would not have been so difficult for Dimple, if she had remained in India. But when faced with the "Other" that is to say America and its open society expedites the hunger in Dimple to refashion her "self" and the amalgamation is not easy. To give voice to her suppressed feeling is not so easy for her because the grooming of "self" has been in a rigid society which considers the act as abhorring. The only way to gain freedom from this fight of duality (which constantly goes on between her heart and her mind) finds its way by stabbing Amit.

> It was only the pre-infidelity stage that was difficult, she'd learned, because there were no rules for that phase. Individual initiative, that's what it came down to, and her life had been devoted only to pleasing others, not herself. Amit had no idea how close she had come to betray-

> ing him completely and not just paying the price for too much fear and loneliness. (*W*, 211)

Her act in killing Amit is more like relinquishing of her "self." Her reincarnation, in a way, exonerates herself from the bondage of repression, the self blending with the "Other" where the other embraces her and gives voice to her feelings. One wonders if Dimple could hold herself in her new freedom or would she end up in an asylum due to the de-ranged thought-filled brain, which does not distinguish between fantasy and reality. Now with all impediments out of the way, she lives a life with Milt or anyone she wishes to be with. But is she attuned into the new world which is crowded with immigrants like Maya Sanyal, who is a free bird yet wants to marry another Indian immigrant?

One needs to wonder what if the novel had continued and, we could have known the fate of Dimple in the New World, but the author ends the novel with the notion that Dimple has finally entered the world of America with watching television and "women on television got away with murder." (*W*, 213)

The new refashioned Dimple is more like "Sita," her idol, refusing to bow down for the second time, and prove her chastity in order to be accepted in the society. However, the circumstances are different. The first time her exile was in the kingdom of the ten-headed demon king whereas being banished in the jungle while pregnant, she is exiled to lead a life with the saints. The long-drawn subjugating factor in Dimple's life is now banished because instead of finishing herself, she in order to resurrect herself, has finished the distress in her life. The question arises: "Couldn't Dimple have taken divorce or left Amit?"

But again, does she have the courage? The decision to kill is in a frenzied state of mind which is momentous. It is not planned. Jasmine kills Half-Face, her rapist, but in a Hindu household where male populace is nurtured with the sole purpose of being the dominant sex, Dimple is unable to retaliate in any other way. She, in a way, has been mentally raped, knowingly or unknowingly, by Amit Basu because he is not able to understand his wife. His purpose in America is to mint money, save it and go back to India to lead a comfortable life.

Juxtaposing the two idols of feminine goddess in Indian culture, "Sita" and "Kali," Bharati Mukherjee is trying to bring out the prominent elements of duality existent in each human mind. "Sita" signifies or rather is an embodiment of patience, love, sacrifice and total surrender of identity for the love of her husband; she is the ultimate virtue incarnated in Hindu mythology. "Kali," being an embodiment of empowered self, a mother, a protector, and in order to protect slays demons and wears the garland of severed heads. Kali's anger is subdued only when she steps on her husband. Both signify the power of women, the intense rigours that are needed for a woman to have a life of her own. "Goddess" is a term which projects the idea that virtues are beyond the human reach. But the basic idea is self-empowerment, which is essential for any human being and one can equipoise between the characteristics and the blending can produce characters like Jasmine and Hannah Easton. Imbalance in personality leads to someone like Dimple and extremities of character can give birth to Frankensteins like Devi but Bharati Mukherjee has managed to maintain the fluidity of each character. Each character has been sustained in a manner that each possesses the characteristics of the above-mentioned idols. It only seems that the male counterparts lack the qualities and they only take out their frustrations by beating and yelling and proving the point that they dictate in order to dominate. The fact is that the male characters of Indian origin have not been given a very strong footage, whereas the American males are shown as being tolerant and broad-minded which attracts the attention of women who come from a culture where they are considered menial. "Dimple laughed at the suggestion, 'I'm sure he wouldn't do laundry! He hasn't washed a hanky in his life. I wouldn't let him.'" (*W*, 70)

The Prologue to *Leave it to Me* is all about Goddess Kali, the demon slayer and saviour of humanity, which empowers Devi who hurtles forward with the sole purpose of discovering her bio-parents. Self-gratification is a characteristic which can be admired in Devi, and Dimple craves it but does not possess because the self-effacing and self-exaltation characteristics in her personality are entwined together to produce a confused Dimple.

The self-consciousness is an intricate part of Dimple's personality which proves to be self-destructive. The forced self-abnegation is not sustained for a very long time. This same self-abnegating attitude empowers the self-educated Hannah Easton and it is the basis of her self-confidence which helps her to spread her wings and the self-mutation is easy. Refashioning of Jyoti into Jasmine and the several incarnations that she undergoes are again born out of self-assertiveness of a one time self-effacing Jyoti. The assistance of Prakash, Jyoti's husband, transforms her into Jasmine but the efforts are terminated in the midst due to Prakash's murder, but as she reaches America, raped and mutilated, Jasmine's self-sustenance prepares her for the life in America. Self-persistence transforms her into Jane and finally into Jase who leaves everything in spite of self-recriminations to have a life with her lover. The transformation is of "self" and an empowered self is persistently enhanced with each character.

> It isn't guilt that I feel, it's relief. I realize I have already stopped thinking myself as Jane. Adventure, risk, transformation: the frontier is pushing indoors through uncaulked windows. Watch me re-position the stars, I whisper to the astrologer who floats cross-legged above my kitchen stove. (*J*, 240)

She is not choosing between men but as her own wish she is trying to choose a life of contentment instead of resentment.

To many, the characters of Bharati Mukherjee can be feminists to some extent, but they are not only feminists but also very realistic, humane and down to earth characters which we come across in our daily life. They are not just a projection of a writer's mind but they seem to live and breathe amongst us. They are feminine, fragile yet have the zest to achieve what they want to. There are few exceptions like Dimple who goes haywire. Tara in *The Tiger's Daughter* to Devi in *Leave it to Me*, Dimple Dasgupta in *Wife* to Hannah Easton in *The Holder of the World* are, or seem to be, a part of the author's early and late life, first as an expatriate and then as an immigrant, Jasmine of *Jasmine* being the adjoining juncture rather than the transit character which seems to balance the character of early and later novels. Jasmine is a mixture of characteristics of both "Sita" and "Kali" flaunting and balancing the inculcated ideologies; she is an epitome of feminism and a human being who knows her mind; her achievements through sheer self-determination are applaudable.

Jasmine lives her life with a zest and a hunger to survive. She makes decision with an open mind but lives a life which can give happiness to her. She leaves Bud after a lot of hesitation and self-recriminations but her belief to flow with life does not let her stay back and stagnate. Her defiance apparently, is her self-determination to survive. She refuses to live the life of a widow, and the aim to self-immolate herself in America pushes her into a new world and the hindrances cannot deter her from her goal. The zeal to live embarks primarily in the mind and the spark of revolt makes her defy all the norms of society and nature. "I have had a husband for each of the women I have been. Prakash for Jasmine, Taylor for Jase, Bud for Jane, Half-Face for Kali." (*J*, 147)

Jyoti, the village girl, widow of Prakash, would not have predicted or visualized the future, what the life would be in America because she had not thought of any life in America. It was death and self-immolation which she had perceived in America.

The characters of Bharati Mukherjee are not, and do not seem at all, fictitious but they are like one of us leading and living realities, going through the pain and torture (mental and physical), and rejoice in happiness like a commoner. Most of them belong to the upper class society. These characters are from various other Asian countries, who are trying to blend into the mainstream of America—hispanics, expatriates and immigrants.

The minor characters, though they do not seem to be minor, are like hinges in the cart-wheel, though their effeminate behaviour somehow seems out of place, as the life-size female counterpart domineers the entire scenario.

Characters like Dr. Rab Chatterjee in "The Tenant" or Mr. Bhowmick in "A Father" are people who believe in taking but never "giving." They want to enjoy the American life, the dreams fulfilled but refuse to change and surrender to the "Other." They are paramounted with male egoism and chauvinism, characters who restrain to transform because to mutate is to lose one's own identity. Their ego can loosen as long as it does not come in the way of their thoughts and expect others to cater to their own ideas and ideologies without question. Dr. Rab Chatterjee like an Indian husband maintains decorum in front of his wife but all throughout, his mind is on wooing Maya Sanyal because he has the egoistic audacity to think that divorced and widowed women are loose and can be taken for granted. Maya's reputation helps a bit but she is scandalized to see him masturbating while talking to her and his pervert behaviour makes Maya run. Her decision to marry another Indian immigrant in order to gain stability is Maya's transformation which she takes in her stride. Rab Chatterjee cannot fathom Maya having a mind of her own. It is her choice to sleep with anyone, be it Fred with no arms or her preference for her other men. "Fran would get a kick out of this. Maya has slept with married men, with nameless men, with men little more than boys, but never with an Indian man. Never." (*M*, 103)

Does Dr. Rab Chatterjee's perverse wooing repulse her or is it her denial of Indian men in general to assert her independence of her home country? But then again she looks for Indian immigrant Ashoke Mehta for her marriage, so it is more like Maya's balancing of two cultures that is apparent. She does not want to lose the American freedom, yet is nostalgic about the Indian culture.

Bharati Mukherjee's characters present a challenge for the readers to sit back and think, not to overlook a single nuance, and to go through the pain felt by them or rejoice with them in their joy and achievements. The tribulations gone through by Jasmine while being raped—what must she be going through, what must she be thinking? Did she abhor her body for being fragile? Did she feel humiliated? The consequences are fatal in most cases. Did she blame herself for instigating the act?

Do we not feel the anger when Jasmine's husband is killed because terrorists have their own ideologies? And do we readers, feel avenged and rejoice when Jasmine kills her rapist? Do we not feel the pain of Hannah and Devi, Tara or Dimple?

One can appreciate the act of Debbie di Martino's torching Frankie Fong's apartment, or when she kills Loco Larry because he is like an animal trying to mutilate a dead body. One can feel the anguish of Devi when she finds about her bio-parents, feel cheated like Dimple when her expectation in marriage is dashed to pieces, feel like kicking characters like Dr. Rab Chatterjee who are psychic lechers in the society.

Devi's belief in "destiny" and "Karma" doctrines extracted straightaway from scriptures of Holy *Gita* and Devi's anguish are evident in the statements that she pronounces in order to shock the readers to apprehend what's going to happen now. Each character of Bharati Mukherjee seems to follow the philosophies of Holy *Gita* in the context of performing of "Karma" without thinking of the end result.

Tara, like Dimple, is aghast to see the transformations which she did not expect and emotions pour in a deluge, everything gets muddled up and she gets angry and frustrated. In the end, she returns to her husband. She could not act and avenge like Jasmine, because she still seems to be finding a foothold for herself. "And Tara, still locked in a car across the street from the Catelli-Continental, wondered whether she would ever get out of Calcutta, and if she didn't, whether David would ever know that she loved him fiercely." (*TD*, 210)

Ravaged and mentally in tatters while going back, being surrounded in the mob and Pronob getting hit and killed, Tara is still not able to come out of her trance-like innocence and face the reality. The only thought in her numb mind is about her ability to let David know that she loved him fiercely. The transformation is instant. Tara is jolted into the world of reality and that reality is away from Calcutta, with her husband. She is running away from a land of chaos to a place from which she had run away to find solace but she is running back to the original place which she feels is more secure.

Devi, in contrast, believes in finding the "tiger-balls," in herself and faces the world which is full of adversaries as well as friends. But then both the characters may be right in their own right. Sometimes to live happily, one does have to back out, find solutions for a better life, other times barging in on troubles can produce solutions.

Each of Bharati Mukherjee's characters speaks for itself, be it major or minor, each one gives a new meaning to life. Her characters reach beyond, are real and some of them life-size. The ethics governing the characters is to treat each one of them individually and again as a whole, in order to facilitate everyone's evolution. As Bharati Mukherjee says:

> In a way, I suppose that's being a Hindu, I mean, this being constantly aware of the existence of many universes, this undermining of biography and individual ego. The cosmology that my characters and I inhabit derives very much from the Puranic tales. The *Puranas* are cycles of tales (think of them as morality tales, religious fables, there are thou-

sands of them) that every Hindu child is told the way that kids in U.S. are exposed to fairy tales and bedtime stories. As "story," they really work, too! Conflict, heroes, villains, obstacles, action, surprise revelation! But the stories metaphorize the Hindu concepts of cosmology, time and space. Current discoveries in astronomy are certainly pointing up the existence of universe other than ours. I believe in re-incarnation, which, too, may be a metaphor for some geo-biological phenomena, why not?[12]

NOTES

1. India Abroad; The New Generation (Jan. 29. 1999)
2. *Indian Women Novelists*, ed. R.K. Dhawan, Vol. I, p. 30.
3. S. Emmanuel Nelson, *Bharati Mukherjee: Critical Perspectives*, pp. 24-25
4. barnesandnobles.com: Author Biography p.1 http://Shop. Barnes and Noble.com/booksearch. Website: J6USH2JUU 00 CONDA Q4 GFWD.VH7 and pcount=o and5refer =
5. *Macbeth, Complete Works of Shakespeare* (Oxford, 1980), V.i, p. 1022.
6. *Transcendental Knowledge*, Chapter 4, Text 22, 249. *Bhagvad Gita As It Is: His Divine Grace*, A.C. Bhakti Vedanta Swami Prabhupada.
7. Gurleen Grewal, "Born Again," in Nelson, p. 194.
8. *Hamlet: Prince of Denmark, Complete Works of Shakespeare*, III.i.56-60, 1046.
9. Reading Group Guide/ *Leave it to Me:*08 by Bharati http://www.readinggroupguides.com/guides/leave_it_to_me.author.asp
10. Fakhrul Alam, *Bharati Mukherjee*, 128.
11. Nelson, p. 60.
12. Bharati Mukherjee, *Holder of the World*: An Interview with Bharati Mukherjee by Chen Tina and Goudie, S.X. 5 of 22 http://www.indiatimes.com

Chapter III

Hovering between Cultures

Once any group of people enter a geographical territory and over generations adopt its culture, language and way of living, they should cease to be foreigners.

> For too long, we have been concerned with the political process in the sub-continent," says Moshed Alam, who was elected to a school board in the New York borough of Queens earlier this year." We have to understand that this is our new *home.*[1]

An easy way and a very significant method to describe the transition that is evident in an immigrant's life in the above statement.

Hovering between two cultures gives rise to split characters, tends to unbalance personalities. Having no choice, the individual takes a decision. It can be totally extreme case of following the emancipated attitude of American culture, or delve into the past and keep hanging on to the former culture. The middle path is difficult, but it has to be decided. Once decided, then the new culture should be accepted. The country which is giving livelihood has to be taken seriously. In elections one has to participate, so that one is accepted in the new environment. "Faced with such alienation, first generation South Asians have realized the necessity of getting involved with local politics to build brighter lives for their children."[2]

Though it might not be so very easy to get involved, one has to lose inhibitions, get more involved in the surroundings. But when one knows what they want, the decision is easier to make. The culture which is inherited should be preserved, cosseted and loved which might be helpful in enhancing one's identity instead of resulting in a broken identity. The rigidity of coveting one's left-behind culture should be changed. Instead one can help oneself to settle in the new culture, learn about the new culture and highlight the best of one's culture. Intermingling can help. One can settle in the new culture without losing one's identity.

At first it might not be so easy but one has to try harder. "South Asian Youth are still trying to determine how they fit into American society," says Madhulika Khandelwal, head of the Asian American Studies Department at Queens' College, "It's hard not being Christian," says Swati Khurana, who is working on a documentary film on Hindi Remix. "In Kindergarten, everyone in my class told me I was a bad person because Santa Claus didn't bring me gifts."[3]

Again it is difficult to calculate everyone's values on the same scale as Bharati Mukherjee herself. Bharati Mukherjee, born in a joint and orthodox family, had the privilege of a father who was of Western thoughts, and a mother who wished to educate her children in English environment. Throughout Bharati Mukherjee was exposed to the difficulties faced by a person of different colour in Western countries. The way was already paved by her experiences in England and later on in Canada. In spite of being experienced, the mental torture she went through is evident in her novels. Her protests in Canada against racial treatment prove that she felt confident enough to raise voice. Married to a Canadian, she knew her rights. But still she decided to leave Canada for the basic reason of having mental peace. Assimilation in a hostile environment was difficult for her. Then again, she had another choice of making a decision to settle in the United States as an immigrant, because her sabbatical period in India taught her that she had to lose her hold on her memories of India, in order to settle in peace in the United States. Acculturation thus became very easy for her.

This situation of uprootedness faced by the new settlers in America is not so very easy. When the immigrants come to settle in America, they are faced with a new culture, a new set of rules and a hostile group of people who do not mix so very easily. It can happen anywhere. Everyone does not have the capacity to attune their feelings and mind.

> The situation faced by migrants who leave their own country to settle in a new one is basically the problem of learning to adapt to an unfamiliar culture. This problem can be dramatic if the new culture is very different from the one they left.[4]

But still it seems that Bharati Mukherjee takes the easier way out. Isn't she an escapist? One situation can make one shrink away into one's own shell. But discarding one culture to embrace another culture is easier for Bharati Mukherjee because she has married a person of Canadian North-American origin. It might not be so easy for an immigrant, because the culture they leave back is something they have it in blood. It is easier for Bharati Mukherjee because from the age of 8 she stayed out of India. She faced the problems which were similar to the ones which she faced in Calcutta. When she returned, she found it to be different from what it used to be. Her embittered life in Canada made her revolt. The experiences of Canada made her react strongly against what happened in Calcutta. Bharati Mukherjee's comments on Calcutta in *The Days and Nights in Calcutta* and *The Tiger's Daughter* show her intolerant nature. Hyphenated existence can be painful. Bharati Mukherjee is critical of her sister who decided to stay as an immigrant, but fails to understand the notion of belonging which is craved for by everyone. The Canadian husband's identity could not help her to stay for long in Canada because of the feeling of racialism, but what about her sister who is married to an Indian. It is a lot to ask for a person to lose one's identity. This feeling of identity leads to broken identities.

It is true that when one inhabits a new country and plans to be there for a long period then it is one's duty to contribute to the nation which provides shelter, but then to be a part of the present nation one has to leave one's own identity and take up a whole new identity and for this, one has to face the humiliation of being a second citizen who is not given enough rights.

Bharati Mukherjee claims herself as an American rather than as Asian American. Her experience and actions show her transformation in America. She believes that this transformation affects both the individual and the national-cultural identity. "A culture is supposed to be something that one should be proud of. Bharati Mukherjee has invested in the present and not the past."[5]

It seems that Bharati Mukherjee is afraid to be accepted as an Asian American. It is more of an adjustment, which might make her feel one of them as she is now a person who is working there. She seems to reject her identity in order to be accepted by her present country. It is a choice which she makes because it is her present and her future. Past cannot help her to reconcile with her new environment. She visits India occasionally, and it is like a married girl visiting her parental home. On the other hand, this is a solution which can be followed by immigrants to prevent broken identities. But to claim a new identity might not be satisfactory to a lot of immigrants, because the inculcated ideas from childhood refuse to embrace the new culture and it leads to dissatisfaction and broken identities. For an individual to say that he is broadminded is one thing, but to practise it might seem another, because after a certain stage one will revolt. Embracing of Western culture by children can be intolerable and unacceptable, especially if the child happens to be a girl as Bharati Mukherjee points out in her short story "A Father":

> Two Saturdays running, he lost badly at duplicate bridge. His wife scolded him. He had made silly mistakes. When was Babli meeting this man? Where? He must be American; Mr. Bhowmick prayed only that he was white. He pictured his grandson crawling to him, and the grandson was always fat and brown and buttery skinned, like the infant Krishna. An American son-in-law was a terrifying notion. (*D*, 70)

Like India, America is a place where people from different cultures and nations come and stay and fight for a living and it has been reflected in Bharati Mukherjee's stories in *The Middlemen and Other Stories*. One can contribute to the present nation's culture but it is wrong to deny the same right to past culture, which nurtured one's identity. The struggle to discover and establish oneself is the same in America, then why deny the same right to past culture which Bharati Mukherjee has always done in her novels. The violence in her inner being and the anger are depicted in her characters. Her claim that her characters speak is one such notion. The guilt of denying her past to establish herself as an American writer makes her claim again and again that she is American and not Asian American. What one contributes to the present is what one's past has given, the self-satisfaction within the self can make a complete person. Indelible memories of the left-behind culture cannot be effaced in seconds. Balance in character is needed to settle in a new environment. Imbalance of character which is depicted in Dimple Basu in *Wife* is something inherent. Dimple Basu's idea of freedom is warped from the beginning. Her mental stability is under question. The ability to transform is not inherent. Insecurity is always a part of her character.

> On dark September nights in Rash Behari Avenue, when the wooden wardrobe cast odd shadows on the scalloped headboard of her bed, she invented desperate schemes. Cosmetic surgery in the West: Transplant Nearly Human Coves an offensively Flat Flesh! On such nights, she looked in bathroom for her father's razor blades, she thought of death. (*W*, 11)

Her desire or fantasy of freedom after marriage and an installed desire to be like Sita has already breached her character. She feels inclined to obey Amit because of her adulation towards the image of Sita but the other part revolts; while she craves to behave like Sita, she hates to let go off her freedom. Feminity in itself seems to be a blocking hurdle in the way of freedom. Being pregnant makes her feel that it would char her future in U.S.A. "Certainly she would not have picked a skipping rope as her weapon. Who would have thought you could skip your way to abortion? Dimple was as surprised as the others." (*W*, 42)

Jasmine seems to skip from one identity to another and gives the impression of an escapist, but she is more stable. She transforms as the situation demands and in spite of a battered body and mind, she struggles to live a life on her own conditions without making a compromise. Leaving Bud might seem to be a selfish act but it is her own decision to drift away from a life which is not fulfilling. It seems that she is defying the predicament of widowhood. The preaching of *Bhagwad Gita* seems to be a predominant factor while Bharati Mukherjee was conjuring up Jasmine. The doctrine of looking forward and living the present is a factor which constantly plays a major role in Jasmine's life. Again and again, in each of her novels, Bharati Mukherjee seems to take out a leaf out of her past life and culture and weaves a character around it.

Devi in *Leave it to Me* is an incarnation of American life and culture, a new version of Jasmine and Dimple but a horrifying version of American culture who exalts in slaughtering her enemies, lives a carefree life, follows the doctrine of "Karma," again, a bond signifying the ties of Indian culture nurtured in the mind of Bharati Mukherjee.

The name 'Devi' has been given to the character so that she brings down her enemies, eliminating them without thinking of the consequences. The non-compromising attitude, or rather the attitude of living only for oneself, is what has been projected in the novel *Leave it to Me*. Devi constantly fights to carve a niche for herself and defies the world. Bharati Mukherjee's new character is totally American, steeped in its culture and it seems that finally Mukherjee has left behind her past culture but the next moment she adjoins the Indian culture and Hippie culture.

The earlier heroines have broken identities. The latter ones slip on American identity, though the Indian ties are still there as if Bharati Mukherjee is afraid to totally let go her own identity; and hence the Indian backdrop in *The Holder of the World* and *Leave it to Me*.

The anger in Devi's mind seems to be the anger which Mukherjee herself might have experienced and suppressed while in Canada. The explanation of Devi's actions seems to be the simmering volcano in Mukherjee, which has created Devi in *Leave it to Me*.

Freedom to live, think and act can be more alluring than being shackled by iron bonding. These are the two basics which apply to American culture and Indian culture. Indian mentality is bound by the patriarchal mentality and male-dominated attitudes.

The choice of having the best of both the worlds is what Bharati Mukherjee chooses for herself: the freedom of American culture, the acceptance of America and yet cling on to the exotic values of bygone culture which is part of her personality. She has a choice but it cannot be applied to her character which leads to produce Dimple and Tara on one hand, and Jasmine, Helen and Devi on the other hand.

It is easier again for her because as wife of Clark Blaise she is not bound to return to India. Every Indian girl married off in any family might return to her parental house, but only as a visitor. The adapting quality has to be there because it is in the tradition. A girl's home is with her husband and if she dares to cross the boundaries, there will be repercussions. Bharati Mukherjee is lucky to have been able to do what she wanted, as destiny was in her favour. Jasmine is portrayed on the same line.

> I see my "immigrant" story replicated in a dozen American cities, and instead of seeing my Indianness as fragile identity to be preserved against obliteration (or worse, a "visible" disfigurement to be hidden) I see it now as a set of fluid identities to be celebrated. I see myself as an American writer in the tradition of other American writers whose parents or grandparents had passed through Ellis Island. Indianness is now a metaphor.[6]

Does Dimple, to some extent, reflect the early conflicts in Bharati Mukherjee's mind when she is in Canada or is it the struggle of her mother which she tries to portray through *Wife*.

The dilemma faced by Bharati Mukherjee becomes a turning point in her life when after her stay in Canada, she decides to return to India and finds it changed. This made her decide to be in America and celebrate being an immigrant. Apparently it is easier for her as she is married to a Canadian—a North American citizen. She says, "For me, home is wherever the people I love are. Making a home—it can be a hotel room or anywhere—is simply setting up my little altar of deities, the chief among whom is Goddess Kali, and hanging up paintings. It provides me the necessary perspectives."[7]

To some it might be a selfish attitude. A person who claims to transform and adapt with situation contradicts this statement. Her world is inside her where no one can trespass. This can be a happy situation for everyone who is fully satisfied in a given situation without bothering for the world. Even while she claims to have an inner world and the umbilical cord has been severed forever, still her novels reflect the Indian culture. It is the self-inflicted wall, which she surrounds around herself in order to prevent pain filtering inside. Child Bharati had created her own world by surrounding herself with books. Today it seems she claims again and again of being an American of Hindu origin in order to make herself believe that she does not have any guilt at renouncing her origin. She says: "I think I would have been a very different person if I had married an Indian immigrant, naturalized citizen let's say from Silicon Valley, than having fallen in love at age of 22 with a fellow student who happened to be white. Life has often necessitated the transformation."[8]

The tendency to emphasize that she is an American of Indian origin is somewhat similar to a situation where an Indian goes to America, still clings to his culture and safeguards it, refuses to intermingle and realize happiness in the new environment. Bharati Mukherjee does not need to point out that she is American. She is not born American but to be accepted there she disclaims her Indian origin. Being ill-treated in Canada has left an indelible mark on her psyche and that's why she criticizes her sister for claiming to be an Indian in America, who still holds on to the fact that one day she will return to India.

In all this chaos the basic fact is lost that one does not change with time, but one should not avoid changes with time. The inner being, the inner self does not need to be changed but to keep with time one has to be a step ahead of time. The first generation of Indian immigrants revolt against the changes that confront them. They feel that they have not been able to inculcate the Indian culture and values in the American born and bred offsprings. To imbibe the cultural values one has to relent a bit, understand the child, act accordingly which happens in India, even in the fast-moving cosmopolitan environment. America changes fast and one has to cling to Indian culture in order to survive in America.

In the words of Indian American writer Vikram Chandra: "After we paint ourselves into corners with these ideas of purity and tie ourselves into knots. It's a self-inflicted damage that's dangerous. If you let the questions fall by the wayside and with the most honesty that you can manage, live your life and be confident that whatever you do it will still be Indian, just be easy. Easiness is the best revolt."[9]

Bharati Mukherjee's refusal to exist in a state of hyphenation is carved out poetically in Jasmine (*Jasmine*), Hannah Easton (*The Holder of the World*) and Devi (*Leave it to Me*). She portrays her pervasion in the new culture, her attitude pertinacious out and out, and she is jubilant in her expressions through her protagonists. Her earlier refusal and bewilderment at her own country's transformation is evident in *The Tiger's Daughter*, where Tara is angry and perplexed with her hometown having been corroded by aliens from other states. She is unable to reconcile with the fact that Calcutta is infested with labour movements and her ego is a direct target for the hurts she incurs during her stay in India. She meets her friends who still exist in the state of buoyancy and maintain total ignorance to the changing city. Not only Tara, but she seems to be the replica of Bharati Mukherjee who is unsettled and baffled by the changes, as is expressed in *The Days and Nights in Calcutta*. Dimple is Bharati Mukherjee's character who exists on the periphery perpetually throughout the novel, undecided, whether she wants to be like Sita because her husband's wishes are so, or whether she wants to enjoy the openness of relationship in America. She is uprooted because she never found her roots. Throughout, her existence is in fantasy, she exists in her imaginary world and a time comes when reality and fantasies become submerged into each other.

As it is, the migration for a female is not once but it is manifold, and with wrappings of imagination, Dimple in *Wife* cannot decide or decipher reality from fantasy. In Dimple's life the existence is always on the periphery. She is always on the extreme end: either she wants to be 'Sita' or she wishes to be Scarlet O'Hara, her evanescent confidence is always on the verge of collapse. Her self-assertion comes out quite late and her anger and exasperation with her existent situations comes out with clarity when she gets angry with Amit from time to time.

> She had expected pain when she had come to America, had told herself that pain was part of any new beginning, and in the sweet structures of that new life had allotted pain a special place. But she had not expected her mind to be strained like this, beyond endurance. She had not anticipated inertia, exhaustion, endless indecisiveness. (*W*, 115)

Amit, a husband who wishes his wife to have freedom but not too much of it, somehow seems to represent the Indian male, or for that matter the feelings of most of the settlers in U.S.A. who refuse to give or contribute a little bit of "self" to the "other"—that is to say, in this case, "other" being America. The mentality of the immigrants is to earn and return home with ample amount of wealth so that the rest of life is happy and spent in one's own country.

> She wanted to dream of Amit but she knew she would not. Amit did not feed her fantasy life; he was merely the provider of small material comforts. In bitter moments she ranked husband, blender, colour T.V., cassette tape recorder, stereo, in their order of convenience. (*W*, 113)

Bharati Mukherjee is pointedly critical of her sister Mira's attitude who plans to return back to her home country after she retires. Mira criticizes Bharati for losing her identity in America. In her essay "Two Ways to Belong to America" Bharati Mukherjee has presented the attitudinal problems of some settlers in America who do not wish to do anything for the country which provides them economic freedom.

> Memory can heighten the experiences of a place, making it far richer, larger, and idyllic than its daily existence. We may also find that our memory can be disorienting and distorted—for example, when we return to an area following an extended absence. Nicolini comments on this collision of past and present in a single landscape: "I fled San Francisco in 1978 and returned in 1982 as a 'new' person, ready to begin a 'new' life. But there's no such thing as a new life; the old one is always right around the corner. . . . Each neighbourhood, each street, contains a different slice of me. . . . I cannot stand on many corners without being at two places at once. In situations such as this; memory conforms contradiction or completely alters our "actual" experience of a place.[10]

Settling in America as a student was naturally not so easy for Bharati Mukherjee because coming from an upper middle class Bengali family, mixing with "other" people—"Other" here refers to people from other communities—was not so very easy and in a way, looked down upon by family, her perspective expanded as she met students of her own country, (but from different states of India or communities), and the affinity grew because she could relate to them.

> I was a Bengali and proud of it, which meant that I claimed as heritage a culture distinct from that of a Bihari or a Punjabi or a Gujarati or a Tamil. That's the way we were brought up in Calcutta in the Fifties. We were encouraged to set ourselves apart from people of other Indian states. In Iowa, where I didn't run into too many Bengalis, I began to see and feel affinities with rather than hostilities towards non-Bengali Indian students on campus.[11]

Naturally, when Dimple goes to America, she already has her reservations about her own culture and to enter the New World she does not want any connections with the old culture, to be continually guided by Amit Basu leaves her exhausted mentally. Doing little work and existing in imagination vexes her into watching Television, a prop to enter the American culture. Eating, sleeping, watching television and imagining Amit in different role models are her favourite pastimes which begin to take a toll after a lapse of time. Existence in unreal world stagnates her to the point that she is unable to judge any situation, even the fanatic attack on her husband. Dimple's attraction to Ina Mullick's personality and her sexual attraction towards Milt Glasser, significantly points out the dissatisfied-self of Dimple who wants to free herself. Here in America, due to her association with people of a very different culture, her wishes to cross the gender space, to find her own identity, Amit is worried to the extent that he gives her the freedom to be a little bit of American but cannot accept her to fully immerse into the culture. It seems to be demeaning, and his male-ego cannot accept his wife to become too American. Amit cannot identify with this new American life invading his Indian security. He wants to be free to earn, to save, and his wife should become modern but not "too American." Her expression of sensuality perturbs him and he can hardly understand his wife's new incarnation. His wishes for her to become Sita, becomes a heavy burden on her and it seems to be a new shackle which is trying to bind her down. The continuous reprimands from Amit lead her to the extreme case of neurosis reminding her of the never-ending bondage that marriage is. Her "self" seems to be lost in the Indian home, which she has with Amit in America. Though Amit Basu is trying to behave and act like any American, he is unable to reconcile to the fact that his wife also needs to express herself and needs an outlet to work out her frustrations. He is physically in U.S.A. but he mentally exists in the patriarchal society of India. To merge into the New World he tries to learn all the nuances of New Society so that he gains his self-confidence—for this he mugs up jokes, which can show his wittiness. His efforts to become American is literal, as he tries to subjugate his wife, which is alien to the New World in which he is so painfully trying to penetrate. Breaking the gender differentiation is far-off from Amit's Indian mentality. For him everything should be perfect, because formality is a part of Indian society, whereas he seems to lose his confidence when faced with the open, informal society in America. He seems to look more self-conscious than self-confident in the company of Indian immigrants in the U.S.A. He is unaware of the changes that overcome Dimple. The individualistic attitude of American society slowly penetrates the secure walls of his home, and suddenly Dimple Basu's horizon expands as she intermingles with Ina Mullick, but Dimple Basu is too passive to change positively. The oppression of the Indian home in America makes her revolt but the clash is mental which surfaces now and then, and with no channelling, Dimple Basu keeps on gorging her vacuum-created mind with fantasies about Amit and how to commit suicide. Her drawing room which Amit tries to protect from the American values is pervaded by the television, as Dimple keeps watching television or sleeps. The journey inward misfires as the fickle-minded Dimple cannot find her true self because of her own mindset and the situation gets aggravated by her husband's attitude. Her self-expression is fantasizing new ways to kill herself or Amit, and she revels in her Americanization through the television. Every time she fantasizes herself being murdered, it is like a "new-birth" for her. The same attitude of despondency continues till the end, resulting in self-destruction. Though it seems like a reconstruction from the point of view of the American society, her release is pathetic and one wonders what happened to her. But naturally her attitude is changed and her belief that America is a place where murderer could escape without hindrance shows the unbalanced mental condition of Dimple. Her revolt is self-inflicted pain in which she rejoices. Her act of self-induced abortion shows a self-willed person who wants to be free of bondage, and the murder of her husband is Dimple's unbalanced mind. Her craving to have freedom in the New World is overlooked by her husband who is enslaved in his own Indian male-dominating world. Dimple is trying to free herself of her old bondage of marriage and motherhood. She becomes bonded to her fantasies and her craving to be free. Her journey of self-realization is never realized due to her own self-inflicted bondage to overworked mind full of fantasies of committing murder. The continuous familial pressure in India leads to a psychological problem which continues in America. Though Amit impels her to go out and mix but the "white magical circle" is always there and Dimple feels suppressed by this. Both Amit and Dimple are victims of circumstances and sudden exposure to a free society where the norms and values are of a different nature. Both of them are bonded to their views and Amit's rigid attitude towards his wife, "not wearing pants" and "not mixing with Ina Mullick," triggers off a feeling of revulsion in Dimple. Dimple is twice-enslaved as she is not free from inside and does not, or, rather prefers not to, assert her freedom due to Amit. Amit magnanimously allows Dimple to drink but advises that the drink should be "weak." Whenever Dimple tries to be creative or channelise her thoughts and actions positively, her efforts are dashed to pieces by Amit's attitude. Though Amit encourages Dimple to engage herself, the question always arises as to whether he would have tolerated the economic freedom that Dimple could have gained. Could Amit's feudal mind adjust to the new developments?

Both Dimple and Amit have submerged themselves into an imaginary world of freedom. Both are enslaved to their own kind of experiences, preconceived ideologies about the virtuous attributes of fidelity in married life. The very "idea of freedom" is warped in the case of Dimple when she imagines her freedom in marriage, due to suppressing force represented by her father. With an over-dominating father guiding her life, Dimple is subdued and her far-off distanced stance from reality exists from the beginning. "His disapproval was torture; all her life she had been trained to please. He expected her, like Sita, to jump into fire if necessary." (*W*, 28)

Dimple walks through her marriage and life, like a somnambulist, always dreaming and imagining herself resisting the bonding shackles represented in the form of her father, then her in-laws, her baby and finally, Amit himself, who initially represented "freedom" for her.

If one looks closely, Jasmine's comparison of Prakash and Taylor in America rings a bell and one wonders if Joyti/Jasmine had gone to America as Prakash's wife, would her life have been the same or would it have been a replica of Dimple's life. Prakash was a perfectionist and Jasmine unknowingly falls in love with Taylor because of his unassuming, informal nature. She is attracted to him because he is not always on guard about how to behave and following a set pattern. The exotic "other" attracts her; Milt Glasser presents a challenging outsider who understands Dimple and pays attention to her with equanimity like a fellow human being, who eats and breathes like the male populace.

The incidents would not have been the same for Jasmine if she had arrived in America as a married woman. She would have ended up living like Professor Vadhera's wife. She feels suppressed in the Vadhera household, what if Prakash had been there? Two options are there: Prakash could have felt cheated when he would have known about Professor Vadhera's profession—the idol which is put on a pedestal would have broken. What course of action could have Prakash taken—the clean-break that Jasmine prefers, or would he have ended up like Amit, murdered as an oppressor by his wife. Though the basic difference between the attitude and mental balance that is depicted with clarity is that Jasmine does not exist in fantasies but her diligence to exist might not have perturbed her to self-destruction. The fluidity in her character is inborn; though floundering in the beginning, still her belief in existence itself speaks volumes.

The transformation in Jasmine is like a rocket changing direction when faced with an obstacle in its decided route. The set rules of an Indian wife, if following the moral codes, the role model incarnation being Nirmala, stifles the soul of Jasmine. The anticipation of new life is smothered in the House of Vadheras and Jasmine is apprehensive of her own future. She promises to pay Professor Vadhera and craves to be set free from the self-created ghetto in the Vadhera household. The determination to free herself from all bondage is inbred right from the beginning when Jasmine broke the rules and educated herself by the "masterji" in the village.

Jasmine continuously keeps comparing everyone's behaviour in America to that of Prakash. It is evident that every Indian girl child nurtures the dream to be like "Sita" and have the virtues of the Goddess.

> The love I felt for Taylor that first day had nothing to do with sex. I felt in love with his world, its case, its careless confidence and graceful self-absorption. I wanted to become the person they saw: humorous, intelligent, refined, affectionate, not illegal, not murderer, not widowed, raped, destitute fearful. In Flushing, I had lived defensively in the midst of documented rectitude. I did not want to live legally if it also meant living like a refugee. (*J*, 171)

The revulsion for a life of repression is evident from the attitude of Jasmine. She, like Dimple, craves for the freedom of "self." The same yearning is there to become what the others see her as. She wants a carefree life, free of bondings and as an illegal immigrant, the sense of freedom is more acutely felt and savoured. She is scandalized at various aspects of life which are new to her. She is not able to reconcile with the fact that subjects of taboo in India are spoken about so openly in the American society. Her blushing at simple mention of male-organs or functioning is hardly noticed by the Americans. The attitude baffles her at first, but freedom allures her to let go herself and live a life which she prefers. Till now she had to go through rigours to express her opinion and to be accepted as an individual and not as anyone's consort is pleasurable to her.

> Wylie said that Duff was adopted.
>
> "Low sperm count," she explained. I blushed, but neither Wylie nor Taylor noticed.·
>
> "Hockey injury," Taylor protested. ((*J*, 170)

A society where all discussion of sex, widow-remarriage is a taboo, where women are considered to be an object of suppression and self-expression is given the name of revolt, the freedom of expression in the New world gives a feeling of exhilaration. Duff, an adopted child, seems strange to Jasmine who hails from a country where adoption of a child mars the parental feelings and is considered a laceration of emotional bondings. "I could not imagine a non-genetic child. A child that was not my own, or my husband's struck me as a monstrous idea. Adoption was as foreign to me as the idea of widow remarriage." (*J*, 170)

To free herself from the ideologies imbibed in her, as it is done through generations, is difficult in the beginning, but defiling of her body by a rapist seems to release a volcano of emotions. With nothing to preserve and cherish, she has a whole new horizon to conquer, which she does; abrading all the set traditional values and moral codes, pacifying her injured "self."

The openness of American society and breaking of preconceived notions liberates Jasmine slowly, and exuberance is evident. Still harbouring the feelings for her husband, she decides to live a life—which might have been abhorred by her relatives back home and Prakash might have objected to, if his life had not been cut short by some unthinking individual—on her own terms. The continuous thinking about Prakash, what he might have done in a particular situation, proves that Prakash is like an idol for her, though he might have been put down from his pedestal once they entered the New World. Jasmine enters the New World after being brutally raped and already having lost her husband. She is left with nothing to lose anymore like Devi in *Leave it to Me*. As she has nothing to lose, she has everything to embrace. Leaving Bud Ripplemeyer after few self-recriminations apparently proves that dilly-dallying and being virtuous is not a quality, which is nurtured by Jasmine. Her decision to profligate her responsibility might be questioned and might not be panegyrized by many critics, because Jasmine seems to be self-centred, but her decision signifies her breaking of the bond and entering the New World completely. She chooses a life of profligation instead of a life full of responsibilities. "Then there is nothing I can do. Time will tell if I am a tornado, rubble-maker, arising from nowhere and disappearing into a cloud. I am out of the door and in the potholed and rutted driveways scrambling ahead of Taylor, greedy with wants and reckless from hope." (*J*, 241)

Releasing herself from all bondages, being a widow, would have been pandemoniac in her own traditional society but refusal to live a life of widowhood, stagnating in a house full of widows, is not a future which is envisioned by her.

Significantly, murdering Half-Face after her rape, Jasmine's sensitiveness to feelings for others seems to get lost in the quagmire of blood. Before she enters the New World, she has to face the murder of her husband, and though Jasmine retains the nurturing qualities of a mother, she has become more individualistic and sensitive to her own happiness. She is not indecisive like Dimple in *Wife* and is free of all bondages. Travelling light is a lesson which is taught by Half-Face and burning of the suitcase full of Prakash's suit and white saree signifies the burning of the old world, its values, wifely duties and the social norms which Jasmine has already denounced by leaving India. "Jyoti of Hasnapur was not Jasmine, Duff's day mummy and Taylor and Wylie's aupair in Manhattan; that Jasmine isn't this Jane Ripplemeyer having lunch with Mary Webb at the University Club today. And which of us is the undetected murderer of a half-faced monster, which of us has held a dying husband, which of us was raped and raped and raped in boats and cars and motel rooms?" (*J*, 127)

Instead of living a life in rut, Jasmine decides to cross all the boundaries of class, gender, race, and live a life which soothes her. She is nostalgic about India but refuses to be caught in the web of events eventually surpassing the earlier characters who still dwindle between the old and the new.

While being with Professor Vadhera, Jasmine feels stifled because of the atmosphere generated in the family. Like many other immigrants, Professor Vadhera seems to maintain Indian atmosphere in the family. His parents are genuinely bewildered when something like English language infiltrates into their Indian home. Though Professor Vadhera is a scientist, his wife is not aware of his profession in America. She is busy watching video-tapes of Hindi movies and working as might be suitable for Indian women, enjoys the Indianness provided by the ghetto existing all around her, never feeling out of place. There is no ambition, no competition, being nineteen, a lot younger than Professor Vadhera, Nirmala is an ideal Indian wife who does not question her husband. She caters to the needs of everyone as well as herself. The only ray of hope for Nirmala is that she thinks of herself. She works where she enjoys keeping away from her in-laws.

Jasmine alias Jyoti, in spite of a protesting feudal father, got educated. Marrying Prakash, she defied all traditional family values. Her modern Indian husband helped her transform into Jasmine. In spite of this, her thoughts and values face a setback, when like any Indian married girl, she wants to become a mother but her husband refuses to help her. His view about young girls getting pregnant and bearing children bewilders Joyti. The exposure to city life in Jullundhar for a village girl from Hasnapur is a culture shock for Jasmine. Prakash opting to move out of a joint family and renting a two-room flat is new to Jasmine who is born and bred in a huge family of sisters and brothers. The emotional upheaval is evident when Jasmine tries to adjust to the changes in life yet remembers the old values. "For the uncle, love was control. Respect was obedience. For Prakash, love was letting go. Independence, self-reliance: I learned the litany by heart. But I felt suspended between worlds." (*J*, 76)

"Nirvana" is a term extracted from Buddhism where it means that one is able to achieve it when one feels one-to-one with other individuals. The feeling of "otherness" is what causes the fear of losing and, consequently, the immigrants keep dilly-dallying between their old culture and the new culture. The fear to preserve the 'Self,' and yet forcefully trying to merge, gives rise to mental tribulation. Bharati Mukherjee's constant struggle to be accepted by the dominant culture seems to be the driving force behind her novel *Leave it to Me*, where Americanism is at its ultimate, violence and killing are the only way through which one establishes one's existence. The Indian attitude of "giving" is nuance for acceptance in the culture whereas America seems to be haven of death and murder, where the individualistic attitude is propitious and the immigrants seem to be baffled. Shaila Bhave in "The Management of Grief," a story in *The Middleman and Other Stories*, after losing her husband and two sons in a plane crash, is unable to express her grief in the American style. The American journalist, not able to analyse her inner turmoil, instigates her to help her to reach an elderly Sikh couple who have lost their son in the same accident. Shaila tries her best to cooperate and reconcile to the demise of her family, as well as consoling the parents to sign the legal document. Eventually something snaps inside and she opts out of the situation.

> "Let me out at the subway," I say.
>
> "I beg your pardon?" I can feel those blue eyes staring at me.
>
> It would not be like her to disobey. She merely disapproves and slows at a corner to let me out. Her voice is plaintive.
>
> "Is there anything I said? Anything I did?"
>
> I could answer her suddenly in dozen ways, but I choose not to.
>
> "Shaila? Let's talk about it," I hear, then slam the door. (*M*, 195)

Her journey back home to India is not fruitful and she decides to return back to Toronto and sort her life out. Her soul is appeased as she feels her dead family around herself. Instigated by a purpose to live, she gets the Canadians to act positively. Shaila writes to editors of local papers and members of Parliament to look into the case of the bombing. Her efforts are in a positive direction. In this way she is able to handle her own grief and it becomes possible for her to help all those who share the same fate. Her step towards renunciation seems more authentic than the efforts of the Canadian woman who wants Shaila to negotiate and help.

What Bharati Mukherjee proposes through her characters is that one has to keep mutating in order to seek acceptance in a new culture. But sometimes it seems that so much justifying is unnecessary and predicts a feeling of guilt on the part of the author who renounces her culture. Though sometimes it feels that it is Bharati Mukherjee's weakness that she claims to be an American, but when looked at it from her point of view, it seems to prove the validity of the principle of assimilation. To dwindle between two cultures can only produce a split personality. India becomes a metaphor for her where she returns to stay for a short period of time. Still somewhere along the line, she reminisces about her link with her home country, the culture which is coalesced with her soul and one cannot cohere between the author and her characters. Evidently, the point which is focused on is, refashioning one's self to adapt in the new world. This concept of refashioning oneself to adaptation, when not followed by her own sister, makes Bharati Mukherjee critical about her attitude of not accepting the new culture as her own. Her sister chose to live as an immigrant for a certain period of time and then returned back to India. Her attitude is that of a person who is not able to adjust to the new culture and like most Indian immigrants of first generation, it seems selfish on Mira's part. The cultural uprootedness is apparent from her attitude.

"In Mukherjee's aesthetic schema, the voice's complexity parallels the endless refashioning of the self, which she claims lies at the heart of the new immigrant experience. Not only does Mukherjee fail to question how this freedom to reinvent one's self stems from her own urban, English-educated, upper class, postcolonial background, but she also conflates the imaginary representation of the American pilgrim-as-quester with the new myth of the eager immigrant ready to slip into such an archetypal role."[12]

The basic emotion that creates havoc is fear of "change," change of lifestyle, acceptance of a culture which is abhorred or rather resented by the first generation of immigrants, the sensibility of losing touch with one's own identity. When one is aware of one's priorities, the decision becomes easier. Is it not selfish on the part of the immigrants to dream of earning a lot so that they can help out the relatives back home? The economic strength gained in America benefits the immigrants. Is it not a loss for Americans? Why not make a choice and not live in a dilemma? A similar situation arises when a resident of a village moves to a cosmopolitan city to earn and enhance his standard of living. The next generation of this same resident, born and bred in the city environment, loses the traditional values if not inculcated by the parents and for this, one has to be on a constant vigil. To keep up with the children, the parents change with time.

Immigrants have memories of their culture and they cling to it. But these memories might not be a reality because everything changes with time. The ingrained memories become distorted when faced with reality and leave the individual bitter and angry.

> Until Atlanta—and it could have been anywhere in America—I had thought of myself, in spite of a white husband and two assimilated sons, as an expatriate. In my fiction, and in my Canadian experience, "immigrants" were lost souls, put upon and pathetic. Expatriates, on the other hand, knew all too well who and what they were, and what foul fate had befallen them. (*D*, 1-2)

The plane crash in the last story of *The Middleman and Other Stories*, "The Management of Grief" seems to be an instant inspiration for Bharaṭi Mukherjee to write "The Sorrow and the Terror" in collaboration with her husband, Clark Blaise. This non-fiction is all about a plane crash of Indian Airlines which caused the loss of many lives. The bomb planted in the plane by a Sikh terrorist is not taken seriously by the Canadian Government and, irked by their complacent attitude, Bharati Mukherjee and her husband wrote this non-fiction to bring to light the attitude of Multiculturalism existent in Canada. Multiculturalism, in the author's view, meant treating the dead as "not-quite Canadians" and was another way of perpetuating the racist distinction between "them" and "us."[13]

This attitude of racism makes Bharati Mukherjee decide to become an immigrant, instead of living a life in a mental turmoil of being an expatriate. Her stories in *Darkness*—"Isolated Incidents," "The World according to Hsu"—depict a life in Canada infested with incidents of racialism. People get assaulted because they are not white. Ratna, the female protagonist, is more comfortable on a revolution-infested island where she has gone for a vacation—than the impending stay in Toronto. The cases of racialism worry her:

> "I'm not worrying about this island," Ratna said from the closet where she was checking the wallpaper seams for roaches. "I'm worrying about Toronto." (*D*, 47)

Antithetical to this is Tara's state of mind in *The Tiger's Daughter*. She goes to India to trace and find out the old Calcutta, which she had to leave at the age of 15 and finds a Calcutta which is infested with revolutions and strikes. Tara is unable to reconcile to the fact that Calcutta has changed and will keep doing so with so many people coming over from all over the country and melting into the cosmopolitan city. Tara feels completely out of place in strike-torn Calcutta. The opulence which is the centre of her orbit is now nowhere to be found. The sense of security is breached and her whole world is trampled down to pieces by people like Tuntunwala.

Tara's state of mind gets a shock while trying to find herself in her home country. Being nostalgic in Vassar, compels her to return home to find her identity, discover her childhood memories; she gets confused and delirious to find a changed scenario. The journey to find "self" is inverted and she comes to terms with the present situation. She returns back being mentally and physically raped by the situation and people who are nastier than those in the foreign land. While Tara's views are obnoxious in the beginning, they seem to start changing after meeting the actual people like Joyonto who seems eccentric in the beginning. The chaos outside triggers off a malaise, blocking her mental clarity, which is momentous but leaves Tara deflated and melancholic. The respite which is in the form of spiritual enlightenment does not equipoise the inner turmoil. It seems her spiritual awakening is based on an issue of denouncing the arrogant attitude of Antonia, and Tara's antagonistic attitude comes forth because she feels Antonia encroaching on her grounds.

> "Race back to the mall," he said over his shoulder to Tara.
>
> He had no advice for Antonia. Antonia Whitehead could look after herself.
>
> As they sped towards the mall, Tara and Pronob felt very close to each other. Pronob seemed to want to do something heroic for her. . . . He was moved by her helplessness. (*TD*, 178-79)

For an expatriate, exile and immigrant, an incident or any habit in the new life and environment might trigger off a memory of the old life and make him nostalgic. Thus both the old and new become a reality, merging into each other, but this does not happen for Tara Moni in *The Tiger's Daughter*. The unreality of Calcutta makes her delirious at times and she loses control of herself. The only reality in her life seems to be her father, but this pillar of strength loses his stronghold when battered by circumstances. Tara Banerjee decides to return back to her husband. The only thought in her mind is to tell her husband how much she loves him. This decision seems to be a justified one and reconciling with reality makes Tara decide what turn her life should take.

Existing in two environments simultaneously might be exhilarating and unassuming but it can be wearying on the mind. Tara still exists in the colonial Calcutta and the postcolonial Calcutta makes her shrivel inside. Imagining the reality and coming face to face with the reality are two different things. Bharati Mukherjee's sabbatical year in India, her decision to shed her life as an expatriate in Canada and merge as an immigrant into the American cultures is impromptu, and so is Tara's decision to return.

Though Tara enjoys all the comforts of elite society in Calcutta and abhors the people of lower class she cannot be blamed because this attitude is intrinsic to her higher middle class mentality. She changes when she comes into contact with Joyonto. The insidious politician innervates her to meet people from different classes and understand the situation existing in Calcutta from their point of view. Joyonto makes her meet people who scare her, whereas Tuntunwala who seems a suave person, leads to the deconstruction of her age-old ideas and memories of safe Calcutta.

Indian families migrating to America are generally sponsored by the relatives or friends staying in America. After reaching the place, they are offered boarding and lodging and as they settle down, they search for a separate place, which might be a step away from the relatives' house. Immigrants from South-Asia and other countries tend to follow this trend or pattern, thus creating small home country in the foreign land. There seems to be little interaction between the majority and the minority. The state of the new culture is very similar to that of Calcutta depicted in *The Tiger's Daughter*, assimilating as many migrants as possible.

> She wanted to tell her friend that little things had begun to upset, that of late she had been outraged by Calcutta, that there were too many people sprawled in alleys and storefronts and staircases. She longed for the Bengal of Satyajit Ray, children running through cool green spaces, aristocrats despairing in music rooms of empty palaces. She hated Calcutta because it had given her kids eating yoghurt off dirty sidewalks. (*TD*, 105)

The immigrants seem to be afraid of interacting, and try to create a homogeneous atmosphere, which gives the feeling of the home and culture that they have left behind, creating a ghetto. Jasmine feels disappointed while staying in Professor Vadhera's house, which is a self-created ghetto. Jasmine gets disappointed and feels that the American scenario changed before she could see it. The vision created by her husband Prakash of a beautiful modern life in America is shattered to pieces. New York seemed to be seething with such ghettos. The lack of interaction with the majority slackens the growth and development though the benefit is in the form of economic independence. The first generation of immigrants are happy but are confused to find their children getting more and more Americanized with each passing day. Mr. Bhowmick in "A Father" keeps remembering his past creating a vacuum for himself. Though his daughter and wife are Americanized, he himself is more of a "taker" than a "giver." He is happy to be earning well, but he cannot feel comfortable in his daughter's company because she refuses to be a model of perfect Indian daughter. He is irritated with his neighbour and cannot accept his lifestyle. But when he comes to know that his daughter is pregnant, he gets jittery at first but slowly starts reconciling, again coming to a standstill as he is informed the source of pregnancy. He cannot reconcile with the fact that his son-in-law is black: "Compromise, adaptability, call it what you will. A dozen times a day he made this small trade-offs between new world reasonableness and old world beliefs." (*D*, 64)

Dimple has to stay in the same Indian community in America as in India. Her friend Ina Mullick is an immigrant in America and seems to be more American than the Americans themselves. The trauma begins when not so Indian Dimple tries to be both. Her notion of marriage being a ticket to freedom is dashed to grounds in India and then again in America. Her affair with Milt Glasser tilts her balance and to gain stability she tries to revert back to her Indianness. The ghetto which surrounds her seems to suffocate her because she wants to be free from the shackles of marriage. The marriage which gave hopes of freedom, now is more like a bondage and to free herself from this, she butchers her husband. Readers are thrown back in time to witness her skipping through her pregnancy to enter a new world. Her wish to be more than what she is, she seems guileless in her fallacious world.

> Every now and then, very reverently, she touched her skin—she thought of it as the shell she inhabited—digging aimless red patterns with her finger nails. At the end of forty-seven minutes, when the alarm went off, the vagrant after-dream returned. She had meant the alarm to go off two minutes earlier; it upset her that she still could not master these small things. She was a pitiful immigrant among demanding appliances. (*W*, 186)

Human mind has to be compatible to changes in order to maintain equanimity in life. Basic difference in America is that life is fast-paced, counterpoised to Indian lifestyle or for that matter all the immigrants from different parts of the world might not be so fast in uptaking. This results in a split personality. The immigrants of first generation, out of fear of losing their identity, refuse to intermingle with the culture they enter. Their apprehension of invasion of new rules into their house forces them to maintain the same code of morals and decorum going to the extent of not letting their second generation merge into the new culture. Marriage is the easiest way to assimilation into a new culture. The tension and stress is undergone by both the genders but women are more responsible for the upbringing of the next generation. Women are the ones who are responsible for maintaining the cultural codes and traditions. The wife in the story "A Father" is an emancipated lady who detests staying in India in joint family. She instigates her husband to migrate. Mr. Bhowmick's dream is to go abroad and earn money but he indulges in the memories of past which are detestable and heartfelt simultaneously. He holds his wife responsible for not raising their daughter according to traditional Indian values and morals. The wife who is so emancipated revolts in the end at the idea of her daughter having a child through artificial insemination. She thinks that the whole process is animalistic. The father who is being very magnanimous acts violently when he knows the truth. The concept of artificial insemination is very much American and it seems like an attack of a foreign culture on their traditional values. Beating his daughter is like beating away the enemy from his home. Economic independence in America is acceptable to his code of values but invasion of the values of America is unacceptable to his Indian traditional morality.

> Lately she had begun to drain him in a wholly new way. He wasn't praying, she nagged; he was shutting her out of his life. There'd be no

> place in the house until she hid Kali-Mata in a suitcase. She nagged, and he threatened to beat her with his shoe as his father had threatened his mother: it was the thrust and valley of marriage. (*D*, 60-61)

Immersed in his tradition, camouflaged in guise of modernity, Mr. Bhowmick exists on the periphery of both cultures. He is dissatisfied in India and he does not approve of American culture. He wants the best of both the cultures but does not relent enough to accept the dominant culture and its norms. The struggle to maintain stability in life, one clings to one's past and one's memories of home. The instability of the new world pushes the immigrants to keep up pace, leaving them drained of all emotions. After so much of haggling in the new environment, some give up and settle down to take life as it is. The others swim in the direction of the tide grabbing the opportunities and faring well in adapting. Mr. Bhowmick's daughter, Babli, disdainfully negates the institution of marriage because of ordained bondage to male populace but the natural instinct to nurture a baby gets her to take an alternate route to motherhood.

> "Who needs a man?" she hissed. "The father of my baby is a bottle and a syringe. Men louse up your lives. I just want a baby. Oh don't worry—he's a certified fit donor. No diseases, college graduate, above average, and he made the easiest twenty-five dollars of his life." (*D*, 72)

The emancipation of single woman in America is not so very unusual but Mr. Bhowmick is unable to reconcile to the fact that his daughter has made a mockery of his beliefs and traditional values. Like an Indian conventional male, he wants a daughter who is respectful towards her parents and Babli is antithetical to his ideas.

Ann in "Isolated Incidents" declares that one has to be ambitious to get deeply hurt. To assimilate, one has to be ambitious to the highest degree, to gain recognition, as does Ann's friend Peppi who lets go everything to gain a position as a singer. Though both of them are childhood friends, Ann works in an immigration office and listens to people pouring out their troubles. Ann, in order to survive, has grown immune to the people's troubles. To adapt one has to get immune to the problems created in changing but Ann is not able to take the insulting comments hurled at her by Mr. Hernandez, whose sister has been discarded by her husband. But then, Ann gets angry and feels that the marriage took place in order to get a passage into

America. Battered by the success of her friend, she sits back in a park to eat and her plans to become a writer are shelved and she reverts back to her present job. Inclination towards a bright future is dashed to pieces as Ann seems to change her mind and is not ready for a complete volte face in life and profession.

> "Nothing is fair!" she shouted. "There isn't any justice. And your sister was never married! It's a trick to cheat Immigration." Her voice sagged with grief, and she sat, a small figure at the end of a long, busy dining hall. She would not stand in line with Donald Sutherland, not Ann; she would remain in Toronto surrounded by Chinese and Indians and Jamaicans, bent over the snack-packs of Kentucky fried chicken. (*D*, 93)

It is not only guilt that she feels at the insults from Mr. Hernandez but the sensitive self of Ann, herself being an immigrant, is touched which is full of pain of not being accepted as she is. In order to be accepted, she had to change like a chameleon, just as her friend does and Ann gets afraid of this new Peppi. Her statements and thoughts about Mr. Hernandez are typical of immigrants who enter the American dreams and culture, unhindered, illegally—some make it and others are denied the opportunity due to circumstances and destiny.

Similar is the case of Dr. Manny Patel in "Nostalgia." Married to Camille from New Jersey, he refuses to think that he is nostalgic about his past. "He has chosen to settle in the U.S. He was not one for nostalgia; he was not an expatriate but a patriot." (*D*, 98) Being called a "Paki scum" by a patient Mr. Horowitz, Dr. Patel is flustered and angry. He had married into the new world and done well for himself, earning dollars, and intended to retire to India and everything was set to his planning.

Like the immigrants of first generation, he is entangled in the emotions that could no longer be retrieved. And he resents New York which, on one hand, he feels has been very good to him but on the other he wants to return before his father dies. In this state of reminiscence, Dr. Nanny meets the woman of his dream. Nostalgia hits him while roaming about in "Little India" and sleeping with an Indian girl makes him very happy but it is a turnabout when he is duped by the same girl and her relative: "The Indian food, an Indian woman in bed, made him nostalgic. He wished he were in his kitchen, and that his parents were visiting him and that his mother was making him a mug of hot Horlicks and that his son was not so far removed from him in a boarding school." (*D*, 111) To take out his frustration, he defecates and with it he writes "WHORE" on the glass in the bathroom.

"Tamurlane" is another story which deals with illegal immigrants in America. They reside illegally under cover and are killed when discovered by immigrant officers. The story depicts the racialism and non-acceptance of immigrants in Canada.

"The Lady from Lucknow" is a short story about Nafeesa Hafeez who has an affair with James Beamish and her way of blending into the American society is a game which she wants to carry to the end with aplomb. Having an affair with a sixty-five-year-old man might be looked down upon in India, but Nafeesa is thrilled to have James's attention riveted on her:

> Love on the decline is hard to tell from love in rise. I have lived a life perched on the edge of ripeness and decay. The traveller feels at home everywhere, because she is never at home anywhere. I felt the hot red glow of blood rushing through capillaries. (*D*, 31)

While Nafeesa tries to get reaction from James's wife—she is treated disdainfully by her like an apparition in her husband's life—Nafeesa gets irked and deflated at the response of the wife. Nafeesa feels like a slave used by a white man and the wife taking it all in a stride. At this juncture, Nafeesa feels the pain of Husseina who had been killed for falling in love. "She has laughed at me. She has mocked my passion." (*D*, 34)

The free society of America has an effect on immigrants very fast and they vociferously embrace the openness of society. Bharati Mukherjee in this story has easily pointed out the shortcomings of Indian men with feudal mentality, who spend their life earning money, neglecting the physical and mental needs of the wife. The affairs are stamped as adultery but it is a natural release from the Indian patriarchal family. The arranged marriages in India face a setback in America and freedom is sought by the wife also.

"A Wife's Story" articulates the life of a cosmopolitan woman who has left India to seek identity for herself. Escaping the stifling atmosphere of the in-law's place in India, getting a doctorate in America, having affairs gives a sense of exhilaration. A visit by her husband becomes memorable because in the New World the husband sheds his old world traditional moral codes and inhibitions, but yet he is unable to lure the wife to leave the job and America to return back to India.

> This has to be love, I think. Charity, Eric, Phil: they may be experts on sex. My husband doesn't chase me around the sofa, but he pushes me down on Charity's battered cushions, and the man who has never entered the kitchen of our Ahmedabad house now comes towards me with a dish tub of steamy water to massage away the pavement heat. (*D*, 35)

Though she feels flustered at the opening of the story where she is watching a play about racism and feels angry, gets hassled by the man who has kept his arms on her chair and in an effortless, mean, well-bred displaced Third World woman's voice, she sniggers at the man and asks him to stop exploiting her space.

Wearing her "mangalsutra" while going to meet her husband at the New York airport, somehow depicts the balancing act of Panna who does not want her husband to notice that the traditional values have been put aside by her. Having shelved her old traditions, this small act of Panna signifies her defiance and is significant in the sense that old habits or old traditions are difficult to be shelved so easily: "The shifting cultural values between East and West and between tradition and modernity are played out within the dialectic between merging and separateness and between self-reinvention and self-suppression."[14]

Women characters of Bharati Mukherjee hailing from different cultures are marginalized in the new culture—being ethnic and being of the female gender, Bharati Mukherjee herself had to face this as an expatriate in Canada. Considered exotic due to her skin colour, facing the problem of racialism and non-acceptance as a writer made her bitter. The same conditions are faced by three of her characters—Tara, Jasmine and Dimple in the initial stages of expatriation in the new world. All of them faced the problems of marginalization and made efforts to carve a niche for themselves. Their quest for identity leads them to several occasions, subsequently emboldening the empowered, emancipated women on the one hand, and confused undecided characters who resort to violence in order to self-assert on the other. The new breed of immigrants who equipoise between the ethnicity and Americanism emerge triumphant and some characters dwindling between two cultures subsequently become split personalities and reside in the self-made ghettoes. As Edward Said remarks: "Exile is life led outside habitual order. It is nomadic, decentred, contrapuntal; but no sooner does one get accustomed to it than its unsettling force erupts anew."[15]

Bharati Mukherjee's journey to India and Tara Banerjee's journeying back home have the same resounding echo of finding the "self" after being battered as the "other" in the foreign lands. Both of them, after the journey, decide to return to this foreign land, home becoming a bygone phase, to which one could return from time to time. The gesture is a basic necessity to anchor their lives. The homeland becomes a land unknown and foreign becomes a place of identity. Married into the new culture, its importance is understood and severing the bonding with old culture is a boosting stimulus to discover one's identity. The immigrant women who find themselves in a fix after their marriage feel vulnerable in new household, a more difficult situation arises when they migrate to a wholly new world, especially the women of colonial India who learn to keep quiet in order to adapt. The inculcated habits of suppressing one's emotions, physical and mental traumas to avoid rift in the family, the obeisant nature is in-bred through generations and the husband is the revered God who has to be served. Amalgamation into the new culture brings forth deluge of emotions unknown to the women themselves, the continuous struggle of changing or to remain the way they were. Intermingling with people forces them to retreat at first but the new format of living with free will allures and attracts. The male, who is used to the wife being subservient, is unable to handle this coercion, and consequently, we have men like Amit Basu, who dwindles between being magnanimous to allow his wife to become American but not too much of change is acceptable, and Professor Vadhera who survives maintaining a decorum at home which is a replica of the Indian home. The ladies have to fight their conscience before they can let go of their "selves." Then there is the struggle to prove themselves on gender basis. Racial discrimination is something which both the genders have to face. Bharati Mukherjee after surviving in the racist Canada for ten years, in spite of being married to Clark Blaise, backed by an educated background and her marriage into the culture, still she is not spared, and bitterness seeps in at the enormity of the situation. Coming back to India to gain stability does not help either, because being considered minority and exotic in a foreign culture batters her spirit but considered as an exotic foreigner in her own homeland is something which is enough to vex her into decision to settle as an immigrant in the United States of America, where she gains respite by losing herself into the hordes of immigrants.

The Indian girls whose identities are never their own, firstly known in the terms of their fathers, and after marriage they are known in terms of their husbands. Individualistic attitude and self-expression in the new world is both new and attractive. To be considered a human being, to be given attention as an individual in their own right proves fatal to most of the Indian women. Nirmala might be able to survive in the same environment but it is not enough for people like Maya, Panna, Jasmine, Tara or Dimple. Each one of the characters flaunts the characteristics of the author herself. The post-colonial Calcutta seems to invade the colonial sensibilities of the elite class and it is more like invasion of new norms into the resentful old comfortable world. This same scenario is enacted in the new culture where adaptation and assimilation is not so very easy, wearies them down into violence and aggressiveness, the corrosive new norms deducing different reactions.

Both Bharati Mukherjee and Tara Banerjee feel cheated in their homeland. Both decide to make a foreign land their home and place of identity, but the initial battle to reconcile with the changes inside and outside is traumatic and results in anger and then passivity and acceptance of new changes. To flow with the time, to live in the present is something which is the foremost criteria for adaptation. The reconciliation comes forth due to education, and the attribute of self-realizing comes quickly to them. The elite background helps to some extent in giving them the self-confidence, in spite of initial hesitation and travails.

> I love these women; I was one of them. But by some fate having to do with my father and with the way I was raised—the intense Bengaliness of my childhood that left me with a horror of its coarseness, and the suspended dream world of my adolescence that shattered so completely I would distrust all attempts to restore it—and the "gift for the pen" that did not take itself like other teenage passions, I became a different per-

> son. Something is fraudulent in the way I live; too little money to give up working; too much ambition to really want to. And I—a Ballygunge girl raised just like Anjali and all the others—to be nodding wisely as intense young ladies at McGill babble on about their lesbian lovers, group sex, and multiple orgasms? (*DNC*, 216-17)

Self-suppression of Indian immigrants gives way to self-expression and one is bound to retaliate to situations in a more fatalistic manner. One tends to loosen up in an atmosphere free of so many bondages. The open society seems to invite changes. Bharati Mukherjee and Tara find solace back home but the stifling situations, the old haggling do not make any difference. They have learnt to speak out and marrying foreigners and being in foreign countries is enough to give them the privilege of sitting and eating with the male populace of the family. No longer they need to sit on the ground and eat. The dilemma for Bharati Mukherjee is that she is born in a society which dwindles between colonialism and freedom from the bondage. The dwindling that occurs in her life is due to this. She is not a patriot as she has not been fed on old conventions to hold on to faith for country, nor too late to renounce the English society completely and be a true Indian.

> But fate sent confusing signal to some of us who were born in the decade in which Britain relinquished her hold on India. We were born both too late and not late enough to be real Indians. In the colonial ambiguities of the mid-Forties we acquired our monstrous habit of loving paradoxes. We loved both the freedom fighters and the red-faced officers who carried bullets and pistols. (*D*, 223)

This upbringing gives a very strong base to build a future for herself in a foreign land. The expansion of horizon does not baffle her in her early years in England. The only thing which baffles her is the feeling of racialism in Canada which batters down her resilient "self" after marriage to a Canadian.

Tara's alienation is not only in Vassar but she is marginalized in her own hometown, creating a havoc on her senses. It is not easy for her to face the expatriation in her home where she has been born and raised like a princess. She feels alienated in the company of her friends who consider her to be a foreigner. Born and bred in a closed environment, always living away from the general class, ambiguities and dualities exist in the very being of Tara. Her condescending attitude towards the lower class is not her fault but her upbringing in a servile atmosphere makes her class conscious. In Calcutta, she is marginalized for existing on the periphery. Sheltered life, all decisions taken by the father, establish the hegemonic patriarchal values existent in the Indian families. Marriages arranged by the elders without asking the concerned person is taken for granted. Born and raised in such an atmosphere and sudden exposure to foreign culture where Tara has to fend for herself leaves her totally confused and the loneliness drives her to reminisce about India:

> The only pollution she had been warned against in Calcutta had been caste pollution. New York was certainly extraordinary, and it had driven her to despair. On days she had thought she could not possibly survive, she had shaken out all her silk scarves, ironed them and hung them to make the apartment more "Indian." She had curried hamburger desperately till David's stomach had protested. (*TD*, 34)

One wonders what her decision would have been. She feels more secure in the presence of Bengal Tiger, and adjusting and adaptation seems round the corner as Tara visits a religious person and participates with full faith. She slowly comes to terms with changing Calcutta but for the riots. Would she have coaxed her husband, David, to join her in India, like Bharati Mukherjee and Clark Blaise visiting India, or would she have been able to detach herself and return back to Vassar with the happy memories as souvenirs, collected to be indulged in from time to time? Rape of her body and mind compels her to take her decision to retrieve her soul and find solace with her husband. A gesture of violence in America makes Jasmine stay and reinvent herself in America. The protagonist in *Leave it to Me* might be a liberated woman of modern America but yet the hunger to find her identity and her biological parents hounds her to go around searching. The characters like Jasmine, Hannah Easton and Devi do not hover between their cultures for a very long time. Hannah's frame of mind is attuned to her mother's act of disappearance with her Nipmuc lover. Thus Hannah never indulges in an extra-marital affair but meeting Raja Jadav Singh releases her from her bondage attenuating her reservations, enabling her to understand her mother.

Inability and disinclination to separate oneself from the past generates weariness of mind and immigrants tend to exist in their diasporic environment. To go out and act by oneself is a difficult course to be taken. Immigrants establish themselves in the new culture, and grow, the very uprootedness of "self" leads to degeneration.

Another factor that arises is that the women of Indian origin detain themselves from expression of their sexuality, suddenly faced by the liberal self-expression in new culture leaves them flabbergasted and they are undecided, not knowing how to react. Nirmala Vadhera is content to have a middle-aged husband and has no hassle about her physical needs because she has hardly been confronted with the nuances of the new culture. Again, one wonders what would be the fate of Nirmala if Jasmine had interacted with her. Would Nirmala, like a dutiful Hindu wife, snigger at Jasmine's unconventional life or would she be lured into changing and leave Professor Vadhera in the lurch? Lots of questions arise with each evolving character of Bharati Mukherjee's novels. Self-purgation might not be healthy in the case of Nirmala because she seems to be more prone to changes. She represents a bored, Indian wife who engages herself to pass time. The only thing is that Nirmala's existence in the ghetto does not instigate much to mutate. She works in a store and watches videos. Back home, she attends to the needs of her in-laws, husband and children. Ambition does not feature predominantly in her life which somehow makes the readers ignore her character.

Dimple is victimized in the ghetto of Flushing and Queens but her ambition does not let her be like Nirmala, and her dwindling, fickle-mindedness does not let her be like Jasmine. The transmigration takes a toll on the immigrant senses and reconciliation and equanimity are not so very easily established. The short stories in *Darkness* depict characters who are still trying to establish balance within themselves before confronting the majority of "Otherness" in an alien country.

Bud Ripplemeyer wants to know only the woman who is his live-in partner. He is afraid to know about her past which might break the image of Jane. Bud's wife Karin finds Bud's code of morals puritan and there is a role-reversal. Bud is like an immigrant in his own country because he is caught in shackles of his own making. His physical incapabilities seem to have imprisoned his soul. Jasmine's soul, ingratiated into the natural instincts of nurturing qualities imbibed by her culture, nurtures him like a mother. But she wonders if she would be acceptable to Bud if he knew that she had been raped and married before. The existence of duplicity brings around the cross-cultural identification of male-egoism. When Jasmine is confronted by the cross-country culture in America she feels let down because the landscape is no different from the countryside of India. "Battered trucks full of produce kept pulling out. More trucks, filled with labourers, turned in. It was as though I'd never left India." (*J*, 128)

The short stories in *The Middleman and Other Stories* have immigrants from all over South-Asia, India, Jews, Afghanis, the immigrants who are illegally in America and trying to establish themselves or melting into the melting pot of American culture. The father in "Fathering," though settled with his live-in partner, still searches for his daughter, Eng. Eng is a traumatized child who has seen her grandmother murdered. She tortures herself to gain attention and epitomizes the pain that she has undergone during the Vietnam War. The assimilation of "Other," Eng with the white father, is the aglimatization of two cultures. The father, Jason, embraces his daughter at the end of the story.

> Then, as in fairy tales, I know what has to be done. "Coming, pardoner!" I whisper. "I got no end of coins." I jiggle the change in my pocket. I jerk her away from our enemies. My Saigon kid and me: we're a team. In five minutes we'll be safely away in the cold chariot of our van. (*M*, 124)

Dr. Vinny Menezies, an Indian physician, proposes to Angela. Angela is an immigrant, an orphan of the old world. Her body has been mutilated in the war. Dr. Menezies provides security in the form of marriage but Angela does not feel any attraction towards the doctor. The doctor is old, bereft of the new ways of Americanism. Naturally he himself wants stability. Angela, haunted by her memories, knows that only a doctor could love her mutilated body.

In "Hindus," the lady protagonist is married to a white man breaking all the Indian ethical values. Being in a party, she is surrounded by immigrants who still exist in a ghetto and their conversation indicates their frame of mind. In order to establish their submerging into the new world, they criticize the Indian society and what it has come to. To assert their Americanism, they flaunt the virtues of the new world which somehow sounds pathetic and Leela finds it amusing. America is seething with immigrants and the ghettos are permanent fixture, which no immigrant can escape. No matter how much an immigrant asserts the fact of being an American but identity cannot be conspired. The stigma stays.

> I speak Hindi. No matter what language I speak it will come out slightly foreign, no matter how perfectly I mouth it. There's a whole world of us now, speaking Hindi. The manuscript of Memoirs was not dynamite, but I stayed up all night to finish it. In spite of the arch locutions and the aggrieved posture that Pat had stubbornly clung to, I knew I was reading about myself, blind and groping conquistador who had come to the New World too late. (*D*, 140-41)

The feeling of being inferior in one's own country, especially with the princely states demolished and the exploited lower classes getting the upper hand is not acceptable to these new immigrants. It is pathetic to watch them renouncing their own culture for treating them unfairly but they opt out to be the inferior minority in the American culture. This seems ironical to the narrator Leela, who though has become American but recognizes her identity as an immigrant.

"By virtue of her own identification with the Indian Diaspora, Mukherjee probes deeply into the inner conflicts of well-educated, sensitive adults whose traditional codes of economy of passion and material desire collapse amid their inadequate comprehension of the American paradigm of life, liberty, and the pursuit of happiness. Mukherjee shows the diasporic Indian as living in between two cultures, constantly journeying into new meanings and fashioning new identities."[16]

NOTES

1. Naresh Fernandes, "Choli to the Macarena," *The Sunday Times of India*, Review, February 16, 1997.
2. *Ibid.*
3. *Ibid.*
4. The Challenge of Multiculturalism for the American Church, <http://www.pioneerbooks.com/multicul.html> p. 6.

5. Bharati Mukherjee, "Classes: Reflection: American Dreamer," 2.11.99, p. 1.
6. Bharati Mukherjee, Bio-Sketch, June 4, 1997. India World Short Stories http://www.indiaworld.co.in/subscribe/rec/stories/bio-bharati.html
7. Lavina Melwani, "India tugs at the heartstrings of Indian American Writers," *Rearview Mirror*, p. 5. http://www.vdashtech.com/achal/ archive/oct98/review.html.
8. *Ibid.*, p. 5.
9. *Ibid.*, p. 7.
10. S. Zohreh Kermani, "Hyper-identities: Relocating Place Indentoty in Narrative and Cyber Space," Chap. One, p. 91. http://www.sirius. com/~zohreh/chapter%20one.html
11. Tina Chen and S.X. Goudie, "Holders of the World: An Interview with Bharati Mukherjee," p. 93.
12. S. Emmanuel Nelson, Bharati Mukherjee: Critical Perspectives, p. 131.
13. Fakhrul Alam, Bharati Mukherjee, p. 75.
14. S. Emmanuel Nelson, p. 33.
15. Reflections on The Exile and Other Essays.
16. Nelson, p. 210.

Chapter IV

Dilemma and Fluidity of the Immigrant Sensibility

"When immigrants arrive in the United States they must decide which of their traditions to continue to practise, which to adapt to their new home and which parts of the mainstream of American culture to adopt as their own."[1]

What they left behind is engraved on their inner being, the culture and traditions, which they are bound to and are secure in, environment in which they are born and bred. Encountering a new culture, new ways of life, coping with adverse situations, shock of a different environment leaves them counterfeiting between old and the new world.

> Below the gleaning crossroads of the world, the No. 7 train begins its journey to Flushing every three minutes at rush hour, welding the most ethnically diverse district on the planet into a coruscating mosaic. Most passengers in the rust red train are recent immigrants to the U.S.: the neighbourhoods in which they live are their effort to preserve the part as they struggle to build a future.[2]

The age-old instinct of being accepted in the new environment while still holding on to the old ideas and culture leads to a life of duality, a split personality, which wants to emerge as a winner in the new world but is still afraid to cut off the umbilical cord, joining them to the warmth and security of the old world. Fighting not only the entire self, they have to fight the colonial sensibilities in order to submerge into the "American Dream."

> My rejection of hyphenation has been misrepresented as race treachery by some India born academics on the U.S. campuses who have appointed themselves guardians of the "purity" of ethnic cultures. Many of them, though they reside permanently in the United states and participate in its economy, consistently denounce American ideals and institutions. They direct their rage at me because by becoming a U.S. citi-

> zen and exercising my voting rights, I have invested in the present and not the past: because I have committed myself to shape the future of my adopted homeland; and because I celebrate racial and cultural mongrelization.[3]

Jasmine in the novel *Jasmine*, meets Professor Vadhera in the United States of America, who is trying to create diasporic scenario of Punjab in his home. Punjab is not the same old Punjab anymore. For Jasmine, Punjab signifies the terrorist infested place where her husband is brutally gunned down by terrorists. For Professor Vadhera, Punjab is the old place where there is greenery, brotherhood, exuberant familial bonding, and happiness. Professor Vadhera is not aware of the new terrorist infested Punjab, or for that matter, even if he knows he acts unaware.

> They had taught me a great deal about surviving as an Indian in New York. If I had been a different person with a different set of experiences, if I had been another Nirmala, as they'd expected, then Professorji's lesson would be life-affirming, invaluable, inexpressibly touching. They had kept a certain kind of Punjab alive, even if that Punjab no longer existed. They let nothing go, lest everything be lost. (*J*, 162)

But still Professor Vadhera is settled in the United States of America trying to fulfill his American Dream. His profession in the United States of America is not so respectable by Indian standards.

> Flushing was not the downtown of dreams I'd conjured from the aerogram back in Jullundhar. And Professorji was not a professor, he was an importer and sorter of human hair. The hair came in great bundles from middlemen in villages as small as Hasnapur all over India. It was not exaggeration to say that the security of free world, in some small way, depended on the hair of Indian village women. (151-52)

Professor Vadhera is not the only one who faces this identity crisis. Each immigrant encounters the same crisis and to protect themselves they build a new world, within the new world, which is a counterfeit of the old one. The existence in duality is an inherent quality in each of them and they deal with the crises in their own way. Some are ambitious to cross over, whereas some still exist in the diasporic ghetto; few of them keep dwindling in between, subsequently ending up as split personalities.

> The immigrants spread out along the train route, building places of worship, stores stacked with imported provisions and restaurants serving up delicacies from home under the elevated tracks. The Astoria neighbourhood, for instance, just past the long Island City ruins, is known as little Greece for the onion domes of Greek orthodox churches and the aroma of lamb kebabs and meaty gyro sandwiches wafting out of cafes.[4]

Jasmine smuggles herself in the United States of America, encounters all kinds of humiliation, in order to fulfill her husband's dream. But unlike a dutiful wife, she is more resilient to her situation. Reality of America is hard and makes her cringe inside initially: "We took the bridge into Queens. On the streets I saw only more greed, more people like myself, New York was an archipelago of ghettos seething with aliens." (140) The disparity between the rich and the poor is very wide in India but it exists in States, too.

The commercialization of social values, hierarchical society, economic consumption has all made the human values go down the drain. As globalization took over, continents around the world came closer to each other and consumerism was the focal point around which civilizations grew and developed, and slowly human feeling became mechanized in the new technological world. The robot took over, life became computerized, mechanical emotions replaced human relationships with one man needing all kinds of machine and techno devices to keep company. The westernized American society and the modern technological culture soon affected the simple normal life of India. The human relationship was whipped away by the whacky modern culture. Acquiring the latest model of products, in order to make life comfortable became the sole ambition. The power emanating from technology advancement of the First World, lured the simple moralistic values of Indian culture. Immigrants feel uncomfortable in both the cultures, because they compare the comforts of America with their own comforts, whereas in America they somehow feel inadequate, exist in the diasporic ghettos and lead a life which is more or less orbitted around their own people. Acceptance into the "majority" is difficult. Though times have changed, immigrants are not allowed to join politics. There might be exceptions, people who excel in their field and help out in raising funds for political parties do get recognised and participate in the mainstream.

"From being a marginal minority who came to America with the sole idea of securing well paying jobs after completing graduate studies and professional training, and saving enough money to settle down in India, and lead a fairly affluent retired life, Indian immigrants are now coming of age, and having second thoughts about returning. The cardholders who came to this country in the Sixties, and had planned to go back to India after fifteen or at the most twenty years, have taken the citizenship, and are now reluctant to leave America permanently."[5]

Immigrants mostly smuggle themselves into the new world or go there to study and get a green card, only after they prove their credibility. In spite of becoming citizens, it hardly makes a difference to the new culture except that it expands and adjusts the filtering-in immigrants. Acceptance is denied on both the sides.

A group of people having entered the geographical territory and adopted the culture, language and the way of living, they should be considered as naturalized citizens and should cease to be foreigners. In the United Kingdom, it is impossible because they don't have the same skin colour. In Canada, a non-Canadian is considered out of bounds. "I am a naturalized U.S. citizen, which means that, unlike native-born citizens, I had to prove to the U.S. government that I merited citizenship. . . . I take my American citizenship very seriously. I am not an economic refugee, nor am I a seeker of political asylum, not by simple accident of birth."[6]

Bharati Mukherjee's sensibilities were ruffled to its maximum as an expatriate in Canada where she encountered not only the demeaning attitude of being treated as the minority, of different colour, having different voice, to the point of being a victim of racialism in Canada. She could not explain this feeling to her husband, who was in his own country and was accepted as an author, while Bharati Mukherjee spending ten years of her life in Canada could not challenge the authority as a citizen, but was always treated as an expatriate.

It is a country where minorities from other countries are humiliated and racial existent fecundity in the system would not let them be accepted in the mainstream. Moving around the world from culture to culture, Bharati Mukherjee's exposure to the outsiders though does not prepare for the situation she has to face in her own country, where she was born and lived till the age of 21. To be considered a foreigner in one's own country, the comparative experience of India and Canada finally makes her decide to move to the United States of America and merge into the mainstream of the American Dream. India becomes a distant country where she could return from time to time. No longer is she an exile or an expatriate. Bharati Mukherjee herself says that she fought for the rights of the Gay community in America because they were the only people who had supported her cause in Canada. Later, when her husband stayed for a year in India, he understood the plight of his wife in Canada, and the emotional upheaval that she had to bear to be accepted.

> In a life of many cultural moves, I had clung to my uniqueness as the source of confidence and stability. But in India I am not unique, not even extraordinary. During the year, I began to see how typical my life had actually been, and given the limited options of a woman from my class and from my city, how even in the West, I have acted predictably. My writing is a satellite of my marriage and profession, I have chosen, or fallen into, the role of a bourgeois writer, limited to a month of writing in a year. (*DNC*, II, 180)

While in Calcutta, like Bharati Mukherjee, Taramoni's sensibilities are in tatters as she is confronted with a new Calcutta, which she had not envisioned in Vassar. She is unable to accept the fact that Calcutta is not what she had left seven years back and as a very beautiful place but was torn to pieces now. The constant comparison of the new Calcutta to the old one in her memory frightens her to the point of getting delirious. Facing the same consequences is not what she had anticipated while journeying back home, expecting warmth and amiable surroundings. Instead, the chaos gets on to her nerves, the moment she boards the train and her fellow passengers keep bickering about their luggage, incidentally Tara's Samsonite being the bone of contention. The chaos at the station throws her into a panic and she seeks out her father for assurance.

The first glimpse of Calcutta at the station shocks her to the core. Used to be protected by her father, he seems to be the only reality around her. Engrossed in her own visions, she is unable to accept the raucous atmosphere at the station. Being with her parents, the house seems the only haven where she can let down her defensive attitude. The strict, masterful disposition of her father makes her feel safe from the distortions of the environment and people around. She literally cringes away from people, who are below her class exhibiting her fear of people. The insulated existence in her father's house, subsequently destroys the impressionistic mind of a child. The fear of mixing with people of different class makes Taramoni react in a strange manner. Blending is not so very easy in India and the wish to blend abroad is not fully granted. "The house on Camac Street began to exercise its hypnosis on her. New York, she thought now, had been exotic. Not because it had Laundromats and subways . . . because there were girls like her, at least almost like her, were being knifed in elevators in their own apartment buildings. Because students were rioting about campus recruiters and far away wars rather than the price of rice or stiffness of final exams. Because people were agitated over pollution." (*TD*, 33-34)

Self-suppression is a quality which comes to the rescue of Indian women very easily and inveigling an expression from Tara is difficult. Being in her parents' house gives a sense of security to Tara which is not there abroad. Being nostalgic about her homeland is obvious and Indian grooming hinders a confession of her love to her husband. David, her husband, is not able to understand her inner being. Intimacy is an expression unknown to her Indian groomed soul and self-introspection gives rise to more confused mind. Self-introspection is forced on her by the insensitive act of Tuntunwala whom she does not understand till the end.

Being in her parental home frees her from her insecurities but does not equipoise her turmoils and Taramoni tends to lose herself, to put down her defences and leave herself open for evil to infiltrate. Continuously protected, first by her father and later on by a loving husband, she is not prepared for the tough turf that she encounters in her own hometown. Relaxed and secure in her father's house, she now starts doubting her husband's love. It is her lack of self-expression that stifles her natural instinct of voicing her love for her husband in a letter because she is surrounded by her father's collection of furniture:

> Tara could no longer visualize his face in its entirety, only bits and pieces in precise detail, and this terrified her. Each aerogramme caused her momentary panic, a sense of trust betrayed, of mistakes never admitted. It was hard to visualize him because she was in India, Tara

> thought. In India she felt she was not married to a person but to a foreigner, and this foreigner was a burden. (62)

Continuous conflict is there in the human mind which is reflected in all the protagonists of Bharati Mukherjee's early novels like *The Tiger's Daughter*, *Wife*, *Darkness* and fluidity in the emancipated characters is apparent in *Jasmine*, *Leave it to Me* and *The Holder of the World*.

The do's and don'ts inflicted upon the mind lead to fickle-mindedness and confusion and Tara in *The Tiger's Daughter* is unsettled. Rather, the transformation or the early exposure to an alien atmosphere of Vassar somehow misbalances her personality. Nostalgic about her home in Calcutta, which is existent in her mind, real Calcutta forces her to self-introspect and decide about her future. Being in her hometown, she starts wondering if her husband loves her. She becomes delirious at times and she doubts that she cannot recall her husband's features vividly. The maladjustment occurs with the realization of changing Calcutta. She is not able to reconcile with the fact that her fantasies are merely bubbles of water, which burst with the prick of needle of reality. She wonders if her husband is real or not. The absence has changed her hometown forever, now she wonders if her absence has made her exist in her fantasies and forget all about her husband. The only reality in this whole chaos is her father, the Bengal Tiger:

> Tara watched his body turn now left, then right, slicing as it turned through that shy and brutal atmosphere of Howrah Station. For a moment she thought she was going mad. For she felt that the Bengal Tiger, set apart from the smell and noise of the platform, had in her absence moved out of the private world of filial affection. He seemed to have become a symbol for the outside world. He had become a pillar supporting a balcony that had long outlived its beauty and its function. (28-29)

A fear constantly grips her if her husband loves her or not, and then she is suddenly struck by the feeling that her mother does not love her. The continuous rejection by the two cultures leaves her bereft of feeling and weakens her power of judging a situation with clarity. The continuous protection by her father smothers her natural instinct of self-protection. Her growth of mind is fashioned by a dominating father, and love is an emotion which means controlling the life of the loved one, till the age of fifteen and the sudden exposure to the Western world of Vassar is too much for Tara to cope with. Return to India to find stability after seven years, married to a foreigner, the whole experience is like a jet lag as she is considered an exotic foreigner married to a "mleccha." Marriage into a different culture makes her an outcast in her own homeland and the immensity of the shock to her system leaves her emotionally weak. Nostalgia in Vassar instigates her to return but the changed scenario makes her hysterical and adaptation to one's own homeland seems to wear out Tara's nerves. Facing the reality of her memories makes her tearful. She finds herself to be naive and is unable to relate with her friends. She is more comfortable with Joyonto Ghosh who claims to have realised his "self" and wants to help the poor. He takes Tara to meet a sage, but Tara runs away scared. Joyonto forces Tara to meet the people who have made a slum of his land. Tara gets hysterical when a woman touches her sari; she is uncontrollable and loses balance as the girl literally pulls at her sari. Tara is unable to camouflage herself in the colours of diplomacy like her friend who zealously goes through the whole village, meeting people as though she is totally detached to the on-goings in the slum area. She struggles to maintain her sanity in difficult situations. Coming into contact with the reality and reconciling is commendable on the part of Tara who slowly merges into the society other than hers. No one is able to understand her traumas. The duality in social values is beyond Tara's apprehension:

> She was not an unpatriotic person, but she felt very distant from the passions that quickened or outraged her class in Calcutta. Her friends let slip their disapproval of her, they suggested her marriage had been imprudent, that the seven years abroad had eroded all that was fine and sensitive in her Bengali nature. (55)

Tara, slowly, starts merging into the social circle and her spiritual awakening and tolerance is evident when she takes her mother to an ashram where she partakes in the rituals enthusiastically. Her self-esteem goes down when her liberal nature is taken for being licentious and is ramshackled to pieces by slimy politician Tuntunwala. Protected by a dominant loving father and never having actually encountered. such people in Vassar, Tara is prone to be duped easily. Her life in a foreign country might add extra leverage to her status in her Bengali Brahmin clan, but her facetiousness makes her an easy prey for prowlers like Tuntunwala. It is however pathetic that Tara believes in Tuntunwala against her own judgement. The first impression of Tuntunwala when Tara meets him in the train is of him being slimy and repulsive. But later on, in spite of being frightened by his audacity she forfeits her own fate. After the incident of rape, Tara no more finds respite in her parents' home because the act of rape is considered a blemish on the girl's character in a conservative family and Tara sought solace in her husband and the culture, which would not point a finger at her or blame her for encouraging the marauder. Guilt results in schism within her self and her own family is unable to provide the balance. Already having faced the traumas of expatriation in Montreal, she has run to her father to find solace and security that she remembers. But even the strength and security represented in her father could not save her from the wily, insidious human being with whom she ventures out, letting down her guards and getting ravished. The sequence reminds the readers of a similar incident when Goddess Sita stepped out of the magic circle and was captured by the ten-headed demon king. Unable to face the trauma of humiliation and self-suppression, finding solace in a new culture where there would be no one to humiliate her and point a finger and say that she herself was responsible for decapitating her virtue, seems a better alternative.

Bharati Mukherjee, in order to keep her sanity, had to constantly fight to keep the "Self" intact from "Others." It began early in the joint family where her "Self" included herself and her family, and the "Other"—the huge family—is a constant pain for Bharati Mukherjee, her mother and her sisters. The rejection of the other crowding members of the family is apparent and can be construed from her actions. Bharati Mukherjee's sensibilities get bruised and she isolates herself behind a wall of her own making. She, in order to avoid the chaos around, surrounds herself with books, thus paving the path of a future as a writer for herself. The wall of protection is to protect her sanity thus creating a vacuum within her self, schism within her "Self" and the "Other." The projection of her feelings and ideologies is evident in her characters who demand or recoil from the situation and create schism within oneself. The two-dimensional portrayal of characters shows her power of story telling where follies of human nature are juxtaposed with superhuman qualities. On the one hand importance is given to Hindu mythologies and philosophies, on the other hand the modernity and punctilious intricacies of American life are intermingled and equipoised, blending into each other with precision.

Bharati Mukherjee tries to blend the two ideologies deftly, and the character created handles the world with propinquity and propitiates the worldly affairs with aplomb. The compelling force behind Tara's decision to leave for Vassar is a volte face for her indecisive frame of mind. Tara is like a child when she runs to her parental home to find solace in the secured walls of the home of Bengal Tiger and she is a seared young woman who runs away to her husband to find security in a foreign world. The attitude of escape comes immediately to one's mind. Tara's frame of mind does not allow her personality to be balanced. But then Tara is not able to handle the aberration caused by her own fault, abrading her mind, soul and body. The rapist in India finds a way out of the situation. Tara, unable to handle the burden on her soul gets hysterical and the efforts of her father to subdue her cannot pacify her anymore. Realisation of love for her husband awakens her to the enormity of the whole situation, innervating her to return to Vassar.

> David's letters during the monsoons also intensified her depression. He wrote that he had been reading Ved Mehta's journals on India, and that even in New York they brought home to him the dangers that surrounded her every day. He told Tara, he saw Calcutta as the collective future in which garbage, disease, and stagnation are man's estate. "Survival to the lower forms, insects and sludgeworms." Though the Bengal Tiger tried to protect her from the excesses of the city, Tara told her parents that she was preparing to return to David and the United States. (201)

Always treated as a misfit in her friend's circle after returning to India, Tara feels let down. Not only had Calcutta changed but had also instigated her friends to change completely. Tara's friends cannot understand her discomfiture and her foreign ways. No longer exposed to colonial atmosphere, Tara has changed into a person who is condescending somehow. Tara gets distracted by her friends' surface chatter and had to listen to them, criticizing and talking about her as if she is not sitting with them. Reminded or rather accused of being a foreigner and not understanding Calcutta irks her but she suppresses any kind of reprisal. Though she feels hurt because she had been suspended in her nostalgic memories for seven years and the shock she receives on seeing the reality is still vibrating with the undercurrents. Her friends still exist in their own world of servility and are unable to understand her strange behaviour. Secure from the worldly hazards and slimy human beings, virtuous in her Indian ideologies, Tara is forced to evolve into maturity, through violation of her body, mind and soul. Old concepts of love and marriage, even after having lived in a foreign culture, are firmly entrenched in her mind.

> When the sandalwood paste had been ground Tara scraped it off the slimy stone tablet with her fingers and poured it into a small silver bowl. But she could not remember the next step of the ritual. It was not a simple loss, Tara feared, this forgetting of prescribed actions; it was a little death, a hardening of the heart, a cracking of axis and centre. (51)

The basic fact of blending of image, of Indian myth in form of 'Kali' and 'Devi,' gives birth to Debbie Di Martino who co-incidentally is rechristened as Devi in *Leave it to Me*, and gets out of hand as she slays her adversaries at random. She has the very attitude of Devi "Kali" who slew the demons to protect humanity. On a second glance, one can easily justify the actions of Devi. Her action is not epochal, but it does affect a few. Killing of her bio-Dad in an action out of revenge and revulsion is an instinct to protect herself. Each of her actions is to save her sensibility. Devi avenges Frankie Fong because he had dared to cheat her of her self-respect whereas Loco Larry had tried to mutilate a dead body which is beyond her comprehension. The action is voluntary as she kills Loco Larry.

> The flaw in the book is that the underlying myth whether Electra or Kali is too weighty for the characters of the story. The escapist hippie generation, the Flower children and the fruit of their amorous adventures, encumbrances dropped and abandoned at will: on such a sensual, hedonistic life style, how does one impose the Goddess Kali, her strength and moral uprightness. And if Debby/Devi is, indeed, the Goddess incarnate, how does one reconcile the divine image with the protagonist's total lack of spiritual depth, her very pragmatic/ materialistic approach to life, and her many liaisons with the men who come

> her way? No, the mythical frame chosen for the story does not fit the bill.[10]

The very action of murdering the marauders is a part of spirituality. The ideologies of *Gita* and the Hindu scriptures are somehow misplaced. Devi, while killing people like Loco Larry, or Bio-Dad, feels no compunction. The "Karma," which is flauntingly expressed in the novel is all about taking action, performing one's own "Karma" without thinking about the consequences. As far as killing of Loco Larry is justified because humiliating the body of a dead woman is something beyond Devi's comprehension. A victim of Vietnamese war, Loco Larry is a psychic case and his act of revenge is repulsive to the humanity. Bio-Dad is killed. After killing Devi's Bio-mom and his act of murdering Ham, the method he resorts to, shows his misbalanced and psychic derangement. Justifying the murders is not something Bharati Mukherjee aims at, but the fact of adapting Indian culture might be suppressing one's feeling but adapting the western culture has a different connotation which is not acceptable. Unnecessary violence cannot be condoned, but violence to save the feeling of humanity might be justified and obviously this factor conjoins the character of Devi with Devi Kali. Electra factor might be existent in the fact that Devi hurtles forward to achieve her goal to find her bio-parents and uses every means to fulfil her ambition, be it sleeping around or torching her boyfriend's house. The ego in Debby retaliates at the injustice done and her belief in herself instigates to kill. It is her ego, which when used and set aside by Frankie Fong, enervates the incident of torching his apartment, thus eliminating the very basis of his identity as an immigrant in America. Frankie Fong uses her physically and mentally, though it is mutual, he discards her for a lady who has an easy way into the American citizenship. Introducing her to his mother as his secretary finally opens Devi's mind to his intentions. The blow on her self-esteem is enough to send her hurtling towards the act of revenge and restoration of self-respect. Taking away his cherished dream house is an act of annihilation of identity as hers was ground to pieces mercilessly.

> A spectacular extravaganza of light, sound, heat. I was an auteur, too. Frankie had no right to be angry. He had a duty to take pride in my accomplishment. Clarity. That's what I prize more than knowledge. In the

> hot harsh light of clarity I saw for myself the difference between justice and vengeance. (*LITM*, 53)

Bharati Mukherjee tries to equipoise the two polarities in each human being by juggling characters under the spell of Hindu doctrines and American life. There has to be a balance in one's life in order to live the life to its fullest and with a zest. Giving vent to one's anger is not wrong and if, Devi, a murderer, killed to take revenge, she could have murdered Frankie Fong instead of torching his dream of merging into the mainstream of American life. "The concept of karma is that fate is very dynamic. Not too many people are understanding that part of it. True concept of Karma is: when on a dead-end street, jump into alternate paths." (80)

Changing from Faustine to Debby to Devi, Debby still searches for her identity and leaves no stone unturned to do so. Her quest for identity puzzles her foster-mom and her reply is that she has to find about her "psychic legacy." What Debby wondered from the beginning is the disparity that exists between her family and herself. She does not hanker after any family ties but wants to find out the people who gave birth to her and left her.

"The whole world has gone into her making and she has to find her place in this 'hodgepodge' of cultural heritage and religious visions," says Mukherjee. "She is an American original and therefore has to decide for herself what it means to be an American in the 1990s. She has been the victim of so many different forms of brutality: political, from the Vietnam war, and from her biological parents who dumped her like garbage on the hippie trail in a desert village in India. The unspoken victim of the Vietnam war is the child of the 70s who had been scarred in invisible way."[8]

Dimple Dasgupta in *Wife* gets entangled in a web of her own making. she gets totally lost when she tries to be a perfect Hindu wife, but her egoistic attitude, her concept of freedom, and her quest of self-identity, all get ingratiated into multiple knots, coaxing her to cross the border of gender and experiment with American doctrines. The misplaced beliefs enervate Dimple to kill her husband. The motive behind Dimple's action is not the same as Devi's. Instead of saving humanity, it is more of an act to save her self. Her self-preserving characteristics drive her to self-assert. Dimple is far removed from Devi, who changes her name and identity like a chameleon. The definition of adjustment changes its priorities when it is in the hands of Devi in *Leave it to Me* or Hannah in *The Holder of the World.* Adoption to outside change is incarnated on the very basis of Jasmine in *Jasmine*. Jasmine seems to be a juncture, where the intermingling and identity transformation changes hands with guilt-ridden Dimple in *Wife* and Tara in *The Tiger's Daughter*.

Tara and Dimple somehow exist in a world which is not real. Dimple right from the beginning conjures up visions of a husband which is a common trait among young girls in India. Her non-acceptance of her own physical attributes is again common among girls, especially in a culture where physical endowments are considered essential in the marriage market. The timidity of Dimple is a characteristic which gives way to aggression and self-pity. To enhance her physical attributes, she consults a beautician. Her marriage to Amit Basu is like a wish come true but she immediately regrets not completing her education. The "present" holds no significance in her life. The future holds promises, an opportunity when she would be revenged upon the mediocrity of her present life. She gains freedom in her dreams, and a place where she is free from the bondages of reality. Dream is an escape from the dreary and paltry existence. The passive existence is forced upon by grooming through generations, and to cross the boundaries and enter the effervescent world of marriage. A simple fact that completely escapes her punitive attempts at freedom is the real fact of married life. A life away from a dominating father is Dimple's aim in life and to achieve this, the physical attraction should be enhanced. She is pretty, but lack of bust (which is an epitome of beauty in Indian culture from time immemorial) fills her with inferiority complex. She works on her skin to make it fairer and learns all sorts of gimmicks to entice her future husband. She always exists for others and not for herself, though preparing herself for the impending wedding concerns Dimple indirectly. She is frustrated when her attempts at being outstanding beauty go awry. Her traditional mind does not set her free to give expression to her feelings and even after being married to Amit, she cannot act extrovertly. She remains passive as expected by a Hindu wife. Later on in America, her attempts to act as a seductress in the presence of Milt Glasser fails miserably and she feels deflated.

> It was not the time to reach for dark glasses and sensible undergarments and make discreet inquiries about the young man's job. She was so much worse off than ever, more lonely, more cut off from Amit, from the Indians, left only with borrowed disguises. She felt like a shadow without feelings. Whatever she did, no matter how coolly she planned it, would be wrong. (*W*, 200)

Her overtures to lure Amit fail to deduce reaction, her physical attributes go unnoticed. Amit is busy working hard to gain a position in America and by the time he is home, he is too tired and goes off to sleep. Her continuous dreams about her having been murdered is rebirthing of a new sensual Dimple who craves attention from Amit.

> She wrapped her blue bathrobe tighter around her breasts and hips and did all the things she normally did between seven and eight on week days mornings, but she knew that she was dead and Amit would recoil from her as soon as he sat down at the table for his wheaties and two fried eggs. (185-86)

Dimple attempts at being the ideal wife, and yet her passivity gives way to aggressiveness, because America defines a new concept of freedom which is alluring to her senses. She revolts to accept the destiny assigned by nature and society but does not have the courage to revolt convincingly. Her nature is already entrenched with the virtues expected of a girl of Hindu Bengali Brahmin origin. The openness of the new culture beckons her to leave behind the virtues and merge into the society promising new horizons. Dimple's guilt drives her crazy with longing to be free of all norms from her past culture, but she cannot muster courage to repudiate the values completely. Divided between the struggle of "self" to go out and to adapt, her struggle is limited to her fantasies, a symbolic struggle to adaptation. Each of her desires gets dampened by anxiety, and pros and cons of each action take priority. She wants to control her future, but is not ambitious and takes her first step towards it by having an affair with Milt Glasser. She wants to flaunt her relationship in order to instigate some response from Amit. In anger, she wants to declare her indulgence in an extra-marital affair but self-expression is something which does not come naturally. She is doomed to her world of fantasies, hiding her yearnings from her husband. She is guilty of committing adultery and consequently is predisposed to all sorts of negative obsessions that ventilate the ambivalence of anxiety and existence in fantasies. Her insecurities due to indisposition of character take refuge into subterfuging her real emotions from everyone.

> She wanted to dream about Amit but she knew she would not. Amit did not feed her fantasy life; he was merely the provider of small material comforts. In bitter moments she ranked husband, blender, color TV, cassette tape recorder, stereo in their order of convenience. (113)

Contrary to this, Pixie, Dimple's friend, seems to have fortuned on a life that Dimple craved for. Her marriage is by eloping with her lover, which seems more romantic to Dimple. Dimple's self-repression takes a negative turn and she is bound to kill her husband. Submersion comes with violence, which is the ethical norm of the new culture. Giving vent to her inner frustration, Dimple gorges herself with food, sleeps and watches T.V. Her favourite past time is visualizing how to kill herself, or how innovative she could be in formulating different methods to kill Amit.

> She would like to make one extravagant gesture in her life. If she only knew where the jugular was! What if Amit were to lie to her? It made nine ways to die altogether. . . . Two hours later, while Dimple was still creating moments of death, Ina Mullick came back carrying a shabby green tote bag. (153)

Lost in her world of loneliness, self-pity and frustration, turns her into a self-mutilating person, instead of self-mutating. Continuously living a forced identity causes a lacerated self. Initially, trying to abort her child, Dimple vomits with fingers thrust inside her throat and she derives pleasure from the action. Giving vent to her frustration is evident when she beats a cockroach or a rat to its death. Her defiance of the norms set by the society is put through with a clarity which horrifies the reader. Fated to passivity, in order to please the husband and in-laws, and exposed to a society which is violent in self-expression makes her more sadistic. Her pleasure in hurting herself and repression of her feelings intermingles and Dimple is unable to handle the situation created by her over-dazed, disgruntled state of mind. Her behaviour towards herself is more or less sado-masochistic as she punishes herself because she lacks the courage to give voice to her inner turmoils. While being in her in-laws' place, she is agitated because she is not able to redecorate her own bedroom. Afraid to break the mould of ideal wife and daughter-in-law, her anger turns inward. Dimple does not face the hazards of the dominant culture, but negligence on part of Amit makes him the "Other." Thus Amit's behaviour puts him away from Dimple. Her desire for economic independence is something which rankles Amit's nerves. Her benevolence extends to words, but never to action. Though Dimple could have easily involved herself in the social circle, or her wish to gain respect among the social stratum could have been filled, but she lacks self-confidence and ambition.

> But she would not begin again, because you could build only on things you had already done. She had learned that simple lesson quite painfully in the last few months and she knew that. While there would be the desire for a hundred new starts, there would never be a real beginning. Sitting in the taxi with the window rolled up, she thought she saw the woman she might have been, a smart woman with pale make up attending a lecture on Introductory Astrophysics (3 credits): stellar structure . . . neutron stars . . . gravitational collapse . . . she wanted the whole goddamn cosmology made accessible to her. (182)

Bharati Mukherjee, after returning to India to soothen her ruffled nerves, is faced with the Calcutta social life and different atmosphere at house. She feels at a loose end. The changed scenario has a very different effect on both the husband and the wife. Clark finds the atmosphere of Calcutta congenial and mysterious, unravelling the mysteries helps him understand his wife. Bharati Mukherjee is unable to relate with the New Calcutta. The adverse conditions faced in Canada have already overwhelmed her sensibilities. Not accepted as a writer in the Canadian writers' world and a continuous struggle to attain acceptance in the culture leaves her harassed and angry. Role reversal of being white in an alien country and his acceptance of the situations irks her to the extent of getting into fights, and he is questioned about how he will feel if he were not accepted as a writer in India. Clark Blaise now understands the traumatic experiences of his wife while she was in Canada. The journey to homeland is more of a journey inward, of soul searching and, by the end of the journey, India becomes a distant country, where she comes to meet her parents from time to time. Bharati Mukherjee, during her stay in India, is cynical while viewing the women of upper class Bengali Brahmins who indulge in maintaining decorum in the society, but refuses to accept the New Calcutta and the strife of labour class. Engrossed in the glossy side of the society, these society women, who are Bharati Mukherjee's friends, are beyond recognition.

> In Chembur, where we spent the first month and a half seeing my family and preparing for the trip farther east to Calcutta, I learned that fear is not an affliction; it merely is a way of ordering a confused world. The wives I met in Bombay relied on fear to give meaning to lives that otherwise have seemed, even to them, banal. . . . These executives' wives thrilled to the lazy salute of watchmen as they drove in and out of the main gate on their way to the bazaar. The salute was reassurance of status. These women were valuable while the millions outside the gates were not. The compound literally isolated them from the world, of unassorted passions. The factory walls gave them their corporate identity, loyalty, and self-respect, created a calming communal village in a chaotic industrial zone. (*DNC*, II, 188-89)

Bharati Mukherjee continuously compares situations in India to that in America, the way things and situations are handled in the town of her birth and the country she married into. The chaos of the hometown seems more irreparable than the place where she had been constantly striving to gain recognition. The sabbatical year for Bharati Mukherjee is a year of indulgence in nostalgia and the situation around her is observed with irony. The atmosphere behind the walls of the factory is servile, free from the chaos of outside world. Not only Calcutta, but Bombay also seems to exist in the same postcolonial nostalgia. "Fear" of existing with "Other" (in this case the labour class) seems to lose the exuberance of the social flitting women who knowingly or unknowingly have the condescending magnanimity as an inherent characteristic, expected by them. The fear existing in the ladies, due to the unrest, seems to generate all sorts of fear. Bharati Mukherjee is continuously warned against mixing with common man. The remnants of being of upper class and the existence of social strata in India are omnipresent and it existed when Bharati Mukherjee was young, but now it is too much of an adumbration to pronounce superiority over the less privileged class. Though the luxury of her parents' house is like balm to her weary nerves, yet emotional upheaval in her house seems to repress her free soul. Facing a different treatment but of the same nature, expatriation to Canada and being married to a foreigner, who is above the Indian norms in her own home country, has the same implication. Both demand her to give her "self" in order to merge. Individuality seems to be an inherent quality of Bharati Mukherjee. Exasperated by "love" which is defined more as a control over the individual in India, and rejection by the "Other" in Canada, seems to be the decisive force which leads her to her own evolution. Decision to merge in the social and economic condition of United States of America seems to hold promises. Being treated as a foreigner in her own country is something which is not anticipated by her. For Clark Blaise, the society of India is welcoming, considering that he is the son-in-law and an exotic guest who is there for a short period but not a threat to the society.

> Clark was astonished by the elasticity of this society, compared to the narrowness of ours in Montreal. As for me, I felt sheepish that I was now so eager to explore the social life I had once regarded with irony. The years of tortured adaptation to other people's attitudes and rhetoric receded, dark and massive like storm clouds, they threatened my simple pleasures. (*DNC*, II, 199)

As a working woman, married to a foreigner, having lived in a foreign land, gives a boost to Bharati Mukherjee's stature in the social circle and the relatives. She is allowed to share the same glory as the male populace of the family, no longer considered the menial housekeeper who is there to cater to the needs of husband and sons. Fluency in English raised her to a pedestal where she is looked upon with respect. But the ladies of the middle class of Bengalis tend to engage in gossip and speculation. The girls working in an office are below their standard. The only concern is to get a groom, the most eligible bachelor with promising future, who would rescue her from this reality of life and give freedom. The same notion becomes the basis for a character like Dimple to be born. Dimple is an incarnation of middle class Bengali Brahmin girl. She literally symbolizes the beauty spot, a dent in the cheeks, epitomizing beauty. Contrary to this, the dent is in her mind and her character turns into a chasm, filled with the illusory expectations she loves to exist in, but never strives to make it a reality. Dissatisfied with her marriage, with her present, with her fantasies, she hates to fantasize about a husband who grates on her nerves. Now and then, Amit quips on her state of lethargic existence, but a new Dimple, who stops watching T.V. after meeting Milt and Ina, seems to provoke him to react cantankerously. When he comments that she has changed, Dimple goes and switches on the T.V. and asks if everything is back to normal.

Tara Banerjee seems to be a replica of Bharati Mukherjee. Being an exile in a foreign country is too much for Tara. Bengal Tiger, concerned about his daughter's welfare, sends her to Vassar to get herself a degree. Her marriage to David Cartwright is a setback to the values generated in her family and the social circle they move in. Acceptance of this marriage by Tara's father naturally upholds all the speculation and sniggering by the society. Tara signifies another incarnation of Hindu Goddess Durga, but the sensitive Tara, seems confused and feels like an alien in her country of birth. The grit in her is visible only at the end of novel where she watches Joyonto beckoning her to understand, to realize her "self." A weak old man but full of inner strength, trying to save her from morbidity, but the only thought, which is inside her head, is to be with her husband and confess her love to him. The breaking of the boundaries and old traditions takes a back seat while Tara sits still, locked in her own world of evolution. The mutilation of her body releases her of her nostalgia. Self-realization seems to hit her as Joyonto Mukherjee is being beaten and Pronob gets killed while trying to save Joyonto. Realizing her potential, she chooses to save her own soul, to retain the feeling of love, yet be free to have a future which is not overshadowed by the past. Sensitive to her surroundings and her feelings, she is able to take decisions with clarity. Once her befuddled mind clears, she focuses on the chaos in her life with lucidity.

Tara is totally unfocused on her own problems and the chaos that exists outside in the surroundings. Repulsed by the poverty in India, she dwindles between her decision to stay and help or leave the irreparable situation as it is. A physical ailment, which is most common in India, makes her sick. In Vassar, she is hit by visions of terror in her lonely hostel room and her emotional crisis is something which she is unable to handle. The emotional upheaval in Calcutta makes her seek out the guidance of her father and later on, in Darjeeling, she feels at peace in the pilgrimage. The continual dubiousness which Tara has to resort to when confessing to her husband about life in India, obviously a trait imbibed into her when she is married to a foreigner, becomes a featured conspiracy, which swathes Tara into manifold layers of strategies she has to go through to maintain a balance between the old traditions and New World openness. David, being a 'mleccha' according to Bengali Brahmin standards, is kept at an arm's length so that he does not invade the sancto-sanctum of traditions. Leading a double life, Tara sometimes falters. Unable to maintain the balance, she revolts by giving in to hysteria and frenzied emotions. This inherent quality of belief in 'goodness' does not warn her against the sanctimonious Tuntunwala, who she refers to as "spider," initially. Always dwindling between maintaining the sanctity of old values and indulgence in the freedom of New (married to a foreigner gives her a licence to mix freely with male populace which otherwise would have been impossible), makes her falter in the judgement of a character. She is easily duped into the web of slinky Tuntunwala. Self-recrimination is not something which Tara indulges in but a new mature Tara is born out of morbidity. Taking firm decision, taking charge of her life instead of any one else, comes to her the same way as feeling of oneness with everyone in the holy temple of Mata Kananbala had seeped in without warning and made her defend the Hindu belief.

> The man was so authoritative, it did not occur to the maid to question the proprieties of his suggestion. Tara knew she should protest. Yet she couldn't. It would be useless to storm out now. She was tired, and sick; she was curious and impatient. She could wait a few minutes longer. If she were a more aggressive young woman, better able to protect herself like Antonia Whitehead, she knew she would have walked out of the suite with the maid. But she was neither forceful nor impulsive. At that moment the Marwari appeared to her strong, sensible and curiously akin to the Bengal Tiger and Harilal Banerjee. (*TD* 197)

Aware of New Calcutta with a veneer of sophistication and tolerance, Tara's evolution is appropriate, and now with a new determination to have a life of her own choice instead of being a victim of nostalgia, her vision has a vastness which can envision a green Calcutta sans disparities among classes. She renunciates parasites like Tuntunwala who are more interested in their own projects. Nuances of life come to her with clarity. No longer impulsive, Tara sits back and maintains her cool, anoints the riots going around. She has made peace with the New Calcutta. No longer caught in the colonial mentality of the upper crust of Bengali Brahmins, she is free of the bondage of slavery to Indian traditions and the hypocrisy of the society, which has dualities in the basic structure. No longer she craves for the bygone times and has no wish to compromise with any circumstance, which is beyond her control. The ingenious decision to take hold of her life, takes a priority, and helps her to evolve. Her decision to leave her past and live for herself, her individuality, which could not be developed earlier, makes a deep impact on the reader's mind. Her father is genuinely bewildered by his daughter's determination to return back to her husband. He is puzzled at her behaviour, but is happy to see her as an individual and feels that she would not return back for a long time. The love for their daughter drives them to arrange all sorts of entertainment so that she gets distracted. Tara, in spite of her love for her parents, goes and gets the air-ticket for Vassar. This incident of getting an air ticket reminds the reader of her initial floundering in Vassar, when she tells her academic adviser that she cannot type because it was never a question to be considered in India, as it was taken care of by her father's staff. It shocks the teacher, because in a culture where everyone does one's own work, it is beyond the apprehension of the academic advisor to focus on and understand Tara's colonial attitude.

> Tara thought a table lamp could throw cruel shadows on the face of a middle aged spinster. "No," she answered, tracing the blotches of light and dark with an imaginary finger. "My father's secretary goes out of his way to help us. When Rajan, our cocker spaniel, died and we were so heartbroken, he even arranged a secret night burial for him without waiting for our permission. He's always done everything, all our typing etcetera. That's why I've never had to learn, you see." The advisor, used to revealing herself only as a liberal missionary failed to understand the import of Tara's remarks. (*TD* 12)

Contrary to this, her father considers her an adult. When he asks and advises her about a prospective groom, she is touched to the heart. No longer considered a child to be protected, treatment as an adult moves Tara, because all her life, decisions for her have been taken by the Bengal Tiger.

> Tara recalled how this tableau had embarrassed her greatly in those days. She was anxious to fall in love, good heavens! There was nothing wrong with her. But marriage meant certain physical mysteries, centering, as best as she could determine, on or near the navel. She had been

> grateful that the Bengal Tiger, so fierce in the business world, had procrastinated in this small personal thing. (*TD* 124)

Tara is not only bewildered at the changing Calcutta, she can also not imagine the modernity flaunted by the female gender in the conservative society of Bengali Brahmin. She, initially, with memories of Calcutta seven years ago, not only fantasizes the same old environment of the life that she had led before leaving for Vassar, but she is also shocked to see her friends in bathing suits. Her sensibilities are ruffled because though Calcutta has changed, her imagination is suspended in the same period of colonial righteousness. Wearing bathing suit in company of the men somehow seems degeneration of values, values which she herself has maintained, even being to Vassar and married to David Cartwright has changed nothing for her.

> Tara's swimming was no good either. She was depressed at this first sight of her friends in swimming attire. She felt there was something unnatural or absurdly heroic about their posture. The soft edges of their bottoms escaping the grip of the western bathing suit had no business being seen by servants. (*TD* 93)

Bharati Mukherjee emphatically points out the difference between her two characters, Tara and Dimple. Tara is engrossed in the memories of her home country and the love of her father, her attachment to her past makes her travel back to her home country to discover her own identity. The journey back is more of a journey inward, more of soul searching and discovering her own potential as an individual and not just an extension of her father. Dimple Dasgupta is antithetical to Tara, renouncing her past and present for her future. She is in a way an apocalypse, epitomizing ambitious young women who are ambitious but do not have enough will power to fulfil their dreams. Her dream to actualize the "American Dream" pertains to violence which is inherent. She is a person fighting her "self" to discover her "self." Always concerned about what the "Other" might think of her makes her sit back and nurture frustration and anger. Her anger is a palpable reality, which surfaces like a volcano and has a negative force which never lets her vent her emotions, but vexes her in renewing new force, which comes out in delusions. It is like an active volcano lying dormant till the fury in her innervates her to kill her husband and exonerate herself of all guilt, because killing is a regular feature in the American culture as shown in the daily soap operas where a killer escapes punishment. The enormity of her act, which is more of self-purgation, does not register on her befuddled mind. Tearing into the new culture, forcing her way through violence, and renouncing the inherent values which are imbibed indelibly on mind, she is similar to the delinquent Dimple evolving into a psychopath who might be acceptable in the American culture but will be disowned by the parent culture. She is unable to tolerate the diminutive attitude of her husband, in spite of his feigned magnanimity, which is demeaning to her sensibilities. Expressing her individuality which is genuine, she goes unnoticed by Amit and vexes her into taking out her frustration by punishing herself. Her favourite pastime is visualizing Amit Basu to be someone else, which in reality he is not, never understanding the fact that she might not have been the woman of his dream. The anxiety to gain success in the new culture is something which occupies Amit to the extent that he is not able to apprehend the forthcoming violence, which is like a seething anger inside Dimple. Like a true successor of patriarchal tradition, establishing himself as the provider of the family, he overlooks the fact that Dimple also might want to breathe the fresh air in the new society. Her continuous vomiting is more like throwing out the embryo, which is the symbol of her enchained soul. Her relishing the act shows how much she wants to control the fate that she faces. Controlling her destiny as a suppressed, weak female is something which she forces herself to accept in her in-laws' place but she cannot tolerate her pregnancy, which is more like a burden than a joy.

> Thus what bourgeois optimism has to offer the engaged girl is certainly not love; the bright ideal held up to her that of happiness, which means the ideal of quiet equilibrium in a life of immanence and repetition. In certain periods of prosperity and security this has been the ideal of the middle class as a whole and especially of landed proprietors; their aim has been not the conquest of the future and of the world but the peaceful conservation of the past, the maintenance of the status quo. . . . The male is called upon for action, his vocation is to produce, fight, create, progress, to transcend himself toward the totality of the universe and the infinity of the future; but traditional marriage does not invite woman to transcend herself with him; it confines her in immanence, shuts her up within the circle of herself.[9]

The affair with Milt Glasser is not only symbolic of her exposure to Western world, invading the sanctity of Amit's house, it also gives a new modus operandi to innervate Amit to wake up to her physical and mental demands, but to no avail, because Amit's struggle to establish himself challenges him to focus on his own life and work, and incohesive about the simmering volcano in the form of his wife's chaotic, emotional bundle of internalized fury, which is waiting to unleash any time. Amit, lost in his own world of dreams of a rich future in India, cannot fathom his wife's emotional upheaval, a result of cultural shock. American dream of a separate house, which she can call her own, is a dream from the stage when Dimple is unmarried. Like any girl who dreams to have her own house, husband and children, Dimple's dream extends to the point where her wishes are fulfilled. Lack of understanding on the part of Amit makes her exist in a state of limbo, a continued struggle to suppress her flighty existence, yet she craves recognition as an individual. Her craving for marriage is to escape the dominating father, and a separate house is significant of her desire to relinquish all responsibility in the form of her in-laws. Her expectations of marriage when crushed to miniscule particles, leaves her bereft of all emotions. Not exposed to the worldly vices, Dimple in a way is like Tara whose revelations to reality are beyond her apprehension.

> She was sure love would become magically lucid on her wedding day. Pixie was lucky, Dimple thought; Pixie did not understand about waiting, she did not worry about the dark unless it happened during a Hindi movie, or about the radio dropping pitch and then dying in mid-sentence unless it was playing a favourite song. Pixie did not know that reading novels, studying for exams, flipping through film magazines were strategies of waiting. (*W*, 9)

Her initiation into the free world is marked by the incident of her trying to get rid of the burden of pregnancy and child-birth and her final renunciation is another act of violence by killing her husband like a cockroach or the rats whom she beats to death. Her mode of killing is kitchen knife; kitchen being a place of solace. A constant duality exists in the life of Dimple where she wants to be Sita and Scarlet simultaneously. Dimple's fluidity into the mainstream occurs with violence against a stimulus outside, that is, Amit Basu, who seems to be a hurdle in the path of self-realization whereas Tara's renunciation is violence against her, mutilation of self into mutation and self-realization. Acceptance of the self, feminity, no longer becomes a hurdle in the path of freedom. Crossing the gender discrimination, violence becomes a common factor in both the cases.

> Formerly, ah, what a conflict between a mentality that seemed incompatible with the present century and the calls of this century itself! Now I seem conscious of a certain calmness. Each new and grandiose idea that occurs to me, instead of causing a painful turmoil, an incessant destruction and reconstruction, is marvellously adapted to what is already in mind. . . . Now I move insensibly from theoretical ideas to life as it is, without a break.[10]

Abandoned by mother, Hannah Easton's soul in *The Holder of the World* is lacerated permanently, with the memories and the environment of puritan society of Massachusetts, which is somewhat a replica of the puritan values safeguarded so ardently by the male dominated culture of India, yet Hannah's renunciation comes to her in India. The violation of moral values by her husband releases her of the "magic circle" that she has drawn around her. The duality of norms is the very basis of her husband's existence. He has several extramarital affairs while he expects a chaste wife and the revelation about his affairs with a black bibi innervates her to finally release herself, and give an expression to her feelings. The final chain breaks as she meets Raja Jadav Singh and decides to become his white bibi. Her realization of love empowers her to break the boundaries of gender and she, like a Goddess, visits the invader king and implores him not to conquer her lover's domain. Her initiation into the flow of life is through her maidservant Bhagmati, who in spite of not being educated, knows the norms of love and is faithful to the memories of a dead man. The expansion of horizon eludes her initially but love for Raja Jadav Singh lures her into the world of dreams, which finally become reality. Release of mental blocks frees her from the self-suppression, which was due to the jealousies of Gabriel Legge and Hannah herself. The illicit relation of Gabriel is not acceptable to Hannah but her love for Raja Jadav Singh finally makes her understand the frivolities of her mother and she is reconciled with her mother.

> Hannah/Pearl stayed on in Salem until her death in 1750 at the age of eighty. Pearl Singh, born in 1701 somewhere in the South Atlantic on the long voyage home, saw in her old age the birth of this country, an event she had spent a lifetime advocating, and suffering for. Hannah/Pearl returned to Salem with the infant and immediately began to search for her mother. She found her in a workhouse for the mad and indigent in Providence Plantations, speaking some tribal gibberish and insisting on wearing her outmoded woollens with the shameful 'I' boldly sewn in red to her sleeve. (*LITM* 284)

Anger against her mother is due to the fact that when Hannah needed her mother she was abandoned, for a Nipmuc lover, an abrasion on a child's mind, who was still unaware of the intricacies of love. Hannah exculpates her mother only after learning to love herself. In the process, she releases herself to embrace life with open arms. Abandoned by her mother, Hannah fends for herself, hardens up with time, learns to treat people medically and restore herself. Her skills of medicine and operation put her on a pedestal and she fashions into a mature woman. Bondaging herself is resultant of childhood remembrance of abandonment and she takes her responsibilities very seriously. Parsimonious with her feelings, Hannah marries Gabriel in order to gain access to the world of adventure and freedom. The enchained soul of Hannah frees itself only when she operates or crotchets. Her life in India is like the wife of English factors of the company, but mixing with the wives of other factors does not hold the charm for long. Quest of the unknown, unknowingly, takes her into the world of Bhagmati and the soul of Indian culture enfolds, layer by layer, under her bewildered and enchanted curious eyes. With this discovery, her own evolution occurs.

> That Hannah was not as malleable as an English factor's wife had to be and that the curbing of her spirit would require diligence and planning must have been clear to Cephus Prynne from the moment she, ignoring his steadying hand, stepped out of the boat that had ferried her. (*HW* 107)

Married to a pirate, a profit maker and a marauder, Hannah exemplifies her duties with honour and respect and is more like an Indian girl who is taught what to do and how to behave in her husband's house. She maintains a distance from slimy people like Cephus Prynne who, like Tuntunwala in *The Tiger's Daughter*, is interested in violating her modesty. Threatened by her calm disposition, he wants to thwart the very strength of morality in Hannah. Repulsed by her, he changes his act with dexterity and finally, he succumbs to the superior strength of Gabriel and is found dead in the waters. Avenging comes easily to Gabriel and to achieve his goal, he enacts the fury itself. He is like the Bio-Dad of *Leave it to Me*, who kills at random, to get what he wants. Gabriel's colonial attitude gets him all the riches that he wants. Looting and murdering comes naturally to him and gratification of the senses takes a priority. He is licentious and cheats on Hannah, but Hannah is unaware to his frivolities until he is discovered due to his own folly. Her nurturing qualities are never satisfied by her husband but Hannah's loyalties extend to him and it seems that she is faithful to her husband due to the feeling of gratitude. He is the person through whom she gratifies her freedom from the puritan society into the new world of India.

> In England, Gabriel had often shocked her with his violence or enticed her with his unpredictabilities. The Gabriel she knew was at his most angry when he manifested an outer calm, as on his return from the dead. As in his patient questioning about men, every man, who had visited her while he was reportedly dead, killed by the Portuguese. But there was a new deliberateness to this assault on the merchant Chetty's umbrella bearer. (*HW* 115)

The infallible Devi in *Leave It to Me* is like a tornado which hurtles forward with frenzied speed to discover the mysteries of her birth. Finding the bio-parents is her sole aim, for which she goes to any length. Indirectly affected by the Vietnam war, Devi is unable to define her uniqueness, her physical beauty which is outstanding amidst a family of people who cannot establish her heretic relation with her foster parents. Scrupulous and unscrupulous simultaneously, as the senses demand, Devi has no qualms about her actions which are violent from any point of view. Initiated into the philosophies of "karma" by an Indian man at McDonalds, Devi moves forward unhindered like a typhoon. Her name given to her by the nuns who raise her is Faustine which means Typhoon. Validating her christened name Faustine/Debby is a deviation and finally the incarnated Devi moves forward without any hesitation to find her bio-parents who are from a generation of hippie culture.

In her quest of identity, Debby merges into the culture of San Francisco. She meets people who are inheritors of the Vietnam war. She meets Ham, who later she discovers to be the lover of her Bio-mom, and Fred who loves her Bio-mom and eccentrics like Loco Larry. She hangs out at Haight Ashbury, the hippie hangout, and easily merges into the street culture. Indubitable in her self-confidence, incisive in her actions, Devi treads towards her goal. Unhindered in her quest, Devi meets characters who teach her the nuances of life. Finally, she ends up working for an escort agency, which caters to the needs of budding authors. Supposedly, the agency is owned by her Bio-Mom and slowly and painfully, she becomes aware of the fact that her lover Ham, is also sleeping with her mother. The person who helps her to get the information from India is also her mother's lover. An heir to her father's violence, it becomes the very basis for re-inventing herself. Ultimately the murder of her father ends Devi's journey in her quest to find her bio-parents though she is not penitent and the journey to quest for renunciation continues. Perforation into the past digs up all the dirt, but it hardly dismays Devi into retrieval of her journey to search for her identity. Instead the violence in the culture that is portrayed in the novel, somehow seems misplaced. The philosophy of *Gita* pervades the actions and reactions taking place in the life of Devi. The rules laid out by Bharati Mukherjee seem to merge into the American society. Violence is peremptory and Devi never backs off or feels repentant at any of her "karmas." It is more like she is destined to the future that she decides for herself and her rechristening herself as Devi grants her the powers to slay the human beings who are below her explications.

> Violent propensities. The sea has them, the Earth rocks with them. I claim my inheritance, kneeing Bio-Dad so hard as he tilt his head back to draw from the tiny bottle that it tumbles him. TAPE ROLLING. The cleaver fuses to my arm. It soars and plunges, soars and plunges "Monster!" I scream. I keep screaming as I cradle Ham's tormented face to my bosom. I am screaming as I dial 911. (*LITM* 235)

Precision and strategic moves on the part of Devi take her to all the right places and she never fumbles or flounders in her decision. Raised in the American culture, she is not hesitant in sleeping with anyone, but never lets herself get ensnared in emotions. The coolness with which she operates is sometimes chilling, and changing jobs and identities with fluidness becomes a second nature to her. With no past, she is hardly concerned about anything which she might lose.

Devi is born to two individuals, who hardly care for the consequences of their passion. Discarded and disowned, Devi has inherited the dubious characteristics, which make her avenge her defaulters from time to time. Belief in executing one's action without thinking, violence is like a second nature and killing of her own father is another violent family tiff, which ends in the gruesome death of Bio-Dad. Working at "Leave it to Me," Devi encounters characters who seem to know exactly who they are. With no identity to call her own, Devi is irked into action. Re-inventing and fluidity are the very essence of Devi's character. Rebirthing herself as Devi, a name ripped off a licence plate, her incarnation in Bharati Mukherjee's novel seems to be the final endorsement on Bharati Mukherjee's evolution as an American writer. Bestowing her character with all the nuances of American life style, Bharati Mukherjee has finally achieved what she has worked for in her earlier novels. Devi is totally American who does not let any weakness or fear deter her. Her weakness for a lack of identity and past is easily camouflaged behind the tough exterior.

> Deep down I envied the Chinese waiter and the Indian student. The guys were geeks, but they knew who they were. They knew what they'd inherited. They couldn't pass themselves off as anything else. No evasions, no speculations, no let's pretends. They didn't see themselves as special or freakish. (*LIJM*, 66)

Till the end of the novel, Jess never acknowledges Devi as her daughter, though Devi has collected all information. Her father, though, immediately claims her as his daughter. He butchers Ham in front of Devi, and he has already killed her mother. Is it the killing of her mother that vexes her into action or, is it the gory murder of her lover that instigates her to kill her Bio-Dad for whom she had gone through a lot. Ham's murder seems to break Devi. He is more than a lover, somebody whom she always looked up to. The killing of Ham makes Devi forget the rules of her own game. Is it love that makes her react violently as she uses the same cleaver to murder her dad? Above all, she calls the police after murdering her father, which is unusual for Devi who has escaped each and every violent act in life. She has never felt repentant, be it torching the American Dream of Frankie Fong, or avenging herself on Stark Swann who considers her a bitch waiting for his attention. Her uniqueness is incredible. Every time she takes revenge, it is wholly new. Drugging Swann, she carves a message on his buttock with a K-bar knife-point and thanks Larry for this new weapon that helps her in taking revenge.

> I nicked an endearment on his left buttock: CW. My homage to my neighborhood graffitiste, cee-Double-you. Because that's what the women who give off their blissful selves of their own accord and for as long as you want them to, the real women, do. (*LIJM*, 163)

The various characters whom Devi confronts in search for her bio-parents, some are bitter about their experiences of the Vietnam war, like Loco Larry, who has shown perverseness in character as a key to assimilation into the American culture. Ham, her lover, who protested against the war, is a man of stature, whom she looks upto, and is a pillar of strength for her. Immigrants like Frankie Fong, who connive their way into the American Dream and Florida writer like Stark Swann who wrote to make reparations for what men did to women though he is a true chauvinist who behaves with Devi as a low being made to serve him.

Her bio-mom finds Ham insipid in comparison to the serial killer who makes her wanton in her needs. Bio-Dad, the serial killer, who has no qualms in taking away lives believes in eat, drink and be merry. Naturally, the inherent qualities of her parents nurtured the killing instincts of Devi. She goes through life infallible, and forages through mysteries to find the centre of her own universe.

> Oh, how the city seduced me! I thrilled to the skylines geometry. Rectangles, cylinders, rhomboids, pyramids, shapes belonged. And I loved San Francisco back, loved its parks filled with lovers, sunbathers, Frisbee tosses, loved its drowsy drunks let alone on streets, its nose-ringed schoolboys riding public buses, its skinny gray ridges stuck with pastel matchbox houses, its lingering Golden Gate and sailboats in the Bay, its streaky sunlight on foggy days, its Day—G10 graffiti inside street car tunnels. (*LITM*, 67)

The fluidity of character is an inherent quality of Jasmine in *Jasmine*, though it is not what is appraised by the members of her family. Surviving the sniping of her grandmother, her future is decided. Survival of the fittest aptly fits Jasmine. She survives the predicament of an astrologer. When Prakash is killed after few months of marriage, it seems that the astrologer's prediction has proved right but the surviving life force forces her to leave the place, which augurs bad spell, and the change of place, culture and identities seems to be a diffident move to prove the prediction false. Leaving India is her first step towards alluding the future curses, and never marrying Bud Ripplemeyer is a part of defiance against destiny. Bud Ripplemeyer is maimed and is destined to stay in the chair forever. The bad spell in her life seems to partly affect Bud. One wonders if the astrologer's predicament might have manifested again if Jasmine had married Bud. But Jasmine seems to be smiling at the fate, because she sidetracks it by not marrying Bud. Leaving Bud for Taylor is another way of escaping a life bondaged to a cripple. Though it seems inhuman on the part of Jasmine to leave Bud, yet, like an American and an individual who has every right to find her own happiness, Jasmine leaves Bud for a person whom she loves. What if something happens to Taylor? Jasmine might be playing a game of hide and seek with the God of Death, and takes pleasure every time she defies the destiny. The wound on the forehead seems to be the "Third Eye" which empowers her to foresee the impending dangers and changing the tracks seems to be easier.

> The incentive, I should have said, is to treat every second of your existence as a possible assignment from God. Everything you do, if you're a physicist or a caregiver, is especially important in the eye of God. When Pitaji died, my mother tried to throw herself on his funeral pyre. When we wouldn't let her, she shaved her head with a razor, wrapped her body in coarse cloth, and sat all day in a corner. (*J*, 61)

Du, the adopted son of Bud Ripplemeyer and Jasmine, is a person who has inherited the vast empire of violence and his detachment to the ongoings around him simply makes him a hermit, for whom happiness and sadness are two facets of the same coin. Adjustment into the life of Iowa comes easily to him. Whereas Karin's life has more complexities, though she, being a white, easily reconciles to the fact that her family life has been intruded into by an outsider and yet she befriends her enemy. Jasmine not only mutates with a fluidity, but unlike Devi, she destroys the marriage of Karin to Bud Ripplemeyer. Her act is defended by Bharati Mukherjee. Jasmine unknowingly encroaches the grounds in order to root herself into the American culture. She destroys, knowingly or unknowingly, intruding into the lives of married men. Taylor is abandoned by Wylie for her own progress, and Jasmine steps in to take her place. Each one of the wives, be it Karin or Wylie, befriend Jasmine. Jasmine's urge to get rooted makes her march forward towards her self-emancipation. Her genuine repulsion to the Vadheras initially shows her desire to go out and embrace the unknown. She feels suffocated in the self-created ghetto in the house of Vadheras.

> Jasmine's temporary refuge with the Vadheras is an encounter with the insubstantiality of identity. But the Vadheras' incomparably pale ghostliness is a kind of vacuity. Mr. Vadhera is frozen in sclerotic lie intended to cover up his humiliating and ghoulish as a sorter of human hair; Mrs. Vadhera is caught between the simulacra of two lives, one in America and the other endlessly rehearsed on videotapes of Hindi films she watches—she dreams of both, having neither.[11]

Shuttling between identities gives a renewed energy, a certain thrill and expectation of new in life instead of stagnation, drives Jasmine to go to America and try to self-immolate. But the violence against herself loosens her moral righteous values and leaves her free to journey light into the unknown future. Rooting herself in one place seems to stagnate her senses. Uprootedness seems to become a habitual trait, which exemplifies her natural instincts to put roots. The ambivalence of dualities in her character is more intoxicating. She turns into a perpetual vagabond, enjoying the unpredictabilities of life. Experimenting with life, instead of living dreary life, thrills the adventurous soul of Jasmine and, one can easily point out that she is the transitory character, a juncture which divides the universe of Bharati Mukherjee into two periods of evolution as an author. The earlier characters like Tara, Dimple and the characters in her short stories compiled in *Darkness* still pay homage to their old tradition and have to be violated and forced to evolve, whereas the characters in *The Middleman and Other Stories* are buoyant characters who are bred on self-empowerment. They cross all the boundaries, break the norms of servitude to the "Other" and surge forward into the unknown to enhance their self. Self-emancipation comes through violence, yet all is taken in stride. The fluidity of these characters itself empowers their bonded self. Fear of consequences is a very great binding force, which does not let the immigrants let go their old beliefs and traditions, which they might or might not cherish.

> Jasmine is innocent, curious; she embraces her new experiences in the New World, even though she is often bewildered by them. Hannah is an illegitimate daughter in seventeenth century Puritan Massachusetts. She has to escape her Puritan surroundings in order to return to it with a deeper understanding of its potential as well as its limits. Debbie is a multiracial orphan, born and abandoned in India, then adopted by an American family in upstate New York. She is confused, hurt, angry. She has to sort through her various racial, cultural, social heritages before she can be at peace with herself. I think of Debby as the difficult sister of Jasmine.[12]

Mr. Bhowmick in the story "A Father" (*Darkness*) is punctilious and unimpressed by his tradition. He cannot accept the nuances of the New World in case he loses his identity. The fear of loss makes him recoil from his very American daughter, for whom Hinduism is "neat" and "is like a series of super graphics."

Going round in circles and finally coming to terms with himself and the world around exhausts him and he takes refuge in Mother "Kali." Due to lack of adventure and fear of unknown, he is sniggered at by his Americanized wife and daughter. To hide his perplexity, he blames his wife of coaxing him into migration but he very well knows that his dream of success was the reason for immigrating abroad. But he blames his wife for forcing him to get permanent resident status in the United States of America, because she could not adapt to the norms of middle class mentality. Towards the end, her middle class mentality hinders her thought in accommodating her daughter's decision to have a child through artificial insemination.

> But Mr. Bhowmick knew at once that his daughter, his untender, unloving daughter whom he couldn't love and hadn't tried to love, was not, in the larger world of Detroit, unloved. Sinners are everywhere, even in the bosom of an upright, unambitious family like the Bhowmicks. It was the goddess sticking out her tongue at him. (*D*, 66)

The opening scene in "A Wife's Story" shows the discomfiture of an immigrant protagonist Panna but as we move further we see a female immigrant from Asia enjoying the freedom and openness in the new world, rejoicing in a platonic relationship with a male friend.

Her marriage, arranged though, does not fall into the tradition of a male-dominated Asian marriage. Though Panna feels the need to justify her marriage bindings to her husband, in case he finds it offensive, she, like Tara, does not feel free to ask about love and freely express her sexuality. Sense of freedom in the New World gives a sense of exhilaration but while preparing to receive her husband, she adorns herself with the garland of black beads, 'mangal sutra,' still tries to equipoise the values of the two cultures, to complete her universe which demands nothing which she cannot give.

Married with initial hiccups and hesitancy, the visit of her husband gives a new meaning to marriage which is beyond her expectation. Laying aside all the traditional rules, her husband indulges her, and their married life transforms into American bliss and Panna is delighted to have her husband at her place. Instead of being obnoxious, America seems to release her husband of all his traditional bondages. Yet Panna refrains from going back with her husband, leaving the New World. Her liaisons with other men are not revealed to her husband, and she shows the positive attitude of an Asian immigrant in America. Contrary to this, Panna's roommate presents a completely modern Western approach towards marriage and love. Charity sleeps with her plastic surgeon every third Wednesday.

> Orientals are supposed to have monopoly in the hands-modelling business, she says. She had her eyes fixed eight or nine months ago and out of gratitude sleeps with her plastic surgeon every third Wednesday. (*M*, 29)

In "Loose Ends" an unwary daughter of a motel owner is raped by a psychopathic Vietnam veteran, who forces his way into the new culture and wishes to gulp it down like a python. "This is what I've become. I want to squeeze this state dry and swallow it whole." (*M*, 51)

Maya Sanyal in "The Tenant" unscrupulously sleeps around with men at random, rejoicing in the freedom of the new culture. She relishes the fact that she has slept with all kinds of men except Indian men who tend to cling and be authoritative. Mr. Chatterji and Mrs. Chatterji are an immigrant couple who seem to be as per rules, clinging to the old values and Mrs. Chatterji is more interested in the lives of others, than to pay attention to her supposed wifely duties. Whereas Dr. Chatterji takes Maya for granted because of her single status, and his licentious behaviour repulses Maya: "Outwardly, she retained her poise, her Brahmanical breeding." (*M*, 107) In spite of a life full of promiscuity, her retaliation is verbalized against the perversity existent in the male mentality, which refuses to mutate in the new culture.

"Fathering" is the story of a white man reconciling with his child who belongs to an Asian mother.

Dr. Patel in "Nostalgia," in order to exorcise his memories of beautiful women, sexually exploits an Indian sales girl in New York. He is shocked to discover that the girl is a prostitute and with the help of an associate, blackmails him into giving all his possessions. Frustrated, he reverts to his Indian origin and defecates into the sink and with his own excretion he articulates anger in writing 'WHORE' on the mirror of the bathroom.

In "Orbiting," Bharati Mukherjee portrays 'love' as an emotion which can save the world and bridge the widening chasm between the two cultures. An Afghan refugee has been forced to live the life of a vagabond, and has been camping in airport transit lounges on and off till now, until he finally enters the New World. His beloved is a second generation Italian American who has had her own share of orbiting. The story begins with 'Thanksgiving' party preparations and a concerned Father asking all about her lover. Having been ditched by her boyfriend Vic, Renata finds solace in her new lover, whose body is scarred but his self-confidence and shyness at once sets him apart from her earlier liaisons. She is ready to get him an American citizenship. He is like a scarred hero:

> I shall teach him to walk like an American, how to dress like Brent but better, how to fill up a room as Dad does instead of melting and blending but sticking out in the Afghan way. In spite of the funny way he holds himself and the funny way he moves his head from side to side when he wants to say yes, Ro is Clint Eastwood, scarred hero and survivor. Dad and Brent are children. I realize Ro's the only circumcised man I've slept with. (*M*, 74-75)

The concept of fluidity means to retain the positiveness and the soul of old culture and then expand one's view to submerge into the new culture. Renata's confession to herself is the realization that she does not want her lover to change except outwardly, in order to blend into the mainstream.

Ratna in "The World according to HSU" is terrorized by the racial discrimination in Canada and feels safer on an Island where a military coup breaks out as soon as they reach the place. Shunned as a white rat in India and scorned as a Paki in Canada, being on the island surrounded by the militants, she feels herself safer. "But conflict," Mukherjee implies bitterly, "seems to be fundamental to the world, not just racial or marital; abrasiveness is embedded in the very structure of the planet."[13]

Darkness is a compilation of short stories depicting the life style of expatriates caught between the two worlds of servitude and freedom. Marrying is the easiest way to merge in the New World, while migrants are there to work their way into the "melting pot." Multiracialism in Canada faced by Bharati Mukherjee is voiced through her characters. The stifling bonded life to norms of society and various other burdens that are still being carried by some of the immigrants do not let them merge easily. Fear of losing one's "self" is the driving force which makes them retreat back into the safety of their own world. "The country is hostile to its citizens who had been born in hot, moist continents like Asia; that the country proudly boasts of its opposition to the whole concept of cultural assimilation." (*D*, 3)

The migrants are humiliated and unaccepted on the foreign soil, linger in their memories, lead a life suspended in time and their attempts at acclimatizing go in vain. The very purpose of being in America is to earn maximum amount of money and to enjoy the economic independence in their own country. To be accepted, they try to be what "Others" see them as, yet trying to retain the values of the old world, makes them exist in a limbo. Unable to establish the equanimity between the 'self' and the 'Other,' they attempt to incite reaction, further exacerbating the situation, Nafeesa Hafeez in the story, "A Lady from Lucknow" is embittered because her affair with a white man fails in getting a reaction from his wife. Taken as a bimbo, and treated as another liaison in her husband's life, James Beamish's wife degrades Nafeesa's sensibilities and leaves Nafeesa nursing her pride. "Though the characters in these stories are, or were, 'Indian,' I see most of the stories of broken identities and discarded languages, and the will to bond oneself to a new community, against the ever present fear of failure and betrayal." (*D*, 2)

The last story of *Darkness* "Courtly Vision" is a detailed description of a painting of Basawan. The detailed intricacies of the painting are vividly painted in words by Bharati Mukherjee. Several narratives interwoven in a single canvas titillate the senses of the readers to applaud the author's hold on her words. Words bring out the beauty of the painting just as painting exhibits several activities, past and present, getting their own dignified place in a single painting. Different people signifying different moods and cultures merge together into one canvas to give voice to greater magnitude, emergence of a new era which is free from the bondages and let the soul free to wander in the realms of the mysteries of life. It is a vision that is envisioned by Bharati Mukherjee as an expatriate in Canada, as is envisioned by Joyonto in *The Tiger's Daughter*:

> I have an obsessive love of Mughal miniature painting. The miniatures that speak to me the most eloquently were painted during the reign of Emperor Akbar. I suppose that's because mine is a writerly love. Each of the Akbari paintings that I'm mesmerized by is so crowded with narrative, sub narratives, sometimes meta narratives, so taut with passion and at the same time so crisp with irony. Every separate "story" in the miniature matters, every "minor character" has a dramatic function. But all the strands and details manage to cohere, that's what's amazing! And each is "framed" by an elaborately pointed border. The border shouldn't be dismissed as the artists' excessive love of adumbration. The border forces you to view the work not primarily as a source of "raw" sociological data but as sociology metaphorized; that is, as a master-artist's observation on life/history/national psyche cast in the aesthetic traditions of the community and transmuted into art.[21]

NOTES

1. "I'm taking the No. 7 train," *The Times of India*, *The Sunday Review*, July 19, 1998.
2. Ibid.
3. Bharaṭi Mukherjee, American Dreamer, p. 4 of 5. (Website) http://www.mojones.com/mother_jones/JE97/mukherjee.html.
4. "I'm taking the No. 7 train."

5. Voices of an Emerging Indian American Consciousness: Bharati Mukherjee and Mani Laxmi Shreela Ray, p. 16 of http://home.eznet.net/hdeleevw/shreelaRay/articles/lakshmitalks.html.
6. "Who Speaks for us?: Bharati Mukherjee's Fiction and the Politics of Immigration," Helena Grice, University of water, Aberystwyth, U.K. p. 85. www.sagepub.co.uk/journals/details/issue/sample/ a031701.pdf.
7. MELUS: *Leave it to Me* (book review), p. 2. http://www. findArticles.com/efom<278/24/63323875/pg2/article.ihtm.
8. Varsity Arts and Culture around the World With Bharati Mukherjee, Shah, Myra p. 2 of 2. Varsity Review: Web Posted On November 17, 1997. http://www.campusme.utoronto.ca/groups/varsity/ archievers/118/Nov17/review/Around .ihtm.
9. Simone De Beauvoir, *The Second Sex*, pp. 447-48.
10. *Ibid*., p. 366.
11. S. Emmanuel Nelson, Bharati Mukherjee: Critical Perspectives, p. 76.
12. READING GROUP GUIDES.COM Bharati Mukherjee, *Leave it to Me*. P. 8 of 8. http://www.readinggroupguides.com/guides/ leaveittome-author.asp.
13. Asian American Literature. "An Interview with Bharati Mukherjee," (1987) Alison B. Carb, *The Massachusetts Review*, Vol. 29, winter 1988-89, p. 362.
14. WAAPA CREATIVE PRACTICES, Bharati Mukherjee, Through Other Prisms; p. 1 of 2. www.waapa.cowan.edu.au/guide/research/ bharati.

Chapter V

Style: Inner Being of Bharati Mukherjee

> The isolated one she just left . . . and the new one she doesn't quite know how to enter.

The earlier novels of Bharati Mukherjee follow the thematic pattern woven around the expatriate Tara of *The Tiger's Daughter*, Dimple Dasgupta of *Wife* and various immigrants's life interwoven in the short stories of *Darkness* and *The Middleman and Other Stories*.

Jasmine is supposed to be the transition; evolution happens with her later novels after Jasmine's metamorphosis into various identities zooming and zipping to carve a niche for herself in an alien country, adopting all means to adjust into a life created by herself, defying the predicament of an astrologer way back in the village she was born. After this novel, the style of Bharati Mukherjee seems to mature and it takes off to unknown realms where sometimes even Bharati Mukherjee herself seems to get lost with her creations especially Devi of *Leave it to Me*. A normal born baby abandoned by parents, Devi turns into a Frankenstein, a forging fury who tramples down all hurdles to achieve her goal. As Bharati Mukherjee says: "I experienced a miraculous emotional break-through. I heard Debby's voice as she spoke the first page and a half of part one. After that, Debby took over, as had Jasmine and Hannah in my two preceding novels. She surprised me. She became my alternate self, the "what if . . . ?" self. The pace, the language, the events all were dictated by Debby. I suppose that sounds a little crazy, but it's the way I've always written fiction."[1]

Hannah Easton of *The Holder of the World* and later on, Devi in *Leave it to Me* take on new ventures, seeking satisfaction in their self-identity. Improvising on the earlier characters, the changing style with every novel marks the evolving self of Bharati Mukherjee.

Each of her novels predicts the evolution of the novelist. The confidence and the comfortable essence oozes out of each of her characters.

The style of the writer significantly adjusts and adapts to the new environment in each novel and her ethical principles mark the emerging and evolving personality of Bharati Mukherjee as an immigrant in America. The journey forward is evident in the maturing style in the later novels like *The Holder of the World* and *Leave it to Me*. The peace within is apparent, the struggle to settle down in the chaotic world around, i.e. to have finally adjusted with new life, comes through in her characters like Jasmine in *Jasmine*, Hannah Easton in *The Holder of the World* and then suddenly her character Devi in *Leave it to Me* sends the reader into a flurry with her daring attitude, raging through every situation with aplomb. The inner turmoils and struggles inside Bharati Mukherjee have been deceptively concealed, to be detonated from time to time, appearing in some of her characters.

Bharati Mukherjee's style may have some basic ethics but the changes in the style clarify the fact that she refuses to extemporize the norms.

> You seem to feel when you come into a Mukherjee novel, a kind of flurry and complexity in the writing. It's rapid, darting, intense and energetic. Mukherjee is fascinated by people who are constantly on the move, who have to live a life in transit, who have to destroy their former identities in other countries in order to live fully in another. It's an astonishingly ruthless understanding of the personality. That the personality has to travel light and move across countries and assimilate other country's culture and ideas and practices like putting on another skin.[2]

Contrary to this, readers of her works feel that sometimes her characters get out of hand. Towards the end of the novel, Devi kills Larry because he ruffled her feministic sensibilities. One wonders if this character gets out of hand of Bharati Mukherjee and turns into a Frankenstein, killing and avenging herself, has the right to punish a person who is another identical twisted immigrant. "That's when I shot him. That's why I shot him. The why and when of that moment are joined like Siamese twins." (*LITM*, 173)

Does Larry not reflect the grotesque personality which Devi herself feels proud to flaunt. Devi never turns around and speculates about herself. She removes anyone who dares to go against her ideology, be it her boyfriend Frankie Fong, or the Larry Loco, who are "bitterness" incarnated into human beings. Larry's sensibilities have crossed the human boundaries and he can be so gross that he has to get sexual satisfaction from a dead woman, whom he kills to take revenge.

The repulsion of the sight makes Devi shoot Larry. The simple word creates the image of inhumanity with a clarity that makes the justified action of Devi very much human. The words conjure up the vision of negativities with harsh clarity. One cannot but get repulsed by what Larry Loco does and the grossness of his mentality is deftly brought out by Bharati Mukherjee. One can applaud Devi's reaction even though on one hand one is bound to point out the shortcomings of her actions.

Style in *Leave it to Me* clearly encapsulates the lifestyle of America. The novel has a variety of characters who help Bharati Mukherjee to capture the various facets of American life-style. With this, Bharati Mukherjee seems to put down her roots in the new culture, fully ingratiated into the seams of new life and culture. As Bharati Mukherjee points out, *Leave it to Me* "is also my way of putting down roots. I feel that I have come home to Haight."[4]

Frankly speaking, it will be little harsh on Bharati Mukherjee and the culture of America, which is depicted in the novel, *Leave it to Me*. The style emphatically points out the fact that Bharati Mukherjee is more comfortable in enfolding her new freedom and life style in America, her style becomes more of an endorsement on the adaptation of philosophies.

"Mukherjee's homecoming is a fascinating story. Her evolution as an author is manifest in the themes she has chosen to address as well as the characters she has chosen to focus on. And this evolution has accompanied an equally momentous journey which has brought her from the sequestered upper middle class Bengali milieu in Calcutta to the cosmopolitan world of North America."[4]

She read various authors right from childhood in order to avoid the chaos outside. She thought that "writing was inspirational" but her going to Iowa to join the creative writing programme made her realise that it was more of an art than inspiration. "I realized as I listened to the workshop and as I did draft after draft of my own work, how much of it is also knowing what you want to say and then how do you best say what you want to say so the reader shares the emotions."[5]

The change in point of the view started right in 1961. The assimilation started as soon as realization struck. The style changed as she evolved as an 'American immigrant.' The phrase 'American immigrant' becomes significant because earlier it was "Indian expatriate" in Canada who had to face a lot for 15 years. The unacceptance in Canada, and then the slow merging into the melting-pot of America, brought forth a change which is evident in her work. She kept on with the flow instead of getting stuck in one place. This is apparent in the flow of her style. The breathing space in America gave a new infrastructure on which she could restructure her life and writings. Acquiescence in the new society gave her the impetus and confidence to assert herself through her writings but then going overboard for acceptance is largely evident in *Leave it to Me*. "Others who write stories of migration after talk of arrival at a new place as a loss," says Mukherjee, "the loss of communal memory and the erosion of an original culture. I want to talk of arrival as gain."[6]

The assimilation was easy because her mind had already been moulded. Right from childhood, she had stayed in European countries. This gave a solid grounding, giving her an edge over her characters. Her characters are more of novices entering a new culture and trying to accept the new culture.

In spite of everything, she had to face a difficult situation in Canada for which even her experiences in India did not prepare her. The bitterness comes through in her early works. This leads to a perfect blending of Eastern values and ethics with Western philosophies. Bharati Mukherjee's style is rendered in such a fashion that it provokes the readers to rethink about their notion of change in life. On the one hand she talks about "Nirvana" in terms of Eastern beliefs when she points out that a person, in order to work, should find happiness inside. "Attaining Nirvana, for Venn, is attaining perfect design." (*HW*, 91)

For Venn, it is perfection in work which gives freedom to his mind. His soul is in the state of "Nirvana." The same term in case of

Debbie Di Martino takes a very different connotation, which is influenced by her attitude towards life. Though this term is introduced to her by an Indian character, for Devi the term catapults into a simple attitude of revenge and aggression. For her "Nirvana" is finding the inner strength which helps her to take action according to her own will. "Nirvana is finding the tiger balls within you." (*LITM*, 53)

Bharati Mukherjee flaunts the Indian ideologies in her style. Indian myth is like an embellishment on the western canvas, just like the Mughal miniatures, which she is fascinated by. According to her, her love for the Mughal miniatures is a blend of so many concepts intertwined into each other to make a whole. Her characters seem to be a part of the whole, the whole being "Feminism."

The style is rendered in such a fashion that when one tends to feel that all her characters possess several facets of feminism, everything falls apart, as if a veil has been lifted and everything seems to be in propinquity with a single theme, and that is, adaptation into alien situation and move forward.

This again holds the reader in awe as each character unfolds in front of his eyes and each one of them seems to be a part of the whole. Each one has a strength of character and it depends which facet of their feminism becomes dominant at a particular time. There are mixed elements of 'Sita' and 'Kali' and it depends which is dominant on an occasion. Jasmine in *Jasmine* is a combination of both. She is full of love and tenderness but refuses to be subdued, be it the prediction of an astrologer whom she defies by living a life on her own terms, or Bud whose child she is bearing. She easily slips into the different roles changing herself like a chameleon. She is "Kali" when she murders her rapist 'Half-Face'; she nurtures Bud and Du like a mother. She again flings off her burden and leaves with another man, to be herself and find happiness on her own terms.

Bharati Mukherjee on a similar wavelength juggles the Eastern and Western ideologies candidly, handling her characters and plots and subplots, bringing forth an awareness about concept of self-identity of a woman, a fact which proves her own zealous feminist identity. Feminism, it seems, for Bharati Mukherjee is more of breaking of the servile existence of self in a male dominant society in Indian context and self-sought freedom of soul in the dominant culture in the Western context. The desire to carve a niche for oneself is evident in every novel of Mukherjee.

The Indian concept of religion and spirituality is also evident in her style. Religion can be only rituals, if not taken in a broader sense whereas spirituality is to feel the freedom within oneself. "Do your own thing, do it proudly, and no one will bother you. Feel free, and you shall be free." (*LITM*, 68)

Clearing the memories of the past is a process of becoming aware of one's own individuality and this is what Bharati Mukherjee points out emphatically through her own experiences and her characters. The incidents taking place in the present have more clairvoyance once we decide to move forward and seek our future. Words used capaciously weave a world of visions for the immigrants. The only hindrance is that some of her characters are still caught in the web of past culture. The nostalgia does not have a firm ground, thus giving a cultural shock to those who return to India to rediscover their beliefs and dreams that were left back. Among clusters of themes that Bharati Mukherjee weaves in her multifarious canvas, one which comes through again and again is the quest for identity. The female characters searching for the Self which is lacerated from time unknown and reasons best known to the male populace, be it India, America (which is supposedly an open culture and grants equality to both genders) or any other country on this earth. The female characters not only face racial discrimination but are also sexually assaulted in order to establish the superiority of the male. But the positive stance taken by Bharati Mukherjee against the violence is the evolution which takes place. Each character evolves with some kind of violent action taking place in their lives. Self-realization which alludes to saints and hermits, is literally forced on the characters. The violence against her authorial recognition makes Bharati Mukherjee recoil and being sensitive right from the day of childhood she turns inwards to lick her wounds. Her earlier vacillation of accepting immigration in the United States is put aside when she reaches India for a crucial, hitherto nostalgic holiday—a period of decisions, which once taken proves apocalyptic for the author. She loses herself in the humbug crowd, yet as a writer she gains an identity which is applaudable. Her form of writing might be put in the slot of immigrant writing but her ideas generated through her characters become a voice of the women who have been degraded for generations, yet put on a pedestal and worshipped. When the same women unleashed their fury, it is not accepted in the Indian culture whereas in the other cultures, women, outwardly self-assured and self-dependent, do go through the same inner turmoils like the immigrants. The difference is that the immigrant women have to bridge the chasm or be divided between duty and family or seek freedom in the New World. The characters in the novels of Bharati Mukherjee portray the various stages of evolution of the author along with the novels. As pointed out in the earlier chapters, the three phases of her work can be divided into three parts marking the rebirth of a new identity for Bharati Mukherjee. The earlier phase marks the early childhood till the age of eight of a child who turns inwards to escape the chaos in a joint family. The next phase of life is marked from eight to twenty one, the attitude of nuclear family and enjoying all the colonial comforts in the compound of self-owned factory of her father. The last stage marks her journey to the West, the problems faced by an Asian expatriate in Canada and later on the joy and exuberance of immigration in the United States of America. In spite of being a citizen by marriage, she is not accepted in Canada as a writer and this is what irks her. Refusing to bash her head against the multiracial discriminating wall of Canadian society, she decides to release her soul from the bondage. As she points out in an interview:

> If you insist, on this beautiful May afternoon in 1996, that I describe myself in terms of ethno-nationality, I'd say I'm an American writer of Bengali Indian origin. In other words, the writer/ political activist in me is more obsessed with addressing the issues of minority discourse in the U.S. and Canada, the two countries I have lived and worked in over the last thirty odd years. The national mythology that my immigration is driven to create, through fiction, is that of the post-Vietnam United States. I experience, simultaneously, the pioneer's capacity to be shocked and surprised by the new culture, and the immigrants' willingness to de-form and re-form that culture. At this moment, my Calcutta childhood and adolescence offer me intriguing, incompletely comprehended revelations about my hometown, my family, my place in that community: the kind of revelations that fuel the desire to write an autobiography rather than to mythologize an Indian national identity.

The transformation of a writer, a human being and a resident of the new world culminates into exuberance with the act of immigration to the United States of America. Married to the Canadian American writer Clark Blaise, whom she falls in love with and throwing all caution to winds, she gets married to him, Bharati Mukherjee breaks the conventional traditions. Her father magnanimously accepts her marriage. No longer aggrieved at her plight in Canada where she is considered an intruder in the white world and tortured by unacceptance of her writing is clearly indicative of her non-existence in the "Other" world—Bharati Mukherjee's flair for writing seems to reach new dimensions in America.

> Suddenly, I was no longer aggrieved, except as a habit of mind. I had moved from being a "visible minority" against whom the nation [Canada] had officially incited its less-visible citizens to react, to being just another immigrant. If I may put it in the harshest terms, it would be this: in Canada, I was frequently taken for a prostitute or shoplifter, frequently assumed to be a domestic, praised by astonished auditors that I didn't have a "sing-song" accent. (*D*, 2)

Her earlier works like *Darkness* reflect the dark side of non-existent status of immigrants and the life of self-imposed exile is reflected in *The Tiger's Daughter*. Her works, *The Tiger's Daughter* and *Days and Nights in Calcutta*, are more of an attempt to identify with the old culture and its heritage. Her own struggle with identity, first as an exile from India, then as an Indian expatriate in Canada and finally as an immigrant in the United States tends to zig-zag its way into the structure of each of her novels.

The stories compiled in the *Darkness* are of immigrants striving to root themselves in North America, the uprooted souls from Asian countries and other countries trying to sublimate their dream in America. Bharati Mukherjee was initially influenced by V.S. Naipaul, another immigrant writer, and later on, Bernard Malamud. What is applaudable about the stories is a conscious effort on the part of Bharati Mukherjee to give voice to the immigrants' feelings and their experiences in Canada and the United States.

> Like V.S. Naipaul, in whom I imagined a model, I tried to explore state of the art expatriation. Like Naipaul, I used a mordant and self-protective irony in describing my characters' pain. Irony promised both

> detachment from, and superiority over, those well bred post-colonials much like myself, adrift in the new world, wondering if they would ever belong. (*D*, 2)

The story "Isolated Incidents" explores the bias of Canadian view faced by the immigrants and the plight of the protagonist, who is tortured by the very thought of staying and continuing with her job. The story depicts how the Canadian government agencies handle the racial assaults. The story is based on parallel lines of immigrants forging forth and claiming their right into the new world, and the people who cower back and stay hidden, who are not ambitious and strong enough to let go and surge forward. The protagonist Ann and her friend Peppi had entered the culture together but separated to carve a future for their respective selves. Peppi was known in the singing world, had the guts to let down her defences and make a success of herself whereas Ann had settled down to desk job in an immigrant office.

> Ann could still detect that old charm, the vulnerabilities of the prepubescent West mount girl who had infected flesh wounds on her shins and calves to set herself apart from the confronting staidness of their surroundings. It should have been entirely predictable even then: she would leave in order to be able to return again and again. (*D*, 87)

Meeting her friend Peppi, Ann breathes fresh air after slogging in the office, listening to the incidents and accidents confronting the immigrants. Obviously, Ann is well-versed in her job and can decipher a genuine incidence of assault. Peppi had become rich and now Ann is completely at loss and wonders how she would meet her friend. Listening to the gory details about immigrant experiences, Ann is totally detached and hardly relates with the experiences of the people. Lost in her reverie, she is not fully engrossed in the work she is doing. Meeting her friend and glowing in her success, Ann also decides to leave the security of rootedness, and work for a new future. But the sedate life style, offering solace from the intrusion of brutal forces co-existing in the universe holds her back.

The story graphically points out the experiences of Dr. (Miss) Supariwala, who has a forbidding resume to back her career in Canada, but even her Canadian citizenship does not help her against the racial insults hurled at her. In spite of the discrimination and insults,

Dr. Supariwala wants to stay back. The novel ends with Ann resigning to the same fate: "That was what amazed Ann. They came to her, cowering, crying, thundering, insulting rehearsed or spontaneous and still they found reasons for staying where Ann herself, on bad days, found few." (*D*, 79)

While listening mechanically to the outpourings of Mr. Hernandez about his sister being harassed on account of not possessing the right to stay in Canada, Ann smiles and reassures him that his case is not meant for the immigration department. Mr. Hernandez's insults thrown her way seem to crack the hard nut and she loses her temper, giving vent to her own frustrations. "'Nothing is fair!' she shouted, ashamed at letting go like that, in a public place. 'You think I have it good?'" (*D*, 92)

Incidents of harassment by the Canadians as well as the government officials are tagged as isolated incidents and no further attention is given. Men and women are assaulted and discrimination goes unnoticed. "Her job had worn her down, She had tried too earnestly to correct the nation's wrongs. Now she saw problems only as a bureaucrat. Deal only with sure things. Pass the others off." (*D*, 81)

A comparison with the laws of America is cited in the story. It is ironical that a person is assaulted in America for his money but in Canada the person is being harassed and assaulted for the simple reason of being racially different. "'Correction, Miss Vane,' said the lawyer. 'If this had happened in New York, he'd have been mugged for his money, not racially assaulted.'" (*D*, 84)

Besides depicting the difference of ethical values in America and Canada, the plots of short stories or novels—fiction or non-fiction—the main plot is nearly every time intertwined with a sub-plot and this technique is used to bring out the crux of matter, and that is, existent duality—the dormant and the dominant factor that makes a person. The two points of view are counterpoised, relegating the difference that can make or destroy a personality. The lives of Ann and Poppy are juxtaposed to bring out the difference: one's attitude, the driving force to seek one's future, can change the future of each person. How you look at life and grab the opportunities thrown your way by fate can change one's destiny forever! Mr. Hernandez's cruel words force Ann to come out of the dazed stupor to realize her own reality but instead of surging forward and seeking a future as a poet, she backs off and realizes her destiny as a listener to the outpourings of pain and remorsefulness of the immigrants. Becoming aware of another facet behind the façade of glamour, the manifestation of hardness in Peppi's stance makes her think twice before abandoning her securities. Fear of the unknown pulls her sails back anchoring her in the job she detests.

Clinging to the security of the past and rigidly holding on to the dreariness of the present, instead of letting go and surging forward, forms the basic theme of all the novels of Bharati Mukherjee. The dualities existent in the universe form the focal point of her writings and ironically, the duality co-exists in each human being The Hindu philosophies have been interwoven into the seams of the plots of each novel. Merging of two cultures to produce a hurricane in *Leave it to Me*. The protagonist, flaunting a violent nature as well as a softness, makes her sensitive to perversity. Quest to find the soul, the self-identity is forced on each character. The tradition of violence existent in American culture seems the impetus which drives the characters on their path of self-realization. As it is, the philosophy of *Gita* is ingratiated in the seams of the American culture. Americans believe in executing "Karma" with a detachment. Devi represents American culture and Asian hippie culture which adjoin to produce a lethal weapon by which she can destroy and destruct and reconstruct herself, rising like a phoenix from the ashes (past which she searches for), to again destroy assiduously and erase the past for a future that is ambivalent. Surging forward, she clears all hurdles without any qualms, to find her bio-parents. Devi searches for her identity, to annihilate it, and move forward. The attitude of Devi in killing her father is more like a hermit who, in order to gain renunciation, disowns his past. Perhaps one of the most striking features of this equipoising of one's life, is evident from the famous line of the Isa Upanishad: 'Find enjoyment by renunciation.'

True asceticism is not narcissistic complacency but the discovery that liberation from the bonds of desires allows us to enjoy things, without being hunted by the fear of losing them or by the anxiety of not getting them. The Hindu philosophy is woven into each character and points to the fact that in spite of declaring herself an American, she still retains the soul of an Indian. This same balance recurs in each novel. The balance is brought into the awareness of human nature by extremities of sorrow. Enduring the unbearable pain, infliction of violent action against the female characters forces them to awaken to their empowerment and self-emancipation and this helps them to lead a balanced, peaceful life.

There are two clearly distinct periods in the Vedic Revelation, the Vedic and the Upanishadic, and they seem to take two contrasting and extreme positions; the one minimizes sorrow to such an extent that one finds it difficult to select pertinent texts, whereas the other radicalizes the nature of sorrow to such a degree, that the only resort is total escape into another form of existence.

"One common trait, however, connects these two conceptions of the sorrowful: namely, both consider sorrow to be an awakening to the transcendent. Suffering brings Man to the point of 'rupturing' his humanness and thus to the threshold of transcendence. Man experiences his own suffering as something foreign to him, something outside himself, as if it came from unknown, from another world, so to speak. This suffering is either the scorpion sting of some evil power or the very means through which he discovers his true nature beyond all the entanglements of the human condition."[8]

Conditioned to the secure atmosphere of Calcutta, faced with the New Calcutta which seems a replica of riot-infested Montreal, Tara is so shocked that she questions the reasonableness of her own presence of mind. She has to shuffle through her memories to find out if she can remember the face of her husband exactly.

A young woman when married is awakened to maturity through physical violence, her husband being the outer stimuli which perforate her body to make her a woman. The deflowerment may be voluntary or involuntary, but is a method to create new family ties. Procreation is the sole purpose but when woman has to be degraded, she is assaulted physically and mentally. The violence may generate a reaction that may be negative or positive. Negative as it is in the case of Dimple Dasgupta in *Wife* or in the awakening of the soul as Taramoni in *The Tiger's Daughter*. Jasmine in *Jasmine*, Hannah in *The Holder of the World*, Devi in *Leave It to Me* are the only characters who manifest the ideology of Americanness where they sleep with men and journey through the realms of mystery to discover their self and the violence is turned outwards creating havoc in the male-oriented society. They are tolerant and sophisticated outwardly but when their anger is unleashed, they act like psychopaths. The fury in Devi is unleashed on wary preys and there is a role reversal where Devi tames the wild animals in the form of human beings.

The physical violence that awakens Taramoni to self-realization has long been understood by Joyonto Mukherjee who knows that even if she has no future in India, at least she has a future in the alien country that she would finally return to. "But now, by the window, watching the electric light skim the tops of flower basket, Joyonto thought again of the sober young woman in the café and his desire to protect her." (*TD*, 70)

Shaila Bhave in 'The Management of Grief,' conditioned to the Indian tradition never confessed to her husband how much she loved him. She loses her husband; her two sons leave her lonely and bereft in the new world but a return home does not give any solace. Being in India, faced with dualities in the moral codes of society where men get married after the demise of wife whom they profess to love, the woman is expected to live in the agony of widowhood and the suppression of their senses. Returning back to Toronto, she acts positively by communicating with the authorities for help and her cause is supported. The element of spiritual awakening is evoked by the character Kusum, who resides in 'Hardwar' and has reunited with the spirit of her daughter and a replica of her daughter forces her into a life of quiescence in the Indian pilgrimage. Again the two paths of renunciation 'Karma Yoga' and 'Bhakti Yoga' are extracted from the philosophies of *Bhagwad Gita*. Shaila Bhave finds herself working towards her renunciation by getting support for her cause whereas Kusum finds her peace in spiritual awakening. The two juxtaposed ideologies bring out the two ways of managing grief by Indian immigrant women who face the same fate, i.e. the demise of loved ones. Kusum returns to India and finds her solace. Her detachment from her Americanized daughter does not deter her from her path of renunciation.

The third character who is a Canadian journalist, mechanically seeks to do her job. Detachment seems to have hardened her feelings. Unable to communicate with an old Sikh couple to sign legal papers, she requests Shaila to help out. Realistic and practical to the core, she is insensitive to the fear of Sikh parents who still cannot believe that their son is dead. Kusum, replicating the immigrant sensibilities, does not accept the frivolous behaviour of her modern American daughter who is disobedient and insensitive in her opinion. The daughter, irked by the difference of emotional treatment, rebukes and insults her mother. Non-acceptance by the mother vexes her into re-taliation while the bereaved mother and wife cannot communicate with her American daughter. The Indianness in the demised daughter allures her into searching the truth of life, that is, the body dies physically but the soul is not destroyed. Finding a replica of her daughter in Hardwar seems to convince Kusum that her daughter has returned.

The hyphenated existence in case of Taramoni occurs because she is not one with her own self. Similarly, the other characters like Dimple and Mr. Bhowmick in *Darkness* remain alienated and the ex-istence in hyphenation is frustrating. Bharati Mukherjee's facing 'ex-ile' in her own home country leads to her bridging the chasm instead of permanent existence on the periphery. Facing marginalisation is not something she expects in Canada as she is a citizen of the coun-try, but crossing over to being an immigrant in United States takes her out of the situation of existing in hyphenation, of being an In-dian-American. India and the old ties become a 'metaphor' just like it is for an Indian bride settling in her husband's house. Self-realization is forced on Bharati Mukherjee when she is treated as a foreigner who cannot understand the sensitivity of people she once lived with. It is like salt being rubbed on an open wound. Tara's self-realisation occurs with physical mutilation forced on her. The hy-phenated suspension is something which initially makes her delirious yet she holds onto her sanity and calmness surrounds her in the af-termath of her physical violation. Her composure is more or less like the Bengal Tiger's on the station, a pillar of strength amidst the chaos. After her reincarnation into her father's image, she takes con-trol of her life instead of dawdling and fumbling like a kid. Joyonto Mukherjee had foreseen the strength in her character to which she had to waken-up. One can hear Joyonto rejoicing in her awakening to herself.

> "After such knowledge . . . tail devoured by head as always. . . . and then. . . ."
>
> "He's crazy you want me to hit a crazy man, Sir?"

> "He's not a madman at all. I veritably believe he's been sent by the other side."
>
> "Dear Madam, you I shored against my ruins. Have you left? Where are the jets?' (*TD*, 209)

Her spiritual awakening comes before she is awakened to the potential inside her own being. Awareness of inner strength is something which she glimpses in the temple of the Divine and she suddenly feels 'one' with all those present in the room. Her 'Nirvana' is momentous, and then the mule-headed Antonia Whitehead seems to be a replica of herself, who had blundered into the Calcutta society with her mind full of economic and social equality. The human righteousness amidst the divine followers especially Antonia, seems a novice to Tara.

> She recalled again her own bad starts and mistakes. To Pronob and his group at the Catelli she must have seemed as naïve and dangerous as Antonia. There was no way to warn the girl, no way they could be friends. "You're being quite idiotic about this thing." Tara repeated as Antonia turned away in disgust. Tara sensed that Pronob had given Antonia a wink, or at the least a fleeting smile. (*TD*, 175)

The experience of the dilemma of immigrants turns into fluidity of emotions. The adoption of mind and the Hindu philosophy of quest for identity through soul searching are intertwined. The understanding once reached, the turmoil of the self gives birth to a new human being who is equipoised with the 'Other' to make a whole. The self-confidence that oozes out of Taramoni is a vast difference from the sensitive one; initially one who used to cower away from physical disabilities. Her sensibilities which were ruffled at the sight of abrasion in human body, look at the situation with a detachment.

> In the car Tara was careful not to respond with cynicism to Sanjay's praise of Tuntunwala as a candidate. She felt she had made her peace with the city, nothing more was demanded. If she were to stay, she thought, there would be other concessions, other deals and compromises, all menacing and unbearably real, waiting to be made. (*TD*, 202)

Her lacerated body no longer a hindrance in her soul transcending, Taramoni is reborn. A better judge of situation, she decides to return back to her husband and face life with a new vigour. The physical aberration no longer worries her soul. As she becomes aware of the inner-consciousness, her inner conflicts disappear. She is aware of herself and the vacillation, a regular feature of her life, disappears. The solitude within herself makes a new person who does not feel the need to make a scene and confront Tuntunwala who is unrepentant in his repugnant self. She no longer feels alone. She has the feeling of love and oneness with David, her husband. She refuses to be an escapist as the love for her husband is more of a dynamism towards the fullness of life, the integration of the self with entire universe.

The hankering after what is unattainable within creates a havoc in Dimple's soul. Throughout, she lives in a hyphenated state of mind. Renunciation comes through violence against the outside stimuli, that is her husband who is unable to understand the traumatic experiences of his wife. Always craving for the unknown and totally engrossed in her own conflicts between reality and fantasies, she is enmeshed into it to the extent, that readers tend to get confused about her state of mind. Repeated actions and reactions give pleasure and the enormity of her actions does not register on her mind. Momentous decision to exist in reality leaves her depressed and deflated. Though talented, she is unable to focus on her problems with no support from husband and herself detesting any sort of traditional servitude, she hesitates to sever the ties for the fear of losing her identity. The salvation comes in the form of killing her husband, the weapon used is symbolic of her Indian mentality. The 'kitchen-knife' used by Dimple is basically a feminine weapon and Dimple uses it to assert her superiority over phallic power. Devi in *Leave it to Me* uses the cleaver to butcher her father, a weapon which is used by her Bio-Dad to kill Ham. Dimple works with precision, keeping cool about the whole situation and knows or rather assumes that she will not be caught as it happens in the American scenario.

Devi who had killed and set fire to pave a path to her success, kills her Bio-Dad in a frenzy (observing Ham being killed in a gory manner) nauseated to the core, and the cleaver, more of a masculine weapon, used by her is symbolic of the hard-core devil in her. When we see Mr. Bhowmick using a 'rolling-pin' to beat his daughter, he seems a weak sort of person, still not reconciled to the modernity of American ideologies yet enjoying all the materialistic opportunities of First World.

The weapon used to defile Jasmine and Tara is more of an assertion of phallic strength on the female protagonists. The renunciation in the first case, comes by getting avenged by slicing the jugular vein with a 'blade' used for shaving. Tara refrains from making any retaliation, instead her humiliation and suffering awakens her to her own powers of soul. Both Tara and Jasmine display two different aspects of rationalist behaviour and American rationalism respectively. Though in the case of Tara, a newly born confidence and self-revelation rushes her into a new but familiar world, where she has to answer no one for actions and reactions.

The reactions of the protagonists are synchronized to the violent acts against them, be it Dimple, Tara, Hannah, Devi or the strings of immigrants whose life experiences are chronicled in the short stories. The violence that forms the basis of each story instigates adverse reactions. Some tend to criticize the glorification of violence, yet each of the violent actions has a firm grounding. It is not necessary to justify the violence but it cannot be called unreasonable. Self-emancipation and self-empowerment provide strength to some people enhancing their decisive powers like in the case of Taramoni. The Hindu myth is intertwined with 'Electra' myth, in *Leave it to Me*, where Devi is avenged by unleashing her violence and fury against her own bio-parent.

Dimple's fury, which could have had a positive solution, leads to a blasphemous act. Turned inwards and unable to handle the pressure from the outside world, her idea of freedom takes a negative connotation. The Indian morals, unlike her pregnancy, are not so easily aborted by the confused Dimple. The abortion of her traditional ideologies happens with the same violence with which the pregnancy was terminated. The psychological apathy that Dimple goes through is felt by the female populace bound to the patriarchal tyranny. Nirmala in *Jasmine* has an outlet which is more in line with her husband's liking.

Bharati Mukherjee's novels do not claim to be moralistic or philosophical but the traumas that are gone through by her female protagonists and immigrants are not an assorted kind of emotional drama. The pain undergone is very much a part of every other Indian girl who lacks the self-confidence to revolt against the norms of the rigid society. Passivity is the only weapon which can give them a respectable life. Dimple is not a singled out psychic case. The violence simmering inside is not directed towards herself but towards the lack of ambition that makes her lead a servile life which she detests. Dimple and Tara are prisoners of their own beliefs. The continuous dwindling between tradition and modernity in the former case, and the comforts and peace of the old world and the pathetic chaos of the New World prove fatal for both the female protagonists.

> Exchange of money embarrassed her, it was a manly ritual, so she folded and refolded her grease spotted paper napkin and devised a third way to deal with guilt. She would kill Amit and hide his body in the freezer. The extravagance of the scheme delighted her, made her feel very American somehow, almost like a character in a T.V. series. Amit's tragedy was that he lacked extravagance; he persevered in the immigrant virtues of caution and cunning. (*W*, 195)

The theme of abandonment recurs in *Jasmine* and "The Tenant" in *The Middleman and Other Stories*, which is not planned but is a capricious escape from the circumstances. This disappearing act cannot be categorized as the feministic liberation from bondage because Jasmine has been an attentive caregiver. She has extended her gratitude to Bud by providing him with the physical release and mental support that he needs, but renouncing her future is not something which she anticipates for herself. Maya leaves her landlord-cum-lover, who has no arms, for a handsome Indian immigrant who does not offer her marriage as a permanence in life but the prospects with Ashoke Mehta hold more exquisiteness than with Fred.

The disappearing act seems to be an act of ingratitude, but doesn't the fairer sex deserve liberty of senses to take priority? The socially-sanctioned relationship which is looked down upon in Indian culture, liberates the female protagonists from enchained selves. Bonded to one man, whether love is existent or not, whether the man is faithful or not, the women are pushed into a corner, living passively all their life without questioning the duality of moral codes in society. The openness of the new society and the living standards initially shocked Jasmine, but later on, to gratify Bud's needs, she takes on the dominant role during physical consummation. It is a vast contrast from Jyoti of Hasnapur who has to be initiated forcefully to become independent of the traditional ties.

Mind fashioned by the American consumer culture, where relationships can be disposed off easily, Jasmine no longer hankers after lost relationships. The eager internalization of American values is complete as she elopes with Taylor. Caring for Du is more of a feeling of loneliness but she never tries to breach the emotional detachment that Du is surrounded with. "I should have broken through, but I was afraid to test the delicate thread of his hyphenization. Vietnamese American: don't question either half too hard." (*J*, 225)

The characters of Bharati Mukherjee are people who exist in reality. They might be fictitious but are very real with their own terrains to cross, a mixed bundle of emotional and mental fixations that have to be overcome through internalization or externalization of mind and soul, trying to carve a future for themselves. The first generation which was forced to cross to earn living had no choice. But the second generation in India with no opportunities within reach, in order to escape the dreariness had to resort to revolutions or to leave the country, cross the border to substantiate their own dreams in faraway continents. America being the land of opportunities, 'American Dream' lured people from all strata of society to merge into the melting pot. The characters reflect the personal experiences of Bharati Mukherjee yet they are independent of her. They are not bondaged to their creator as Bharati Mukherjee herself claims.

> I didn't know she was going to leave Bud at the end of the novel. She just up and went! Because she got bored with the situation. Not bored. She felt it was a regression, like going back to village life, a life of duty and devotion, to stay on caring for this crippled fellow. The frontier was out there, beckoning. She just left. (Mukherjee to Connel, 31)

Bharati Mukherjee, in conceiving her characters and nurturing them to the point of making them real, somehow reminds one of Shakespearean characters who are full of human follies and are not put on pedestal to be worshipped.

> When he conceived of a character, whether real or imaginary, he not only entered into all its thoughts and feelings, but seemed instantly, and as if by touching a secret spring, to be surrounded with all the same objects, 'subject to the same skyey influences,' the same local, outward, and unforeseen accidents which would occur in reality.[10]

The motif of sexuality and carnality in the female characters as they enter the new world might be obnoxious but it symbolises the self-mutation of the female characters who not only cross over the boundaries of gender and race but their crossing over marks the transnationalistic attitude. The freedom, which is legally sanctioned and the basis of the new society, throws them into a frenzy. They are either bound to progress and flow with life or regress and reach the psychological break-down, which Amit Basu associates with habitual psyche of the American women. His way of merging into the American world is memorizing jokes to be cracked to mark his wittiness. Dimple continuously compares him to Milt and Jyoti who are so self-confident whereas Amit seems like a wimp standing besides them. Though Amit realises his shortcomings, Dimple refuses to acknowledge them and blames Amit for all the confusion in her mind.

Professor Vadhera in *Jasmine* and his family attitudinal behaviour encapsulates the Indian diasporic ghetto. The feelings that lead to creation of such environment are a mirror of the existence of many other such ghettos in the realms of American Dream. The self-created existence in hybridization is not a fate forced on them. Closely observed, one can justify Professor Vadhera's working as a hair sorter by looking at it positively. Instead of backing out, his resilient power can be categorized as his way of surviving in America. He lives in the world of duality or rather being the provider of his family, he maintains the same atmosphere as in India. His wife, a contemporary of Jasmine, finds a way out by working in a shop and watching videos. The parents's expectations are traditional and they detest any intrusion in their house. The mother-in-law expects her daughter-in-law to stay back at home so that she can take out her frustrations on her. Looking at the Vadhera family is like looking at any other Indian immigrant family who shuttle between the two cultures.

The various immigrants in *The Middleman and Other Stories*, who have smuggled themselves into the new world, reflect the traumas and tribulations they undergo in order to merge in the American culture. Illegal marriages for the sake of getting citizenship are common among such immigrants. Remaining undercover is their main concern, and if discovered they are deported. The stories in *The Middleman and Other Stories* emphatically point to the changing

America with infiltration of immigrants from so many variegated cultures. 'Danny's Girls' brings into focus the huge number of Indian immigrants' presence in New York. The protagonist imports girls to be used for facilitating legal immigration in the United States of America. The story narrator is a pimp, and is initiated into the world of sexual maturity by one of Danny's girls. The use of "Danny Sahib" is ironical because in India 'Sahib' is a term used with respect for persons who are rich, affluent and have honourable jobs, whereas Danny is literally involved in selling female bodies to earn his living.

The narration of each of the stories is in first person, be it a boy of thirteen in "Danny's Girls" or Renata in "Orbiting." The first person narrator of the first story 'The Middleman' is also the central character who gets involved into a racket of terrorists. A professional gunman, originally from Iraq, he is saved by the lady love of Andreas. Maria, the girl is depicted as a nymphomaniac. "She has made love to me three times tonight. With Andreas today, doubtless more. Never has a truth been burned so deeply in me, what I owe my life to, how simple the rules of survival are. She passes the gun to Andreas who holsters it, and they leave." (*M*, 21)

Refashioning of self is used as metaphor by Bharati Mukherjee. The traumas and pain undergone during the birth of a child are compared to the new-born immigrants who refashion their self to reinvent a new identity like Jasmine, Devi, Hannah and Tara. The severing of the old ties with the old culture is more like the umbilical cord severed as soon as an infant is born. The process of rebirth, once started, the women in Bharati Mukherjee's novels cannot revert back nor can they stop it. The only thing they resort to is to be delivered into the new world with violence, rupturing the body, mind and soul. "I wanted that moment when he saw me above him as he had last seen me, naked, but now with my mouth open, pouring blood, my red tongue out, I wanted him to open his mouth and start to reach, I wanted that extra hundredth of a second when the blade bit deeper than any insect." (*J*, 118) The narration of *Jasmine* is in first person and the use of 'I' is emphatic and Bharati Mukherjee is able to make the impact she wants.

Bharati Mukherjee has created a constellation of characters who, while experiencing the pangs of rebirth, seem to stand back and observe their own reactions. Tara in *The Tiger's Daughter* and Dimple in *Wife* seem to be continuously involved in a conversation in their own mind. Dimple constantly conjures up the negative images from the darker side of human beings. There is a continuous dialogue going on inside her mind, where her mind is busy in inventing and fantasizing new methods of killing herself and Amit Basu. Her heart flutters to go out and seek the freedom that it craves. The use of interior monologue, emphatically ascertains the fact that Bharati Mukherjee's characters decide their own destiny. Stream of consciousness is woven into the fabric of the novel unpretentiously. It is more like soliloquies in Shakespearean plays where a person speaks out his mind for the audience's sake.

The multiple narratives enmeshed together in *The Holder of the World* are inspired by the 17th century Moghul Raj in India. There is a role reversal in this novel where the lady protagonist travels to India to seek freedom from the puritan culture of Massachusetts. Seeking adventure, she marries Gabriel Legge who is a pirate. He plunders to gain richness and a position for himself as an English Factor during the British Raj in India. Parallelled to the main plot is the story of the narrator Beigh Masters, who somehow feels related to Salem Bibi. Venn is a data collector and an immigrant from India and helps Beigh in her quest with the help of his Time-Machine. Bharati Mukherjee seems to juggle with the technical terms with a finesse as if she herself is a part of the data programming. The insertion of universal truth of life and reality is weaved into the technicalities, and the efforts seem unpretentious. "Every time-traveller will create a different reality just as we do now. No two travellers will be able to retrieve the same reality, or even a fraction of the available relatives." (*HW*, 6)

Just as the time machine traveller travels though past, present and future, so does the narrative of the novel shuttles from the present to the past and finally the future. The future envisioned by Hannah Easton materializes towards the end. The future is represented by her love child Pearl Singh. Beigh Masters associates herself with past history. The journey into the past through the time machine is like a regression which gives a glimpse of the incidents in the past which change and decide the future for Hannah. While in the quest of the diamond, Beigh travels into the past and in a dream she seems to be the part of action and yet she is not. Experiencing the events, she sees herself as Hester Hedges who is injured in the battlefield and the diamond that is retrieved from the Emperor, is thrust deep into her own body. As she experiences the death of Hester, Beigh knows where the diamond is. The quest for Beigh is again through a violent out-of-body experience. "Venn says he was about to pull me out of it, the screaming, running, writhing, my tears, my adrenaline and heart rate and endorphins all indicated a near death experience; even the plunge in my blood pressure and pulse was consistent with mortal trauma. He understood me apparently I was shouting partially in his language, which, of course, I don't know." (*HW* 283)

The characters of Bharati Mukherjee are made to mouth the ultimate high philosophies of life, which on the surface might seem very vague but the depth in each word hides in itself manifold layers of philosophies. Bharati Mukherjee claims that the use of mythological philosophies is not through reading but listening to the oral narration of Hindu mythologies. This finds a way into the very structure of her plots.

> Much as Mukherjee seems to insist that she belongs to the ghetto American traditions of American literature and as easily as she is able to fit into that tradition, there are aspects of her work that are derived mainly from her cultural roots in India. She has spoken of the important influences in her life, of the images and ideas of her childhood in India and the sounds and sights of the great traditions of Indian mythology and literature. Her awareness of these influences enriches her stories and novels. For example, she can give the impression of a larger work even in a short story such as "A Wife's Story," which carefully meanders from one place to another and in which stories live within other stories. This technique of winding stories and embedding stories within stories dominates the Sanskrit epics, the *Mahabharata* and the *Ramayana*, and much of Indian literature.[11]

Her characters present a challenge for the readers to sit back and think twice. Not a single nuance about their behavioural attitude can be overlooked. One is bound to go through the pain felt by them. One experiences the tribulations gone through by Jasmine, while she is being raped by the monster, Half-Face. A kind of detachment is there in her mind while her body is being mutilated. She keeps thinking about her dead husband, and she can feel his presence in the room with her. When Jasmine retaliates, she slices her tongue and incarnates herself as "Kali," the empowered Shakti that resides inside the soul.

> No one to call to, no one to disturb us. Just me and the man who had raped me, the man I had murdered. The room looked like a slaughterhouse. Blood had congealed on my hands, my chin, my breasts, what a monstrous thing, what an infinitesimal thing, is the taking of a human life, for the second time in three months, I was in a room with a slain man, my body bloodied. I was walking death. Death incarnate. (*J* 119)

Did she regret having a female body, her weakness, which is a social stigma? Catering to the needs of the male populace is an expected fact in India, even when the woman regrets or detests doing so. Self-suppression comes to her as second nature. Leaving India, raped and mutilated,. she enters the New World. One can feel the anguish Jasmine goes through. The act of avenging the gruesome murder of the rapist is an act of long-awaited expression of anger that is suppressed at the time of her husband's murder. The murder in cold blood is thought out with a total detachment to avenge her husband's death. Being physically weak does not prove cumbersome as Jasmine takes her revenge and slays the wrong-doers. The action or "karma" is performed without any attachment to the reaction.

Bharati Mukherjee's characters follow the path of renunciation, reaching it by performing their action (the most basic ideology of the *Bhagvad Gita*) with a detachment that shocks the readers into feeling that violence is justified and advocated by Bharati Mukherjee as the only path for ethnic women to retrieve their lost selves. Born to life of servility to the superior male, the woman is castigated for renegading her conventional values. In order to assert, she has the weapon of tears which she uses to destroy. The slicing of tongue by Jasmine is more like severing all ties with the old traditions. The act of burning the white sari along with Prakash's suit is symbolic of Jasmine's renouncing the past which she leaves. 'Travelling light' has a metaphysical ring to it. In order to transcend, one has to be pious, and lesser the karmas, quicker he/she attains transcendence. Cutting of the tongue before killing is symbolic of the piousness of Jasmine's revenge. Throughout the novel, her actions have an essence of piousness. Her relationship with Wylie and Bud are congenial. Even her extravagant act of disappearance is marked with self-recriminations. Jasmine is more a 'giver' than a 'taker.' Devi in *Leave it to Me*, a true American individual, is more of a 'taker' than a 'giver.' The two characters are juxtaposed to bring out significantly the ideologies represented by them, though Jasmine is a character balanced by retaining the values of both cultures. Devi's act of torching Frankie Fong's dream-house or tattooing Stark Swann's back, murder of Loco Larry and Bio-Dad might be gruesome, but all acts are carried out with a feeling of detachment. Her act of revenge brings forth a feeling of peace.

In *The Holder of the World*, Hannah Easton, for the love of Raja Jadav Singh, risks her life to protect him. Her love for the Raja changes her perspective towards life. She is a generous woman, a medicine woman as she is called by the people she has cared for. She leaves Gabriel Legge after she becomes aware of his infidelities. He always expects Hannah's fidelity which enrages her. Hannah refuses to stay with her husband and tries to return back. But destiny has something else in store for her. She is washed back on the shore and discovered by Raja Jadav, changing her life forever. Releasing herself from the old shackles, Hannah is able to accept him as her lover. No longer does she feel an outcast in her own trappings. Acceptance of herself as a mistress to the Rajput king is a step towards her moral, physical and mental liberation.

Tara in *The Tiger's Daughter* is angry and frustrated, unable to fathom the present Calcutta and her friends with sophisticated and cool countenance. Rape of Tara exemplifies that the once-peaceful Calcutta has been raped and mutilated, and is beyond recognition. New Calcutta destroys her memories to the extent of frightening her. Even riot-torn Montreal could not prepare her sensibilities for the changed scenario of Calcutta. Forced to transform like Calcutta, she shrivels inside. Bharati Mukherjee's mind, while writing her earlier novels, depicts the mental confusion and infliction of pain pertaining to deciding her stay in Canada. The forced exile and feeling of expatriation in Canada (her husband's country) makes her feel like a stranger in her own birthplace also. Tara's decision to find solace in her husband's arms is a decision pulsating with pangs of self-realization. "After fourteen years in Canada, she found life as a 'dark skinned,' non-European immigrant to Canada very hard."[12]

Ironically, Clark Blaise who has no inkling of what to expect from India is a welcome change from the traumatic experiences back home. He is filled with wonder, and is totally bemused because the new culture seems to be flamboyant. Contrary to this, Bharati Mukherjee feels detached and confused; her mind becomes the voice of her earlier characters who go through rejections and yet come out of the situation self-empowered and jubilant.

Later on, she, in an essay about herself and her sister, Mira, depicts the feelings of the two sisters and their separate ways of merging into the world of freedom. Bharati Mukherjee as an immigrant goes out and embraces the New World with a feeling of belonging, whereas Mira, still attached to her former culture, is determined to return back home after a certain period of time. Both sisters blame each other, as their points of view differ.

Unable to fit into the culture of Calcutta, which is more of confinement, where emotion of love is protective to the point of stifling natural growth, Bharati Mukherjee decides to go to United States of America. India becomes a metaphor, a home away from home. Her husband is now more understanding to her need for self-expression and acceptance as a writer as he himself goes through the pangs, adjusting in a new culture.

> Other than that, I had my books, my notes, and my husband's heart to say yes to anything my wife's city offered me. Not to hold back, not to judge, not to be shocked, never to say no. I was the 'jamai,' the son-in-law, collecting all his wedding gifts ten years late. Though we'd been married ten years, it had been ten years of knowing Bharati on my terms and in my language. (*DNC* 96)

Dimple in *Wife* is an emblematic projection of upper middle class Bengali male-oriented society, a confused Bengali Brahmin virgin, who awaits her marriage. To her consternation, she finds out that her marriage to Amit Basu is not a bed of roses that she had fantasized. Self-suppression of feelings and yet craving to give voice to her feelings, she grows desultory with no interest in her day-to-day activity. Each activity is performed mechanically and the only thing she is interested is in her fantasies. Her mind is negative, reflexive and symbolic of her inner turmoils. Unable to give expression to her imagination, her behaviour turns into perverseness against herself. The continuous conflict between being 'Sita' and still needing to be free, keeps her going around. Symbol of modernity and free life, Ina Mullick titillates her senses to awaken to her surroundings but lack of courage hinders her from breaking the cage. "Again and again, among middle-class Bengali women I would hear, 'She is a lovely, docile girl, she's never given us any trouble,' or 'She is not at all independent, she'll do what her husband tells her.'" (*DNC* 231)

This is a universal statement cooed into the unsuspecting ears of the girl-child in Indian families, dooming them to a life of passive servitude to the male populace. It is like a tribute to age-old tradition, dubious norms laid out by generations, a blockage is created for the girl becoming economically and socially independent. Bharati Mukherjee is chided for her independence; her attitude of equality with her husband brings about deluge of criticism from friends and relatives:

> Clark had poured the tea, few actions in India seem to be regarded as matters of simple convenience. Clark's pouring the tea was regarded by the playwright and several other readers as emblematic of power relations between the Blaises. In a Bengali home, I was reminded by friends, a husband would consider it demeaning to get himself a glass of water (especially in front of guests) or to pour his own tea. (*DNC* 230)

The Holder of the World is divided into four parts and there is subdivision of each part into chapters and each chapter begins with a new happening in the life of Hannah Easton. The multi-division of the novel somehow reflects the Vedic writers and Hindu scriptures which have innumerable parts and chapters and sub-divisions within the chapters. Each part has been adorned with patterns. In fact, most of her novels are divided into various parts, but *The Holder of the World* has been adorned with lines from Keats' "Ode on a Grecian Urn." Each line marks the essence of the novel. The first part significantly marks the childhood abandonment of Hannah and her silent suffering, her passive existence as a bride; the second part marks the period when Hannah's adventurous heart craves for a journey into unknown lands. The third part marks her journey into the unknown realms of love and sacrifice; and the last chapter ends the journey of quest of Beigh Masters. In his ode, Keats has attained the highest degree of philosophy of thoughts. The philosophic sensuousness and beautiful depiction of emotions like love, which encompasses Hannah's soul into unfurling itself has been aptly adorned by Keatsian ode.

The multi-division in the novels indicates the interest of Bharati Mukherjee in Mughal paintings. As she herself claims in an interview, she was attracted to the Mughal miniatures and paintings which are woven around meta-narratives depicting the multifarious activities in the society. The poetics used in "Courtly Vision" is a smaller version of *The Holder of the World*. The language used in "Courtly Vision" is full of reverence for Mughal paintings and the border that surrounds the paintings is more than an adornment for Bharati Mukherjee. The flow of language in the story seems like "spontaneous overflow of powerful feelings."[13] The tone of language used in the diaries of Gabriel Legge marks the crudeness and unsophistication, a blemish marking his inferiority to Hannah Easton. "'Go,' Salem Bibi whispers, her kohl-limned sapphire eyes cleaving a low-hanging sky. Fly as long and as hard as can my co-dreamer!'" (*HW* 19)

A fisherman's child mouths poetic language, which marks the language of society. People speaking in poetic diction indicate Bharati Mukherjee's in-depth study of the dialects spoken in the social strata, not only in India but the puritan Massachusetts and England of 1660s.

The novel ends with reference to Nathaniel Hawthorne's (the great grandson of Joseph Hawthorne) association with Salem Bibi. Nathaniel Hawthorne was born in Salem in 1804. His mother's mourning of the death of her husband, a sea captain, in seclusion draws a parallel to Hannah Easton's life of puritan dilemma. "And so all of this had happened a century before the writer's birth, a century and a half before he wrote his morbid introspection into guilt and repression that many call our greatest works. Preach! Write! Act! He wrote against the fading of the light, the dying of the old program, the distant memory of a shameful, heroic time." (*HW* 256)

The morbidity of violence of weather in India wears her down. She is rescued by the Raja. The event is described in a vivid fashion in *The Holder of the World*. The language is full of similes and metaphors and turns the prose into poetic diction. "She squeezed her sari end; the water hit the ground in hissing droplets. The horses were scraped for leeches, which seemed to rise like locusts from the very grass. She thought: If the earth can melt from heat and humidity, it will today: she could brew her tea by waving a cup in the air and setting it in the sun to boil." (*HW* 241)

A genius with words, Bharati Mukherjee's novels depict the violence striving to be voiced in *Wife*. The inner-conflicts in the conjugal life, Dimple's act of violence against herself, the strains and stresses of an Indian wife, have been verbalized, painting the melodrama that takes place in an Indian couple's life in New York, striving to root themselves. Both are unsure of what to expect in the alien country, blaming each other. The bickering between them has two separate effects on the two individuals. Remorseful, Dimple is unable to express her traumas and Amit Basu can hardly understand her.

Shuttling between the old and the new world, the old and new beliefs, balancing between several identities is the basic structure of narrative technique in *Jasmine*. The novel is again divided into parts, but the sub-divisions are not done in this novel. "Though Jasmine attests to an eye for meticulous observation and an ear for contemporary American slang, it becomes clear that Mukherjee is less interested in giving us a realistic depiction of one woman's peripatetic life than creating a fable, a kind of impressionistic prose-poem, about being an exile, a refugee, a spiritual vagabond in the world today; and in this she has eloquently succeeded."[14]

The veneer of sophistication, juxtaposed with the crudeness of riot-torn Calcutta, forms the basis of the novel, *The Tiger's Daughter*. The difference in the two levels of social and economic disparities is depicted with clarity. The scenario seems to be a replica of Bharati Mukherjee's own experience in Calcutta. As Nelson says: "Mukherjee uses other images to emphasize the division between inside and outside, which contradict Hindu philosophy's insistence on the transparency between Brahman and Atman. For example, the riots on the streets as opposed to the calmness within middle-class households, the poor outside, as opposed to the rich within, and the surging crowd outside the theatre and the glitter of wealth within, all emphasize division."[15]

Leave it to Me depicts the violence in the American society. The novel is full of American slang and four-lettered words. Idioms and phrases used are reflection of the language used in America. "And why not ole! Fuck the Haeight, it's strictly for white breads!" (*LITM* 100)

The social, political and cultural background is specified, emphatically pointing to the conditions existing in America of 1990s. The hippie-culture is blended into the structure of the plot. The self-searching souls—who believed in free life with no ethical background and shelving off responsibilities, shirking from the responsibilities in the name of 'Karma,' free sexual relations established for carnal purposes—form the background of this novel. Against this backdrop, the protagonist of the novel, heir to a serial killer and an individual answerable to no one but herself, an avenging angel or devil incarnated into human form, carves a path for herself.

> She invoked this thing, this snake-thing. This snake-god or snake-devil, whatever it was, just rose right out of the cracks in the dry soil and rocked her in his arm.
>
> A trip?
>
> "You had to have been there, Devi! There's no describing that erotic moment.
>
> My beginning, I thought. I've just heard my beginning. (*LM* 155)

The art of ventriloquizing becomes an innate part of Bharati Mukherjee's style. The words articulating from characters seem to be the author's voice. Like Jasmine, Devi is made to jettison in and out of identities in search of her original identity. Continuous monologue is used to describe the surrounding environs from the streets to the various agencies that she works for and the contacts that she makes into the higher strata of society.

The colonial tone is evident in the novel *The Holder of the World*, a period of co-existence of Moghuls and the East India company. Raja Jadav Singh is the Hindu king, a representative of the Hindu regime. Aurangzeb represents the end of the golden era of Moghul regime and the British representing the initial intrusion of Outsider into the realms of Insiders, three cultures co-mingling with each other. In spite of the struggles going on, people co-exist in harmony. The society benefitting from the marauders and the invaders, insidiously creeping into the very being of the conventional but rich heritage of the then India.

> The chain of multinational factories stretched up and down the Coromandel like condos on the Florida coast. And the wealth they generated! Even with the Europeans' enfeebled head for business, as the nawabs charged (so enamored were the liquor-swilling *firangi* with legalisms and book-keeping, being apparently incapable of keeping accounts in their heads or of acting decisively in obvious self-interest), they could hardly go wrong. Everyone grew rich—the shareholders back in London, the sharp trading, black-marketing factors, the various local nawabs and, finally, the Great Mughal himself, old Emperor Aurangzeb in his Deccan war tents." (*HW* 102)

The cross-culture encounters inevitably give birth to apprehension in the mind of the expatriates and immigrants. The confusion, misunderstandings and ambiguities in the new culture are obvious.

> When he had married, he burned his India Society membership card. He was professionally cordial, nothing more, with Indian doctors at the hospital. But he knew he would forever shuttle between the old world and the new. He couldn't pretend that he had been reborn when he became an American citizen in a Manhattan Courthouse. (*D* 105)

The motif of unacceptability in one's own home country is brought out with clarity in the character of Tara, who at the beginning of her stay visits Aunt Jharna and meets her son. Her impromptu question instigates a feeling in Aunt Jharna which is incomprehensible to Tara's unpretentious frame of mind. The violent anger in Aunt Jharna, her pain and frustrations, come out pouring like a volcano erupting after being suppressed for a long time.

> Aunt Jharna's quietly violent response to Tara's innocuous suggestion can be seen as a paradigm of the response many Indian critics have had to this and other Mukherjee books on India and Indians. Aunt Jharna rebukes Tara thus, "You've come back to make fun of us, haven't you? What gives you the right? Your American money? Your mleccha husband.[16]

Later on, in the slum area, Tara's behaviour is counterpoised with her friend Rina's poised countenance, going through the paraphernalia with a practised ease. Getting an attack of paranoia, when a woman (who is stunted in growth) touches her saree, Tara screams in a frenzy, her behaviour shocking her friend, but Joyonto Mukherjee seems unrepentant and unmoved.

> It would have been a relief if he had been like other old men, intact though weary. He could have retired and gone on a world cruise, taken up gardening or bird watching or some other hobby. But Joyonto, the owner of foothills in Assam and estates in Tollygunge, felt trapped by his assets. He had to know too many people, remember too many details, see too many things. Yes, that was it, he had seen too much. (*TD* 70)

Shaila Bhave plays the pivot in "The Management of Grief," a point where one culture merges with another, instigating a change. The rigid stance of the Sikh couple and the confused white journalist are unable to communicate, as the Sikh couple cannot understand the language spoken by the white journalist, and the white journalist is not able to fathom the feelings of the old parents. Shaila acts as a bridge. Tara and Bharati Mukherjee face a similar kind of dilemma, though the self-amelioration in both the cases helps them out of the difficult situation.

> Shaila's dilemma is to some extent that of postcolonialism. Her role, and that of the Sikhs, is of colonists in the New World, the Western world that for so many years exported its cultural values to her nation. However, the same problems apply to the members of a culture that has been colonized, or even, as Mukherjee points out in several stories, to the returning soldiers who fought in Vietnam and absorbed cultural values there. Hybridization is the issue, the flux that exists when disparate cultural discourses come into contact and influence one another. The individuals who reside at that point of flux must deal with the violence that is often inherent in such contact, and must also deal with the fact that they become hybrids, alternately regarded as outcasts and valuable bridges.[17]

The disparity exists due to the rigidity of few people in each culture, who detest the intrusion of "Others," impurifying their culture. The stories in *The Middleman and Other Stories* have an array of characters like Shaila Bhave, through whom Bharati Mukherjee enables her readers to understand the disparities that exist. The borders are crossed through interracial marriages and romance. The love for Ro instigates Renata to step out of her Italian American background to embrace an Afghan lover who is exotic and whom she can use to heal America.

The immigrants in the various stories of *The Middleman and Other Stories* belong to different cultures which are trying to immerse themselves in the American culture. Acceptance of norms and perceptions of old culture are no longer possible. In 'A Fathering,' Jason, in order to embrace the 'Other' (his daughter), denies the validity of American perceptions to the extent that he denounces the western ideas and medical treatment given to Eng.

In 'Fighting for the Rebound,' an American man has an affair with a Philippine woman Blanquita. He tries to change her. Blanquita, renouncing her own culture and trying to merge into the American culture, has her own perceptions to deal with. They both have to change in order to create a cogitable balance in their world.

Panna, standing between the two cultures, sidetracks the assertion of protection extended by her traditional husband but wants to enjoy the freedom of both worlds. She gets flustered at the jokes cracked on India evident from the "Patel" jokes, yet, she has usurped the American ways of life to the extent that the jewellery seems a burden and a symbol of bondage to her. She embraces her men friend in public and is confident enough to navigate to her own needs in the New York city. The problem arises when her husband wants her to go back and she refuses to comply. As a hybrid, she is free to pick and choose and balance the two cultures in her personality. Her feelings are sensuous and carefree as she admires her nude body in the mirror: "In the mirror that hangs on the bathroom door, I watch my naked body turn, the breasts, the thighs glow. The body's beauty amazes. I stand here shameless, in ways he has never seen me. I am free, afloat, watching somebody else." (*M* 40)

Jasmine, a cultural uproot from Trinidad, renounces her culture in order to fulfil her American Dream to an extent that she is unable to decipher the change of events in her life. In order to merge, she sleeps with her employer, not knowing that she is just a plaything for Bill. She is used and discarded. Naturally, this concept of sexual freedom is equally acceptable to the American female gender but the colonized Jasmine hardly notices that she has been sexually exploited: "His hand moved up her throat and forced her lips apart and it felt so good, so right, that she forgot all dreariness of her new life and gave herself up to it." (*M* 138)

The idealized image of American Dream allures aliens to infiltrate the borders. The dream of earning money in dollars brings about the degeneration of cultures. People get exploited and they do not realize it. The subjects of taboo, sex and narcissistic attitude to one's own body are prevalent in most cultures. The freedom to express delight in one's own body and sex being legally sanctioned in American culture is an infallible part which facilitates the female gender from getting exploited. The images of physical beauty and freedom appear in most of the stories, especially the end of *Jasmine* collides with 'A Wife's Story,' as Jasmine lies on the rug submerged in a sexual embrace with her employer. It is symbolic of the subjugation of the colonized to the imperialistic culture of America.

> She felt so good she was dizzy. She'd never felt this good on the island where men did this all the time, and girls went along with it always for favors. You couldn't feel really good in a nothing place. She was thinking this as they made love on the Turkish carpet in front of the fire: she was a bright, pretty girl with no visa, no papers, and no birth certificate. No nothing other than what she wanted to invent and tell. She was a girl rushing wildly into the future. (*M* 138)

The idols of 'Sita and 'Kali' are used very cleverly by Bharati Mukherjee to bring out the qualities embodied by each of the idols. The patience and self-suppression of Sita (the only time Sita voices her desire is for the golden deer and steps out of the white magic circle, she is kidnapped by the demon king) and the qualities of 'Kali' who is a mother but can slay her own children if they are wrong. The qualities of the two idols have been balanced and internalized as a collective force, empowering Jasmine and Hannah Easton. Devi and Dimple resort to extremities, radicalizing the characteristics into the imbalance in personality. Devi, who is a self-empowered individual, exhibits the killer instinct inherited by the serial killer bio-dad and killing with detachment comes as a second nature. The existence of 'dualities' is a part of Bharati Mukherjee's constellation of multi-dimensional and multi-faceted characters who display the universal truth of such dualities. The extremities and disparities being a part of Indian as well as the American culture are full of such polarities that split into disconnected multiplicity. The intertwining of the Hindu philosophies within the structure is not an attempt to be evangelistic in her novels, but it emphatically points to the different experiences of separate individuals having a separate reality for each one of them. Each has his/ her own universe to deal with and surmount the hurdles to crossover as a winner.

The style of the author marks each phase of her own evolution. The earlier novels depict the emotional upheaval that she goes through. The evolving is distinctly clear with the novel *Jasmine*. The style of *Leave it to Me* marks the rootedness of the author into the new world. The liberation of soul from the feeling of "Otherness" is finally vanquished. The firm belief in herself is blended with new norms (taken or discarded, as she wishes), gives a new outlook to life, and the author authenticating her views through her characters is validated. Devi's intermittent expletives define her individuality and the blending of ideologies extracted from Hindu scriptures and the American ideologies.

"Nirvana is finding the tiger balls in you." Bharati Mukherjee uses aphorisms to shock the readers into awareness. The novel *Leave it to Me*, at first glance, is like any other novel exhibiting Americanism but the second reading compels the readers to venture out of their own practicalities to journey through the realms of the protagonist's mind. The action and reaction of the heroine may be violent but the events backing such violent acts clarify her actions.

> You can get a rough idea of the bloody scenario in prospect from the strength of want and envy in Devi's style all that use of 'I,' all those lists. Repeating the Frankie-move, she becomes the lover of a 1960s survivor named Ham and the furious rival of his long time girlfriend, Jess, who may or may not be her mother but deserves to pay anyway for being there and being in the way. It's Jess who gives Devi her motto, "Leave it to Me"—a pun on the name of her Media Escort Agency, through which Devi's Devil Dad himself tracks them down.[18]

The female protagonists are so vivid and come through with a power that the minor characters take a back seat. The subordination of the male characters seems ironical because the male-orientation of being the powerful individuals is very much evident in the majority of the cultures that coalesce to become one in the American culture. The female protagonists carry triple forces of burden on their shoulders, fighting to cross the discrimination on three levels, that is, racial, class discrimination and gender-crossing. The traumas confronted by them are psychological, as well as physical. Self-realization of their inner being, the emancipation comes through quickly. The women protagonists in the short stories, flaunt the flamboyancy of the major characters. Each one of the short stories is structured in a way that they can be turned into novels. "The Management of Grief" is a smaller version of "The Sorrow and the Terror," a non-fiction. Written in joint effort by husband and wife, it brings into notice the horrors of the plane crash taking away innocent lives. The multi-racial policies of Canada become the basic structure for the non-fiction.

"Courtly Visions" is an appreciation of Mughal paintings and also a plot for *The Holder of the World*. Jasmine inspires the plot to be expanded in form of novel. Jasmine, the protagonist hailing from the interiors of Punjab and not Trinidad.

> It does not do to think of Bharati Mukherjee primarily as an Indian or an immigrant or a foreigner, even though she was born in Calcutta and migrated to the United States (via a long detour in Canada) only as an adult. For Mukherjee writes prose so indelibly, effortlessly American that I, a fellow immigrant, occasionally have trouble keeping up with her rapid colloquial pattern, in something like the way I could never follow the dialogue in the Rockford Files when I first came to this country.[19]

Chitra Banerjee Divakaruni, a fellow immigrant writer, contemporary to Bharati Mukherjee, writes about the Indian immigrants in America. The difference between the styles of the two authors is apparent. As for Bharati Mukherjee, America is a place which she embraces with open arms and is accepted. As an expatriate in Canada, she looked down upon the immigrants as lost souls but glorifies America as a positive place for expansion of horizons. Divakaruni evokes the strangeness of the foreign land. The theme of their writings is similar and their female characters are navigators, juggling the two cultures, to find a new one for themselves. Retaining or discarding the nuances of the old culture and blending it with their new identities, failures and successes are taken in their stride.

> Violence is very connected with Diaspora and the transplanting from one's original culture into a new country, no matter for what reason we've come to the new country, implies or necessitates death of one's former self or mutilation of one's former self and so I want to think that the physical violence in my novels is really my metaphorical or artistic way of showing the psychic damage that takes place.[20]

Bharati Mukherjee detests the very idea of feminism and sort of brutalized feminists from other culture like Antonia Whitehead in *The Tiger's Daughter*, Karin, wife of Bud in *Jasmine*, Levi Anspach in *Wife*. These feminists are just extreme cases of Americanization who blunder into other cultures in order to impress their imperialistic attitude. Levi's outbursts instigate Dimple to react vehemently, whereas Tara admonishes Antonia for being rude to the traditional Hindu beliefs. Shaila Bhave is vexed at the incomprehensible, mechanical attitude of the white journalist and in a very Indian-American way she retaliates by banging the car-door without any explanation.

Extreme cases of Feminism are detested by Bharati Mukherjee. Her characters flaunt equipoised feminism, a paradigm celebrating fluid identities, centred and focused, journeying towards the transcendence of soul. Feminism presents a very different sort of connotation for Bharati Mukherjee: "It's certainly not a conscious decision to write as a woman writer but I find that quite naturally my main protagonists are rather strong women who assert themselves sometimes physically and always very emotionally."[21]

NOTES

1. Bharati Mukherjee, *Leave it to Me*, Reading Group Guides.Com 2-3.
2. Bharati Mukherjee, Style B.B.C. World Service. 1.
3. Swapan Ashfaq, Passage to India, *The Week*, San Francisco, August 31, 1997 1.
4. *Ibid.*, p. 1.
5. *Ibid.*, p. 1.
6. *Ibid.*, p. 1.
7. LITR 4333: *American Immigrant Literature* (University of Houston Clear Lake, Spring 2002. Recorder: Perkins, Andrea 1 of 4 http://www.motherjones.com/mother_jones/JF97/ mukherjee.html.
8. Raimundo Panikkar, ed. and trans. with introduction and notes, *The Vedic Experience*, Mantramanjari, IV 460 A 461.
9. Shankar Dhingra, "Activism, Feminisms and Americanization in Bharati Mukherjee's *Wife* and *Jasmine*," *Lavina, HCM A Journal of Asian American Cultural Criticism*, p. 4. http://socrates. berkeley.edu./~critmass/v3n1/shankar5.html.
10. D. Nichol Smith, *Shakespeare Criticism: A Selection*, 307. The World Classics.

11. Bharati Mukherjee (b. 1940), 2 of 4. Contributing editor Rustomji-kerns, Roshni, 2. http://college.hmco.com/english/heath/syllabuild/iguide/mukher.html.
12. World Literature in English: Bharati Mukherjee, 1. http://www.eng.fju.edu.tw/worldlit/india/mukherjee.html. *Days and Nights in Calcutta*: PART I
13. M.H. Abrams, *A Glossary of Literary Terms*, Third Edition, p. 132.
14. Michiko Kakutani, "Third World Refugees Rootless in the U.S.," *New York Times: Word and Image*, Tuesday, September 19, 1989.
15. S. Emmanuel Nelson, *Bharati Mukherjee: Critical Perspectives*, p. 28.
16. Fakhrul Alam, *Bharati Mukherjee*, p. 25.
17. Insecurities and Hope: Bharati Mukherjee's Hybrids and the Role of Divider/Bridge. 1 of 7. http://www.legendmud.org/raph/pupers/ mukherjee.html.
18. Lorna Sage, *Wrath of the Goddess, The New York Times Book Review*, p. 33.
19. Notes from A New America Ward, Elizabeth Book World/ July 3, 1998. 3.
20. Mukherjee's Works 1 of 2. Her Story BBC World. http://www.bbc.co.uk/worldservice/arts/features/womenwriters/mukherjeework.shtml.
21. Her Story /BBC World Service "Being a woman writer" 1 of 1 http://www.bbc.co.uk./worldservice/arts/features/womenwriters/ mukherjeework.shtml.

Chapter VI

Sensibility of the Uprooted in *Desirable Daughters*

> Woman is the earth, air, ether, sound; woman is the microcosm of the mind, the articulation of space, the knowing in knowledge; the woman is fire, movement, clear and rapid as the mountain stream; the woman is that which seeks against that which is sought. To Mitra, she is Varuna, to Indra, she is Agni, to Rama, she is Sita; to Krishna she is Radha. Woman is the meaning of the word, the breath, touch, act; woman that reminds man of that which he is and reminds through him of that which she is. Woman is kingdom, solitude, time, woman is growth, the woman is death, for it is through woman that one is born; woman rules, for it is she, the Universe.[1]

The female protagonists of Bharati Mukherjee are a blend of modern and traditional qualities and they believe in creating their own universe, but then they keep oscillating between their inner and outer universe. Tara of *Desirable Daughters* keeps oscillating between modernity and traditional ties. Though the female protagonist is comfortable with her American identity, still she identifies with her Indian roots. The catalyst creating havoc in her life is an outsider who leads her to questioning her upbringing and the imbibed values. Always questioning her exotic status in America, she is faced by upheavals in her life. She is not certain about the breaking of the values in which she feels herself sacrosanct. Unable to handle crisis, crying and getting agitated is the only way she can handle her emotions. She is ridiculed by her son Rabi. He has even written a play about two sisters who give in to histrionics and melodrama. "Our sister act sets off Rabi's anger like nothing else. He promises me some day to write a play about two Indian sisters on the telephone."[2]

Yet we find that Tara Bhattacharjee is fluid and adapts to both the traditional culture and her adopted American ethos. She is like

Hannah who reconciles in the end her past; and her future merge to reconstruct her present.

Tara Bhattacharjee tries to reconstruct her present by searching her roots and questioning it. She tries to juggle between both the cultures, her past and present.

> She vacillates between two lives: "maybe I really was between two lives." Yet to strike roots, yet to belong to any of these lives, she exemplifies the "existential dilemma" of diasporas and the problems an immigrant who has a fluid identity associated with mobility and plurality rather than stasis and singularity.[3]

Tara Bhattacharjee drifts from her husband to her lover and back to her husband as a lover. She feels lost as an Indian immigrant's wife. She leaves him to gain an identity, but she is dependent on Andy for emotional and physical nurturing. She has had affairs with many lovers. Andy leaves her because Tara disobeys him by going to New Jersey to find out the identity of her sister's so-called illegitimate child. Her contacting Jack Sidhu infuriates him. She returns back to San Francisco to be with Bish and Rabi. The night before the bombing of her house she plays the role of a seductress, lover and a wife to her husband.

> Bish might be the reigning genius of Silicon Valley, but he could not reverse the cosmic order and return to marriage and the status of a householder at a time in his life when all that should be drawing to a close. "All of that" meaning what we'd done that afternoon and again that evening and, so far as I was concerned, would do again as soon as I could drag him back inside. (269)

Being with her husband and while trying to resurrect her life, she is thrown into an inferno. Bish is badly hurt. After destruction, resurrection is bound to come and she goes to India. In India, she is faced with a different atmosphere but both she and her son move fluidly. Rabi, a child of American inheritance, is quite comfortable and is like a kid who is at home in India looking around from a tourist's eyes, trying to acquaint himself with the immense depth and knowledge of Tara Bhattacharjee's ancestral culture and to which Tara is re-introduced. Bharati Mukherjee's protagonist cannot be judged as an immoral individual who has had affairs because it is not prevaricated in the American culture. Yet, she is scandalized to be introduced to Chris Dey, the illegitimate son of her sister. Her sister has always been looked upto due to her beauty and intelligence. So why is she unable to accept her sister's infidel affair with Ron Dey? In fact her sensibility has been ruffled beyond expectation. The rootless exuberance of the immigrants is focused on giving the plot a two-dimensional vision. The emotional ebullience of Rabi and constrained one on Tara's part as she reacquaints herself to the mystifying culture of her native land. The mystical environs of Rishikesh seem to soothen her senses, which have been impaired after her confrontation with the realities of life. She is like a child who is lost in a jungle, as the world, which she felt secure in, comes crashing down, her values that were instilled during young days seem to be debased and defiled. *Desirable Daughters*, the first novel in Bharati Mukherjee's trilogy, reveals an exuberant character of Tara Bhattacharjee who questions her own identity. The identity crisis and a longing to define one's own identity is triggered off when she is faced with the illegitimate son of her much idolized sister, a role model for the younger sisters. An imposter forcibly enters her life, shattering the icons of family ideologies.

Debbie di Martino in *Leave it to Me* has nothing to lose. Discovering that she is illegitimate, she has nothing to lose, she forages forward searching for her roots. Debbie, belonging to the second generation does not need to be cautious, partaking all that she can. Tara Bhattacharjee is happy floating rootlessly in the country she adapts but due to delicate sensibilities, she is taken aback as secrets of her past seem to unravel in front of her eyes. The imposter who claims to be her nephew, barges into her secure world, trying to disrupt her tranquil existence. The safe haven seems to crumble in front of her eyes and she is unable to stop. Switching on the lights every evening to ward off any evil is a habit inculcated from old culture. "In describing the cross-cultural impact on Tara's identity partly Indian and partly Americanized, the novelist portrays her as a hybrid subject, a mimicry of the American socio-cultural ethos."[4]

Floating rootlessly, both the sisters are self-empowered, questioning their identity. Tara questions her very existence while her sister tries to unveil the family secret as saving her heart and mind. She tries to reconnect with the past to give authenticity to her present existence. Debbie's exuberance emanates from her being as she creates a havoc around her avenging her wrong-doers. She embraces life without any qualms. Tara's life takes a complete turn when faced with the realities and her values are up for questioning. She questions her sister who is happy in her South-Asian American status and then comes to the conclusion that the imposter cannot be a kin. She uses self-denial to pacify her fretting soul. Evasion of facts though, is not her style. Instead of simmering inwardly and maintaining the dignity of the high class good Bengali family, she chooses to bring forth the wrath of her sister.

The novel is not only a nostalgic-romanticisation of the past, but a reconstruction and revalidation of Tara's identity. It is "her inverted story of mobility." The events and locales that form a part of Tara's identity have been nostalgically delineated by Bharati Mukherjee. The spatio-temporal construction of Tara's identity is based on "fragments of place memories, on desires and experiences."[5]

Bharati Mukherjee's novel, *Desirable Daughters* analogues her own life. Real life corresponds to the life of the protagonist in the book. Experiencing the state of an exile, Bharati Mukherjee is more exuberant and tolerant about the fact that she is an Indian American writer (linguistically, Indian). Her family is more or less a blend of nations. "When I first started writing, people didn't know how to categorize me," she said "you can't be Canadian because you didn't grow up here, they said. They didn't have a concept of diasporic writers. It wasn't until I came to the States that people realized this was a whole new area I was identifying."[6]

Fully assimilated into the American culture, Bharati Mukherjee is tolerant about her past culture. She refuses to exist in her past, tearing herself apart from memories. Bharati Mukherjee has two sisters, and in her early immigrant days she could not understand her sister Mira who lives in America but her heart belongs to her motherland. Contrary to this, Tara Bhattacharjee is more tolerant to this fact that Padma has made her own choice. Tara's visit to New Jersey and Jackson Heights is more of a re-acquaintance with her South-Asian American sister. The novel explores and reveals the alien society and culture of America in a more congenial atmosphere. Her work illumines the mental stress that Tara goes through, but unlike the earlier characters in her novel *Darkness*, she refuses to give in and floats rootless in her adapted nation. She is not like Dimple of *Wife* who is not able to decide if she wants an affair with Milt Glasser or not. Tara takes her lover Andy, accepting him with all his philosophies and her son is more like Jasmine who floats rootless in the adapted country. *Desirable Daughters* focuses on the refashioned and reinvented culture of America and the globalisation that brings the world closer. After 9/11, *Desirable Daughters* flaunts introduction of underworld network and terrorism on the American scenario.

The story of the novel somehow loses its tight reins, as many themes have been incorporated into a single fabric. Tara Lata Gangooly had inverted the tragedy in her life, the death of her husband and imposed virginity throughout her life into selfless sainthood. But her namesake, Tara Bhattacharjee lives her life on her own terms. Married to Bish and their immigration to America, Bish's preoccupation with his software leaves her bereft in the New World. After living up to the instilled values of patriarchal Bengali 'Bhadralok' society, she divorces her multimillionaire, Silicon valley entrepreneur husband, to drift along rootless, having many affairs and finally finding solace in the arms of her live-in-partner. Andy, a Hungarian immigrant, who believes in Buddhism and its philosophies, comforts her through her travails with back rubs and sayings of the Zen.

> Mukherjee is ever conscious of the force of memory. Though her heroine Tara Bhattacharjee, estranged from the millionaire Silicon Valley entrepreneur Bish Chatterjee, lives a Westernized life in San Francisco—where she feels free "to make myself over, by the hour"—it is her Calcutta roots that shape her reactions and actions when she's confronted by a family problem.[7]

Bharati Mukherjee deals with family ties, feeling of belonging and identity crisis in *Desirable Daughters*. Acceptance of the "New" and the values influenced by the American culture, the second generation and their values in the domicile country and easy acceptance by the first generation are few of the themes dealt in the novel. Manju Kapur's *Namesake* also deals with the acceptance of "New." *Desirable Daughters* is a tale of immigrants and the attitude of three sisters and their ways of dealing with situations. Desirable daughters, as the title suggests, are kind of daughters that parents would be proud of, and for whom every parent would crave. The three sisters, who are the daughters of Motilal Bhattacharjee and the great-grand-daughters of

Jai Krishna Gangooli, belong to a traditional Bengali Brahmin family. The most desired and coveted belonging to the "Bhadralok," they part ways taking their own course of voyage towards their destiny. Padma, Parvati and Tara—symbolic names of Shakti (Goddess of Hindus)—do not flaunt the same ethical values but have the grit to carve a niche for themselves. They are a blend of traditional and modern outlook. Padma and Parvati do not regret their choices, the former an immigrant of ethnic origin in New Jersey, and the latter married to a boy of her own choice and settled in the plush locality of Bombay with an entourage of servants to cater her. Tara, the narrator of the novel, takes the readers deep into the intricacies of the New World (America) and seems to float rootless with time. The fluidity of her identity testifies not only her own but also the fluidity of the immigrants. She values her traditional upbringing but takes pride in moving forward in life. Her image of her family values forms a wall of security around her camouflaging the fragile vulnerable self.

> When you go to a new environment through immigration, you are vulnerable because you have left the protective cocoon of your own community where there is a certain identity, mingling or co-mingling of identity. You go to a new society or a new community, you don't have that co-mingling of identity. Suddenly you see that protective layer is gone.[8]

Tara as a young wife stays for ten years with Bish Chatterjee, but his preoccupation with his software leaves her yearning for companionship and care. She finds solace in Andy's arms but again, when Andy leaves her she feels threatened and comes back to Bish. Her rhapsodized soul takes a dip as she is confronted with the realities of terrorism. New revelations unfurl as her son declares that he is a gay, tearing apart her cocoon and, the final blow is her house being bombed and Bish Chatterjee is crippled and dependent on her. Bharati Mukherjee reanimates her alter ego Tara Banerjee of her first novel *The Tiger's Daughter* to create Tara Bhattacharjee. Like Tara of *The Tiger's Daughter*, Tara Bhattacharjee returns home to find solace at her father's house. She further probes into her family tree to unveil the life of "Tree Bride" her ancestor. The retrospective journey is more like a journey inside to correlate the chaos outside with the peace inside.

> The bride is named Tara Lata, a name we almost share. The name of the father is Jai Krishna Gangooly. Tara Lata is five years old and headed deep into the forest to marry a tree. I have had the time, the motivation, and even the passion to undertake this history. When my friends, my child, or my sisters ask me why, I say, I am exploring the making of a consciousness. Your consciousness? They tease, and I tell them, No. Yours. (5)

Bharati Mukherjee begins the novel with Tara Bhattacharjee, the namesake of Tree Bride Tara Lata, to narrate the tales of India and its traditions. Tara Lata, who is just five years and is being carried on a palanquin, all decked up in the finery to be given away in marriage. The older sisters, seven and nine, are already married.

In Hindu culture it was authenticated that a father should give away his daughter in marriage before she reaches puberty and if the father is not able to do so he is bound to go to hell and all his good deeds would go astray.

> In a palanquin borne by four servants sit a rich man's three daughters, the youngest dressed in her bridal sari, her little hands painted with red lac dye, her hair oiled and set. Her arms are heavy with dowry gold; bangles ring tiny arms from wrist to shoulder. Childish voices chant a song, hands tap, golden bracelets tinkle. I cannot imagine the loneliness of this child. A Bengali girl's happiest night is about to become her lifetime imprisonment. (3-4)

Not only is the similarity uncanny when the names are similar, but destiny seems to infer a similar destiny onto both. The tradition has continued through ages and the great-grand-daughter follows the same footsteps and her father fixes her marriage. The daughter who cannot raise voice against her patriarch, a graduate with M.A. degree in hand, is handed over to her groom, a suitable match in the form of Bish Chatterjee alias Biswapriya Chatterjee. She has to get married because she cannot follow her heart and marry a person whom she might like. She cannot follow in the footsteps of Parvati who marries a boy of her own choice. The boy is suitable in accordance with the psycho-social set up of Indian Bengali Brahmin family categorized as the "Bhadralok." Obviously the girl's consent is contingent. Later on, she feels like an outsider among the Silicon smug Indian wives' groups and divorces Bish to move to Cole Valley in San Francisco with her teenage son Rabi. She takes on a teaching job which gives her satisfaction till her world is turned upside down with Padma's illegitimate son barging in on her safe haven.

> Innocence taken out of context, turned against you. I didn't have a husband, and Andy was remote. I feared my son and his friend. My sisters wouldn't take me seriously. . . . "Rabi!" I shouted out when I heard him come in, "tell that Chris Dey to come back here. I want to talk to him again. (114)

The child bride, Tara Lata is headed towards her destiny. She prays to God to save her groom. Before marriage God and Goddesses have been invited, nurtured and pacified. Goddess Manasha (Mother of the snakes) has been prayed to, but unfortunately, the Goddess is not pacified and she strikes. The groom dies on his way due to snake bite. The groom's father is greedy and wants Jai Krishna Gangooly to give the dowry. Jai Krishna Gangooly, instead of baulking down to the groom's father's demands, puts his foot down and refuses to hand over his daughter to her in-laws, dooming her to a life of servility. A Sanskrit scholar and a Brahmin, he decides to marry his daughter to a tree (symbolic of eternity; God), so that she can overcome the curse of widowhood. She is united with God, and now she is eternally doomed to be a married woman leading a life of purity, sainthood and lifelong virginity.

> Tara Lata the virgin, the untouched, who opened the house to beggars, then to the sick, then to the young soldiers fighting the Raj. . . . Tara Lata the saint, the freedom fighter. What ever the bond between us, it is less than obvious. (17)

One tends to question if, there is any karmic connection between the two Taras—Tara Lata and Tara Bhattacharjee. Tara Bhattacharjee and her two sisters, are born on the same date. Is there a significant connection? Tara Lata represents the old patriarchal world where child marriages were rampant. As her groom is struck by a snakebite, instead of letting the daughter lead a life of widowhood, her father prefers to get her married to a tree—the immortal. Is it a way to defy destiny or is it to protect his daughter from being marginalized. Jai Krishna Gangooly, on the other hand, goes on marrying girls in order to sire a son. Is Tara Bhattacharjee's move to divorce her husband and move on with her life a defiance on her part or is it a revolt against the patriarchal mind set, which is a part of immigrant life style in the New World of America? Tara Bhattacharjee, unlike Dimple in *Wife*, believes in staying afloat like Jasmine. She frees herself from the shackles of marriage of 10 years and the symbolic phallic power, to live a life with her live-in partner Andy, a Hungarian immigrant, and her son who is a gay. Her Indian sensibility takes a nose dive into abyss as this fact is revealed to her, but then she refuses to disown her son on the grounds of his sexual preferences. Does this novel emboss purgation of emotion—a cathartic experience for the protagonist as well as the authoress.

The novel to a certain extent seems to be an autobiography. Bharati Mukherjee has two sisters. Mira refuses to become an immigrant and is happy with her identity of South Asian American just like Padma. The retrospective journey to India to find more about the Tree Bride somehow analogues Bharati Mukherjee's trip to East—Bangladesh—to find her roots. The novel traverses through incidents to end where it begins—the marriage of Tara Lata, which took place in 1879—the marriage which was doomed and the bride was married to a tree. The Tree Bride stays in her paternal house throughout her life cherishing her bridegroom. She becomes like the tree, nurturing the freedom movement in India, healing and praying for the people around. She reminds the readers of Hannah Easton in *The Holder of the World* who is a healer. Tara is free to live as she wishes, but she prefers to be bondaged to the patriarchal house. Tara Bhattacharjee tries to find the facts about Tree Bride and like Hannah she tries to resurrect her present and future by unveiling the past. She stands on the margin, vacillating between the two cultures, trying to hinge on her rootless existence. Bharati Mukherjee's heroines embark on the principles of existentialism, trying to authenticate their identities in a subtler manner except Debbie di Martino in *Leave it to Me*, who leaves nothing behind her. She destroys. She is Americanized, verbalizing the American linguistics and mannerisms. She wants to find her real parents so that she can question them and ends up killing her Bio-Dad. But with *Desirable Daughters*, Bharati Mukherjee is more at peace with herself. No longer is there a hassle to break out from the conformities of her values of past culture. Pacified with both—her past and the present—she looks onto her past culture without any qualms while fully enthralled in her new identity of being an immigrant in America. *Desirable Daughters* is seeped in the Indian culture which is juxtaposed to American culture. Indian feminism is juxtaposed to American feminism—Tara Lata, the Tree Bride alias Tara Bhattacharjee, the great grand-daughter.

The former is an epitome of Indian feminism, a virtuous lady with inculcated qualities of tolerance, a freedom fighter of yester years, a widow and a virgin. She is a Devi, a Goddess, who has not brought defame to herself whereas the latter, Tara Bhattacharjee, a divorcee, tagging along a live-in partner, a Hungarian immigrant mistry (whose profession is looked down upon in Indian culture), a believer in Buddhist ideology, and a son who is gay. Tagged as a slut, she feels out of place in her immigrant existence, especially when she visits her sister and finds the same attitude in people around. After reconciling with her sister and her life and her own destiny of being hounded by a terrorist and a bomber, feigning an identity which is false, she returns to India at the end of the novel to search for the roots or familial ties.

One can recall Bharati Mukherjee's existence in Canada and her house being burnt in a fire accident, returning back home to Calcutta and chronicling her experiences in India in *Days and Nights in Calcutta*. Bharati Mukherjee enjoys a happy existence after a long period of exile. She visits India frequently and is way off from the days of her sabbatical year in India. Tara's sister Padma and Bharati Mukherjee's sister Mira (who is an expatriate and refuses to contribute to the domicile country), seem to be one and the same. No longer caught in the conflict of separate existence, Bharati Mukherjee claims and authenticates her identity of American writer of Indian origin (linguistically). This statement gets validity in the novel *Desirable Daughters* where her female protagonist authenticates her "Voice" and enjoys her feminity. Parvati, who married a boy of her choice and settled in Bombay, fully enjoys her life with a feudal outlook to life. She might have resisted her father to marry a groom of her choice but the attitude remains the same, though she refuses to reveal secrets of the family, especially about Padma. She refuses to give details about Padma's illegitimate child but writes long letters explaining all the Indian nuances to Tara. Parvati's character is again like Bharati Mukherjee's sister who is an Indian resident. Parvati frets about the dangers lashing around the corner, just like Tara

Banerjee in *The Tiger's Daughter* who is hounded by crime in the sub-ways in America.

> Now I was regretting my sanitized upbringing. The plot and the participants in my San Francisco drama belonged more to Bombay than to Calcutta, and the India that had alarm system, but not an armed chowkidar outside my door, no half-wild dogs inside. (114)

Bharati Mukherjee has woven a plot around globalization, which has given an access to everyone, anywhere. Biswapriya Chatterjee has innovated a software 'CHATTY,' a computer programme, which makes him a millionaire. The introduction of Chris Dey, the illegitimate child of her sister Padma and Ronald Dey, creates a havoc in her life. The search begins by Tara writing to Parvati and her visit to New Jersey to meet Padma. The American search cultivates into unravelling of family secrets and Tara's creed taking a dip. "No man would consent to be a woman, but every man wants to exist."[9]

Tara Bhattacharjee acclimatized into the values of New World, accepts the new changes in her life and zealously tries to solve them instead of sitting back and praying for everything to make itself right. Bharati Mukherjee asserts the Hindu philosophy of "Karmayoga" as she has done time and again in her novels. A gay son would have caused a furore in India, but she accepts her son's choice as normal talking it out with her ex-husband. Rabi's character might be cloned by Bharati Mukherjee from her Canadian days, when she was supported by the Gay Union and she in turn had supported their cause. The issue of Gay is no more questioned after the formulation of New law in America. Bharati Mukherjee authenticates their existence. Rabi is a normal person with a difference and Tara's acceptance of her son's choice is significant. Even Tara's choice of Andy does not cause any problem with Biswapriya Chatterjee. Her assimilation is complete, yet she is bewildered to see her sister's immigrant status from a different point of view.

> Didi was sitting just inches away, a firm identity resisting all change, at least from a distance, on a brief inspection. But under scrutiny, fractured, like cracks under old glaze. Up close, I didn't recognize her. I didn't know who she was. I was following the cracks, fascinated by their complexity, not the simple, shining face. "Puffles and Piffles,"

> Andy once called them, but I never thought that previously unidentified fault lines could refer to my sister, or to me. (196)

Bharati Mukherjee's protagonists are no more judgmental. She gets agitated but opens her mind to accept the new. Her book reveals Tara's angst and the terror inside but she refuses to give in. Her character is more balanced like Hannah.

> "I've done nothing of the sort," I said. "This 'hand' of yours is a claw. Your demands are threats that I reject, and you've made claims that no one was verified. The 'evidence' you've presented is clearly manufactured." (196)

Her son is the bearer of family's name who brings renunciation to his family beyond this illusory world. This brings out the conflict of sensibilities of Asian Indian immigrant set against the backdrop of American democratic ideals and the Indian consciousness. The Bengali Brahmin lady is unable to reconcile to the fact that the "desirable daughters" had their weaknesses. The Pandora Box is open and Tara Bhattacharjee is totally confused. Tara of *Desirable Daughters* is very different from Tara of *The Tiger's Daughter*. Filled with superiority of belonging to patriarchal familial bondings, both are rudely awakened to facing the rude realities of life. Tara of *The Tiger's Daughter* tries to detach herself from the lurking dangers infested in the society around, to be in the warmth of her father's feudal set-up, but Tara of *Desirable Daughters* tries to chain the bull by holding it by its horns and does not waver from the consequences. She does not cringe away dissociating herself from the "Other" (the terror-stricken society).

> As I walked, I wondered: was this my final neighbourhood excursion? Was this what it was like to be marched in the company of the man who would kill me? All those articles in the paper, the irate husband or boyfriend with a court order against him, suddenly showing up. "I just want to talk, honey. Just let me in for chrissake. What's the harm in that?"
>
> He asked, innocently, "Have you spoken to my mother?"
>
> "And who might she be?"
>
> He responded with a nasty laugh. (119)

When Tara Bhattacharjee goes to meet her sister Padma, she is introduced to her sister's world where she is considered a royalty and had her flings and affairs. Her husband lived under Padma's shadow. She, with her friend Danny Jagtiani, and few others, runs varied types of business. Tara is asked to have a make over. She is tired and looks haggard and old by Padma's standard and naturally, Padma overlooks the point why Tara is looking tired. Tara's confrontation with the imposter leaves her drained and she easily succumbs to her sister's demands. She is treated like a mannequin, where she is made to drape an expensive designer sari and wear heavy gold jewellery to the party organized by her sister. Tara is introduced to the South-Asian immigrant society and the regulars at these parties. The irony of the situation is that Tara does not realize the motives behind Padma's generosity. She keeps on calculating her budget: if she would be able to pay for the sari and jewellery, little realizing that she is being used like a mannequin on display for people to look and buy the commodity. The detached tone and attitude of Padma is a setback for Tara, as she is taken to a corner and asked to take out the set because it is sold. She feels bereft, naked and feels thankful that she has not been asked to open her sari. All these incidents happen in good zest and Tara encounters the new persona of her sister who is beyond recognition.

> She let me know she couldn't be seen with me in public ("My reputation, Tara") and couldn't introduce me to New Jersey Bengali society in my present bedraggled condition. She'd have to take me to her hair-and-nails girl, her masseuse and studio trained make-up man, and her Calcutta-Chinese hair stylist, then unleash me on the sari shops and jewellery stores of Queens, where even movie stars came to shop. . . . If you fixed yourself up and resurrected your flirting skills, there are dozens of catches out there. (186)

Tara had not met her sister for a long time though they stay in the same country. She is more in contact with Parvati in India. Talking to Parvati is difficult as she is busy with her patriarchal feudal set-up in India. She is busy with organizing her home, children, servants and fretting about the conditions worsening in Bombay. She keeps talking about her cavalcade of servants, terrible experiences in Bombay and its cruel culture. The long letters that she keeps writing to Tara reveal her world where she rebukes her sister for doubting her heritage and slowly reveals the intricacies of the family secrets, pushing Tara towards a crisis of identity.

> The dilemma of emigration is viewed by Bharati Mukherjee in Freudian terms, without passion there is no movement in life. This is the inference, which the novelist for a typical immigrant draws from Freud. It is only passion which drives one to be an immigrant. Reason settles the issue once for all whereas passion promotes life and puts it in progress and conflict. A crisis teaches a person more solidly than affluence and leisurely life.[10]

Reinventing herself with aplomb is a special aspect of Tara's persona. Each protagonist of Bharati Mukherjee reinvents herself, but Tara Bhattacharjee is opulent and applaudable. Acceptance of a son who is gay, Tara is way ahead of Bharati Mukherjee's other fictional characters. Her unconditional love allows her to accept her son, and her re-invented acclimatized self is more prone to accepting the new ways of the new world. Even Bish Chatterjee is not like Amit Basu of *Wife*. He accepts his wife's lover and does not hesitate to appreciate his capabilities. He keeps an open mind towards the happenings in his life. In fact, Bish Chatterjee is modern in his views and acceptance of the new world and its ways which is evident in his persona. Bish is a great improvement on the other Indian male characters of Bharati Mukherjee. He is more like his American counterpart Taylor in *Jasmine*. Bish does not hesitate to bow down to his wife's wishes and instead of getting oppressed by her husband, Tara is allowed to spread her wings. She sounds like D.H. Lawrence's Elsie in the short story "White-Stocking" who likes to take her flights to return back to her nest in the evenings. Bish Chatterjee is portrayed as a balanced personality who does not believe in subjugating his wife. In spite of the divorce, both keep a track of their son's progress. That her son is a gay is an information that the father already has and he pacifies and settles her nerves. Bish accepts Andy as easily as a friend.

Bharati Mukherjee has always concentrated on how the immigrants and exiles have re-invented themselves, shedding their husbands and lovers like a snake's skin undergoing metamorphosis, their re-incarnated selves celebrating the freedom and rootlessness in American culture. Tara Bhattacharjee enjoys the best of both the cultures. Considered as an unrivalled "queen," she possesses everything provided by her husband. She is a constant feature on magazine cover page. Leading a life on her own terms, she does not need to sever her umbilical cord from her past culture. She is at peace with herself and her habitat till it is forcefully disrupted. She lives with her lover and her son, gets a job as a school teacher and then haplessly meets the intruder. She is agitated and on her tether's end when she finds that her son is associating with the imposter in spite of her asking him not to. But it is Rabi who tells her about the suspicious behaviour of the imposter. Tara takes control of the situation and turns everything upside down to find out the facts about the imposter, who fakes the identity of her illegitimate nephew. This incident makes her go around asking about her own status, her uprooted identity in America. She visits her sister Padma and then writes to Parvati, consequently discovering that her image of her sister is under question. Even her own status as a divorcee is under scrutiny when she faces the South-Asian society:

> Tabloid Headline: Tara's great retrofitter! Honey, are you actually living off a generous divorce settlement from one man while playing around with another? And still keeping the first one on the leash? That's so cool! That's so trashy! Can you talk about your connection to terrorists and international criminals? (275)

The two cultures flaunt two different sets of values about marriage, partnership and many other things. Resisting the ethnic ghetto of Jackson Heights, she does not question their identity nor does she give in to the pressure of being categorized as different. She faces the same situation in India. It is not only her own identity that she scrutinizes with the foreign stimuli in her life, she is also introduced to the barbaric world of dons and underworld kingpin Dawood's gang. It is the new world of criminal miscreants and the globalisation and glamour of terrorism that is faced by Tara. She tries to save her family but realizes that she, the lovely rich lady, and not her family, had been the target. As she goes about finding about the imposter, truth reveals itself:

> Andy had felt the danger, Rabi had felt it, Jack had felt it, and I'd been sailing through a minefield like a self-appointed Joan of Arc. Rabi and Bish were roaming round without a sense of caution or a care in the world. My house was empty and just sitting there, dark and inviting. (221)

The old myths of Indian mysterious mystic world are revived, contrasting it with a very modern American world. Bharati Mukherjee has drawn real characters into her fictitious world establishing the fact that she is comfortable with both the worlds.

Rootless in America, life endangered due to the imposter who claims to be her nephew, Tara floats endlessly dithering from sister to sister belonging to two different worlds. Isolation makes her shiver, yet she dauntlessly marches forward with the sole purpose of discovering the intruder's identity. The three sisters, Padma, Parvati and Tara, are descendants of the son of the ninth wife of Jai Krishna Gangooly—a lawyer in British court which he renounced later. He is a Sanskrit scholar and a staunch follower of Hindu spirituality, a patriarch who goes on to marry again and again to sire a son, a father who married his youngest daughter to a Sundari tree to save her from widowhood, a man who belonged to the 'Bhadralok.' The oldest sister Padma was born eighty years after the marriage ceremony of his daughter, the Tree Bride Tara Lata, in Shoonder Bon. Parvati and Tara were also born on the same day with a difference of three years between each of them. The story of Tree Bride, Tara Lata, which begins in 1879 and whose namesake is the female protagonist of *Desirable Daughters* reveals the severity of the influence of traditions and conformity to societal norms on the lives of Padma, Parvati and Tara, as well as their cultural and traditional patriarchal inheritance. Born in Calcutta's "Bhadralok" family of Bhattacharjees, sensitized to the socio-cultural norms, they are bound to share a tradition of leadership, achievement and refinement, of beauty and sensitivity—reasons that were the envy of the world. These cultural, socio-political and economic bonding make her glued to her husband, who is busy expanding his business, which will make him the richest in Silicon valley. Feeling neglected, Tara decides to live her own life, and in the process, she divorces Bish, leaving behind a marriage of a decade, moves to San Francisco and leads a typical California style life with a live-in-partner, who like any male chauvinist dumps her at a crucial point in her life. He is a Buddhist and his Koan advices to Tara Bhattacharjee go haywire when he feels that Tara has rebuked his ego by going to Jackson Heights and contacting a policeman. The earthquake-proofer could not deal with the fissures in his life. For Andy, love is having fun with someone symbolic of American culture. The detached attitude when he leaves Tara without a backward glance is way off from Bish's attitude for whom love is indistinguishable from status and honour. He supports her emotionally throughout and symbolizes the Indian culture. Tara extricates herself from the twists and turns in her life to face an imposter who creates havoc in her life, bringing her the realization that her secure world based on her past and present experiences is not so safe. Her continuous efforts to assimilate in the present, secure in her past bonding, is literally bombed by the revelation of family secrets, jerking her into the realities of the world around. Tara wants to be free of the past and assimilates into the flow of the present and is confronted by the terrorist from the past reshaping her future. The sedate life in India—married to a boy of her father's choice, her duty to feed her husband and in-laws and be flaunted in front of guests—makes her frustrated. Her condition is more like Dimple in *Wife*. What else could she crave for. In America she is a queen, but then she drifts towards Andy. She is unable to identify with her 'Self.' She is attracted and fascinated to Andy because he is exotic like herself, a Hungarian immigrant. "I'm feeling just a little alien." (75)

Tara Bhattacharjee epitomizes the hyphenated self, who is suddenly faced with a question mark on her identity. This crisis is forced on her by Chris Dey who claims to be her nephew. He is an outcome of an illegitimate liaison between Padma and Ronnie Dey. Tara and her sisters, descendants of Jai Krishna Gangooly, are the "desirable daughters" who are held highly in the society, and they cannot commit a blasphemous act like begetting an illegitimate child. When and where did Padma got the time to commit such hanky-panky? The feudal society did not allow girls to meet boys and girls; yet the desirable daughter Padma had an illegitimate son. The revelation brings back snippets from the past, when as a child Tara remembered her father going abroad with Padma. Her maternal great-grandfather Jai Krishna Gangooly married nine times to get a son.

> The son eluded him until the ninth wife, a girl in her mid-teens whom he married at the age of sixty-eight. . . . She remembers the shock she felt when she discovered that her paternal grandmother, a woman of autocratic will and sour temperament, wasn't her late grandfather's only wife. (19-20)

In her search to find the truth about Chris Dey, Tara contacts her sisters, Padma in New Jersey and Parvati in Bombay, to track her stalker, because attack is the best way of defence and one has to be fully geared up to face the atrocities of this world. "Their voices drift through time, they penetrate the thickest stone fortress, I open myself to them. Bishey bish khai, only poison delivers us from poison." (310)

Andy is a big man who is in search for softer roots as his life has been fed on anger, violence and brute force. In order to find solace, he has turned to Buddhism and meditations. Through the short span of their time together, Andy is in the role of a pacifier, relating anecdotes about Zen Koan from Buddhist beliefs, somehow reaching the heights of spirituality, providing answers for a difficult situation with an ease. But Tara does not embrace her lover's religion. She keeps remembering his anecdotes and does not follow the belief that everything gets solved on its own. "His search has been for softer way, kinder speech, gentler company and (he says) I am in possession of the best Andy ever, the final version in a series in reinventions." (77)

Tara hounds her pursuer after initial setback, to find out about Chris Dey. She goes to Jack Siddhu, another Indian Sikh immigrant policeman, who helps her in finding out about Chris Dey. When Andy finds out about her going to Jack Siddhu, he retaliates by leaving her in a huff. He severs the contact with a blow, leaving Tara in an emotional lurch. She is left bereaving for company and support when she needs it the most. Her former beliefs about her sister already broken, she is left to bereave her loss. The exotic Andy's betrayal leads Tara to finally search for her roots from the past to bring some authenticity to her belief in her 'Self.'

Old mythical mystery of India is revived, contrasting it with a very modern American outlook. Tara Lata, the Tree-Bride is married to a Sundari Tree after her bridegroom dies of snake-bite. To save her from life-long widowhood, she is married to the tree, her groom symbolic of eternal life. Contrary to this, her great-grand-daughter divorces her husband, the Silicon Valley king. In her journey of "root-search" she unravels many secrets about her family.

While her namesake lives in her house and never comes out of it, she lets her house to be a place for meeting of freedom fighters, devoting her life to serving the nation. Tara Bhattacharjee divorces name and fame to be with a nobody like Andy. Free with her choices, Tara has had many affairs. She sleeps with more than one man and the readers come in contact with the free culture of American living. Body is not sacred to be revered as believed by Tara Lata of yesteryears, but feminine sensuality and passionate urges are fulfilled in the new world. But then, the close brush with Chris brings her back to Bish. She does not marry him but she sleeps with her ex-husband before the bombing of her house. Cell phone, a medium of communication, is used to blast her house, which cripples Bish Chatterjee but her encounter with Bish impregnates her. A new life is born after the destruction. Bharati Mukherjee blends past with present and future, blends tradition with modernity, the juxtaposing of two cultures—Indian and American—blended in the same bloodline.

> "I did not know I was capable of all that, not at my age," he said, to which I laughed, not at the 'all that' of which there had been a considerable amount, but at his professed amazement. I realized that for Bish his "age" was not chronological, but mythic. He was seeing himself as fitting into the ancient, discrete divisions of life. . . . By his age alone, Bish should still have been a householder. But the State of California and my lawyers had aborted that phase much earlier than it should have been. Rabi was still a child; more children might well have followed. (269)

The protagonist, a South-Asian immigrant questions her identity, if she is an Indian or an American? Where does she stand in the new world? Though immigrant, expatriate and diasporic (South-Asian) are different aspects of the same term, the psychological and the cultural origins are disintegrated. The dilemma of identity is born due to conflict between psychological and cultural inheritance.

> In the postmodern climate, the notion of America as melting pot for different cultures and the need for assimilation into what was thought to be the American culture is passé. Today the American attitude towards ethnicity and foreignness has changed. Ethnic difference is no more a matter of embarrassment. It is a matter of pride, instead. The metaphor of the melting pot has been replaced with that of a mosaic—an image used by Joan Morrison and Charlotte Fox Zabusky. . . . The emphasis in the last three metaphors marks a shift from the paradigm of assimilation to the acceptance of what used to be perceived as alien, and ethnic as part of the larger whole.[11]

Searching for identity of Chris Dey, who claims to be the illegitimate child of Padma, her elder sister, and her old flame Ronnie Dey, Tara tramples on many toes. Padma, the most beautiful and charming of the three sisters, had an affair with Ronnie Dey—son of a convert and thus considered an untouchable. While pregnant, she had gone abroad and got married to another man. Today she enjoys a coveted life, her "New Avatara" in New Jersey, but she curses her father for making her miss the chance to act in Satyajit Ray's movie. She could have been a star, but now in America she has carved a niche for herself as an anchor on a TV channel airing programmes for the South-Asian immigrants. Besides this, she has multifarious other jobs, supported by her boyfriend Danny Jagtiani (a gay), whereas her husband, a weakling, basks in her success and is happy to live in her shadow. Harish Mehta knows his limits and enjoys all that he can get. He wishes to forget his own Indian identity, of being a nobody camouflaging his failure with his wife's success. As Manju Sampat writes:

> Mukherjee decries hyphenation that is thrust on most South-Asian immigrants. European immigrants are never referred to as Polish or German Americans, so why should an Indo-American, she questions. European immigrants, because of the colour of their skin, easily blend in. Despite feeling totally adjusted to being an American immigrant, Tara is frequently asked, "Who are you really?" She feels 'tired' of explaining India to Americans. I am sick of feeling an alien.

Being to New Jersey, to Padma's place, makes Tara realize that she does not belong to that society also. Her sister refuses to answer her questions about Chris Dey but Jack Siddhu, the detective, a Sardar, sends a fax on Danny Jagtiani's fax number. The photos sent are of two people and one of them is identified as Abbas Sattar Hai who has facsimile resemblance to Tara's intruder and is somehow related to Dawood's group, the underworld don operating in India and Dubai. This discovery emphatically brings into focus the concept of globalization of terrorist activities. The world seems to have shrunk and Tara's privacy is infiltrated in San Francisco. She calls up Bish and finds out that Bish and Rabi will be going to her house in San Francisco. She immediately leaves everything behind to be with her husband and son. Tara oscillates between the old and the new world, trying to co-relate the two.

> Tara says, Bish it was my fault, my head was turned. I was so naïve, I had too much time and not enough to do . . . my parents are fifty years together. Even our house servants, forty, fifty years. One time you mentioned the loneliness inside of marriage and I did not understand what you were saying. Two people are together; they have come from the same place; they share the same values, the same language. Practically speaking, they are two halves of one consciousness. They eat the same food; they have a child; they sleep in the same bed, how can they be lonely. . . . Bish what you eat, what language you speak, where you sleep—in our world they meant everything, but we're not there anymore. Here dharma and duty, they do not mean a damned thing.

Tara Lata led a life of virginity whereas Tara Bhattacharjee seems to search for the feminine sensuality. Tara, a young girl, and married to a man of her father's choice, is introduced to sex on her wedding night, a shy bride who fills with wonderment that her touch could awaken and arouse her husband's anatomy. When she meets Andy, she wonders how big he might be. She has had other American lovers and sounds like an exuberant individual in her new-found freedom. She is the Indian counterpart of Debbie di Martino in *Leave It to Me*.

Tara Bhattacharjee does not draw a 'white line' around herself like Hannah in *The Holder of the World*, nor does she camouflage her sensuality like Dimple Dasgupta of *Wife*. She does not wait to meet her Raja to awaken her sensuousness as does Hannah in *The Holder of the World*. Like Dimple, Tara is married to an engineer, who is the wealthiest person to reckon with in Silicon Valley. The similarity ends here. Tara assimilates in the new world with an ease as she knows that Bish is always there. Tara Bhattacharjee criticizes Padma for revolting against her father but Tara's own choice is also a transition that takes place and she lives life on her own terms. Padma might associate with Danny, a Sindhi (a community looked down upon by the Bhattacharjees), and if it is a revolt against her father and the oppressive patriarchal socio-cultural set-up, then Tara's associations with a Hungarian immigrant, Americans and other European immigrants can be categorized in the same class. Is it the duality in her nature? Anyhow, she takes her sister's attitude in her stride.

The new persona of Tara is the final stroke of Bharati Mukherjee's evolution as an immigrant writer, who is comfortable with the new ways of life in America. She accepts her son's choice of sexual preference and so does Bish. Rabi, a second generation child, is born in America and is a natural citizen of America, imbibing the ethos of his nation (rather motherland). Instead of a conflict ensuing between the first and second generation, Rabi's secret is accepted by his parents with an ease, authenticating the close mother-son relationship. Rabi uses abusive language for his aunt, which is fully Americanised. Linguistically, the novels of Bharati Mukherjee flaunt colloquial language and the American influence on language is more evident in her writings after *Leave it to Me*. Expressing his sympathies with Chris like a true young American youth who is well capable of taking responsibilities, he yells at his mother.

> I can't believe you are treating Chris like a liar and a criminal. You have decided he is the liar because you called all the way over to Bombay to talk to your lying bitch of a sister—do not shush me, ma, I'll call her that as long as I live. I am getting to know you very well, ma. You will believe anything she says, and you will play along with the big bitch's cover-up and she will not lift a finger to help him. (90)

Tara, the desirable daughter, who never knows about such confrontations in her younger days, reconciles to this outburst of anger because show of emotions is not looked down upon in American culture but this sort of display of emotion is uncalled for in the Indian culture as offsprings should pay obeisance to the parents. Parvati is the desirable daughter from Bombay who married Aurobindo, a boy of her own choice, and is supposedly the richest and the most well-settled sister among the three of them. Rabi accepts Chris as his cousin at first and is angry with his aunts for concealing the truth. Though later on, he himself tells his mother that Christopher is not what he seems to be. The long letters written by Parvati to Tara reveal a few family secrets which make Tara doubt her own beliefs. Parvati warns Tara not to become too Americanised in her ways.

> Our family's "Westernization" was superficial, confined to convent school, Metro cinema, and movie magazines, which overlaid a profound and orthodox Hinduism. Brahmos were scary to us; their knowledge of western classics was thorough, their Bengali proud and chaste, their Hinduism ruthlessly reformist. (178)

The universe is energy and man seems to create his/her own negative or positive energy. To say 'yes' to everything that comes your way is accepting your destiny and Karma. Rootless immigrants own nothing and as a consequence they own everything. If one goes against the flow, it creates friction. The second and third generations accept each and every event as natural and accept or reject it in America as Americans do. Acceptance of 'present' is what matters the most. Andy explains this fact again and again to Tara and so does Rabi. The people around Tara seem to have accepted their fate, except Tara. Is it the detective in her who wants to find out about the imposter, or is it her search for identity that instigates her to go to the agency and Jack Sidhu, which aggravates Andy, making him leave, or is it fate and destiny that brings Bish back to her? Is it fate or human materialistic attitude, which leads to bombing of her house? It leads to a Sabbath in India, and her search to find more about her namesake Tara Lata. The bombing of Tara's house and her Sabbath in India are few incidents that conjoin to the burning down of Bharati Mukherjee's own house and her year-long Sabbath in India. Tara and Rabi leave for India to take care of Tara's ailing mother and come in contact with Hinduism—its belief and faith. In Rishikesh, Rabi is introduced to the intricacies of Hindu faith and philosophy. Tara's mother is an example of a disciplined person who takes responsibility of her Karma and tells her daughter that one has to face the consequences of one's own Karma. But she hates the fact that Rabi should be introduced to spiritual books. Mummy fakes horror, "Get that book from him, we don't need another Sanyasin in family. Daddy's doing enough praying and giving up life's good things for all of us. Home is where you belong, Rabindra. Tara, don't let him get bad ideas in the head." (297)

Rabi is faced with a new culture in India, but like a true American individual, he accepts all the facts on face value without refuting them. The acceptance is natural. He is astonished at first, but he is fluid in his assimilation in the new culture. He reads the books provided to him by his maternal grandfather but is rebuked by his maternal grandmother. She wants him to stop reading Vivekananda because generally old people believed that young people should not read scriptures. They fear that the young would walk on the path of asceticism, leaving behind the enjoyment of this world. In Indian culture, young are prevented from getting acquainted with religious scriptures. The readers glimpse the mystic ambience of Rishikesh and Haridwar, the names having significant meaning. The former means the habitat of saints and the latter, a passage to God's abode.

Tara like Tara of *The Tiger's Daughter* finds solace at her father's house in Rishikesh and chances upon the mystery of Tree Bride, the enigma in her family. The novel takes a 360^0 turn and the readers are taken to the world of Tara Lata, the Tree Bride. Tara goes to the old house in Mishtigunj with Rabi in search for the story of Tree Bride. It parallels Bharati Mukherjee's visit to East Bangladesh to trace her own roots. *Desirable Daughters* is more like an autobiography where Tara and Bharati Mukherjee's life seem to be in a collateral flow.

> After the night of her marriage, Tara Lata returned to Mishtigunj and, at least by legend, never left her father's house. Unburdened by a time-consuming, emotion-draining marriage and children, never having to please.a soul, she grew up and grew old in a single house in an impoverished village in the poorest place on earth, and in that house, the world came to her. She lived there seventy years and gradually changed the world. (16-17)

Tree Bride becomes a heroine in rural Bengal, as a spiritual healer and a martyr, a freedom fighter to the core. Tree Bride in this sense makes the readers remember Bharati Mukherjee's earlier protagonist Hannah Easton in *The Holder of the World* who is a healer, a medicine woman, who fights like a warrior to save her lover.

> The house of Tara Lata Gangooly (1874-1944), known to the world as "Tara-Ma." Behind these walls lived an untrained nurse, spiritual healer, and inspiration to generations of peace-seeking individuals from around the world. During the Bengal Famine of 1942 she fed the town and the outlying villages. She rallied the cause of an Independent India and United Bengal and protected young freedom fighters from British arrest, she herself was dragged from her home on the night of October 12, 1944, by colonial authorities and never heard from again. (20)

The narrator, Tara, associates herself with her kin and namesake, Tara Lata and compares her own stance. Tara Lata is a part of their traditional familial bonding and each in the family associates with her and her feminine empowerment. She is known as Tara-Ma. Co-incidentally, Tara is one of the names of Goddess Durga. Tara Lata never left her paternal house and she becomes the saviour of humanity. "Each generation of women in my family has discovered something in her new. Even in far-flung California the Tree Bride speaks again." (289)

The narrative is like a bedtime story, a part of oral tradition through which the stories of heroism are handed down to generations. The narration connects the past, present and future of the protagonist, her familial bonding with Indian traditions, her past which affects her future in California, the 'present,' which was shaped under patriarchal guidance has somehow boomeranged, bringing her back to India to find a foothold. Tara takes everything in her stride. 'Now' matters more. Resurrection becomes the basis of her life.

The novel ends with Tara finding the house of Tree Bride which forms the theme of *Tree Bride*, the next novel, second of the trilogy. The life and culture of America finds its voice in this novel, blended with and seeped in Indian culture. Bharati Mukherjee's transition into her present life is more fluid and easy. She does not need to look for an identity any more. She claims to be American and it is proved in the new novel: "I am an American writer of Indian origin, not because I'm ashamed of my past, not because I'm destroying or betraying or distorting my past, but because my whole adult life has been lived here."[13]

Darkness, the short story collection by Bharati Mukherjee, was a gallery of people still caught up in the conflict of the two worlds, existing in ghettoes, but *Desirable Daughters* flaunts people who are happy to exist in their South-Asian immigrant status, especially the South-Asian community at Jackson Heights and, of course, Silicon Valley of America.

> Mukherjee draws a portrait of an ethnic area Jackson Heights, to where all Indian immigrants must make their pilgrimage: Jackson Heights is not a China town or even a Japan town on the San Francisco model—Indian people shop collectively, but they don't live together in tight little communities. . . . They travel from distant suburbs . . . or from neighbouring states. We are a billion people, but divided into so many thousands or millions of classifications that we have trouble behaving as monolith.[14]

Bharati Mukherjee's characters do not bow down to the situations they are faced with, however demeaning or dehumanizing that situation might be, they refuse to bow down. Tara Bhattacharjee and her namesake, Tara Lata, face a similar kind of situation but they belong to two different ages and live in two different environs, but both are fluid in their existence. Confined to the house and following the conformity of the society, Tree Bride Tara Lata excels. Empowering herself by educating herself and existing as a parallel to the male-dominated society of pre-Independence India while Tara Bhattacharjee in her new world of postcolonial-postmodern age does not bow to the destructive force in her life. She faces the company of terrorism, very evident in America after 9/11 bombing. Losing everything does not make her lose her confidence. She gives voice to her identity in the white world as well as her feminine vulnerability. Tara, like Jasmine and other characters, post-Jasmine, does not give in to her fears. She tries to be invisible as she is afraid to be visible. Her weaknesses become her strength. She accepts the values of her new society instead of resisting them and so does Tree Bride in her environs.

Bharati Mukherjee's ability to delineate her characters and the way she handles the tangled relationships, give the readers a glimpse into her genius as delineator of characters like Shakespeare. Bharati Mukherjee takes up issues that are of national and international concerns and brings out their significance through her characters. The secrets of Tara's family are revealed through the long series of letters written by Parvati to Tara where she warns her sister of the pitfalls of American life. Central to the theme is Tara Bhattacharjee's quest for roots. She portrays the elemental contradictions of two cultures and the dilemmas of the immigrants. Though the plot-line is very thin and seems to be weak, the thriller aspect loses its veracity from time to time and is not so confining, but it does not drag. The plot is engrossing.

> The author has ended up writing a book with typically American feminist ideas about housewives, sexuality and worth. Having settled for American feminist issues and avoided the aforementioned Indian feminist ones, the author ends up with a nearly familiar tale of female victimhood and females on the verge of personal enlightenment and freedom from oppressive well-meaning husbands. So many passages seem

like polemical arguments that are simply added to make a feminist American point. For instance, there is the introduction of homosexuality. The main character accepts the sexual orientation of a homosexual character fairly readily. . . . The author glosses over the issues of Poppy Dey's dark skin and the Indian desire for light-skinned desirable daughters. Perhaps because she is light and that isn't American feminist issue. But is not lightness of skin something that is immensely desirable in daughters? How does acculturation, hinted at in the story of the father of the first Tara Lata, connect with American imperialism?[15]

NOTES

1. *The Image of Woman in Indian Literature*, ed. Yashoda Bhat and Yamuna Raja Rao (1993), p. 26.
2. Bharati Mukherjee, *Desirable Daughters* (Rupa, 2004), p. 93
3. S.P. Swain, *Self and Identity in Indian Fiction* (New Delhi: Prestige, 2005), p. 62.
4. *Ibid.*, p. 58.
5. *Ibid.*, p. 58.
6. Duelling Cultures in a World of Change online Milwaukee Journal Sentinel
7. www.jsonline.com http://www.jsonline.com/enter/books/may02/40569.asp p. 3.
8. Jasbir Jain, ed., *Writers of the Indian Diaspora*, p. 211.
9. Simone de Beauvoir, *Second Sex*, p. 141
10. *The Commonwealth Review*, Vol. XIV, No. 1, p. 104.
11. *Ibid.*, p. 109.
12. Manju Sampat, "Expat Exuberance," *Biblio*, July-August 2002, p. 15.
13. Bharati Mukherjee, Interview, March 28, 2002.
14. Review of *Desirable Daughters* by Luan Gaines. www.indiatimes.com
15. *Ibid.*

Chapter VII

Convergence of Past and Present in *The Tree Bride*

> We lived the Tree Bride's courage. We were child-soldiers in Mother India's army. We knew from our history books the consequences of being caught by the Raj police. Mummy chipped in with her war-time memories of cheering the Japanese planes and of a Calcutta swarming with refugees from the fall of Burma. . . . Proud Bengalis, we hated Mahatma Gandhi, that worm of a Gujarati. We thrilled to the martial cadence of our homegrown hero, our netaji, our leader, the martyred Subhas Bose. His Indian National Army would march with the Japanese to plunge a dagger into the retreating back of the British Raj. No Gandhi, no partition, no loss of our beautiful, green and golden East Bengal. The blood of our martyrs would be avenged. Women in our family, however distant and legendary the connection, had been beaten by colonial police.[1]

The Tree Bride is a sequel to *Desirable Daughters* in which a gallery of characters and their identities are interwoven. The "root-search" links the past incidents with present happenings in Tara's life. The search to find out the identity of her stalker leads to several revelations. The terrorist kills the real Christopher Dey and camouflages an identity of being her nephew. The sergeant reveals the name as Abbas Sattar Hai, a hardcore terrorist, a member of Dawood's group who stalks Tara's life. Tara Bhattacharjee, instead of cringing back, bounces back into action and rises like a phoenix from the ashes of her burnt house. The bombing of her house destroys her on surface. The incident adjoins two worlds together and the link is evident, live and kicking in Tara's womb. Tara Lata was married to a Sundari Tree to save her from life-long widowhood. As her name suggests, Tara, the Star, and Lata, a creeper, are eternal. Even when the creeper is destroyed, it plunges back into life. Sundari Tree is like 'The Casuarina Tree' that bears the creeper like a scarf around its neck. Toru Dutt's "Casuarina Tree" must be an equivalent to Sundari Tree, the husband of Tara Lata. Tara Lata and her namesake, the great-granddaughter Tara Bhattacharjee's destinies seem to merge, giving birth to the tale of Tree Bride. The story of "The Tree Bride" moves back and forth in post dot.com San Francisco and her ancestor in a mansion in pre-Independence East Bengal. Bharati Mukherjee's novel, *The Tree Bride*, deals with colonialism in India, terrorism in U.S.A. and the British Diaspora in India. As Sandip Roy writes:

> Bharati Mukherjee certainly never thought in 1961 that she could be both Indian and American in quite this way. "When I was a child, we were wary of Bengalis who had moved out of Bengal," says Mukherjee. "To be a "probashi" (diasporan) Bengali, was to be a sorry creature, cut off from true Bengali culture. . . . She remembers at that time, even in a place like Manhattan, Indians were so few that when passing each other on the street, they nodded and smiled. "By the time I came to write *Jasmine*, Indian immigrants were far more visible as a community, but the rhetoric for talking about immigration was struck in the old melting pot versus rejection of American culture," says Mukherjee. "That meant either you had to reject wholly the culture that you had come from or you became very American and gave up something in order to acquire the other."[2]

The socio-cultural and political history of Bengal is tightly sewn into the fabric of Bharati Mukherjee's novel, *The Tree Bride*, blended with the family saga of generations handed down to the younger generations. Bharati Mukherjee in her novel, which is more of a "historiographic-metafiction," enmeshes the impact of colonialism on the minds of the 'Bhadralok' Bengali society. The expatriates are the officers of Company who had come to rule India and the story chronicles the life of British officers and their atrocities. *Desirable Daughters* revolves around the after-effects of colonialism on minds of Bengalis. The conflict that is part of the psyche of the Indian immigrants in America is reflected in *The Tree Bride* but in inversion. India is the place where British officers are faced with different circumstances. While in America the confluence is of the Orientals and the occidentals, in *The Tree Bride*, the confluence is of the Colonial masters and the servitudes. The cadaverous journey takes the readers into the deep realms of atrocities inflicted by some of the officers, while some with their attitude of empathy, emphatically point out the process of assimilation of the conquerors in the conquered country. Bharati Mukherjee presents the nineteenth century Bengal as a place of contradictions and ironies. The beauty of the place comes along with desperation, its suffering emerging partly due to its socio-political and psychological situations and the British Rule in India.

> Plenitude is its feeble precaution against starvation. In all that water, there are droughts. In all that wild profusion, starvation looms in shades of green. Muslims can take four wives and Brahmins from my subcaste any number, all in the hope that a single son might survive.

Bharati Mukherjee quarries into the conflicts faced by the ICS officers of British origin who left home with good intentions to subjugate the colonized serviles. Immigrants, like John Mist who denounces his mother tongue and his roots completely to carve a new identity, an outcast in his homeland becomes a Mogul in the deep interiors of Bengal in Shoondari Bon, is juxtaposed with the character of Vertie Treadwell, an ICS officer of British Raj who insulates himself from the Bengali culture and refuses to embrace the norms of the new culture. His self-denial leaves him in a state of dilemma, making him act harshly. A simple game of cricket played by the Indian children enrages him beyond control leading him to fall and break his nose. The bleeding nose is more of a symbol of breaking stranglehold of British in India and their bleeding souls, which does not apprehend their situation in the free India.

"Cricket is an Indian game accidentally discovered by the British," wrote political psychologist Ashis Nandy. "But then the ideas and practices of colonialism too were discovered and deployed in England, and elsewhere into Europe, much before the Europeans introduced those aspects to South-Asia. Does this mean that colonialism is an Indian reality which was accidentally discovered in England? . . . But the congenital affinity between colonialism and cricket in South-Asia is not merely a historical accident. Cricket was a part of the colonial paraphernalia of the British Raj."[3]

The novel begins with Tara Bhattacharjee speculating on the past events and then she links her brush with death to Hindu philosophies, the seed in her womb and the place of renunciation, Kashi alias Varanasi. She speculates on the cosmic convergences and destiny of soul travelling through births. The Prologue of the novel clarifies the content of the novel—linkage between Karma, destiny, immortality of soul, the basis of Hindu Dharma, faith and philosophies. "Abbas Sattar Hai: I pray we do not meet him again." (3)

With her discovery of being pregnant comes the knowledge of her carrying another soul in her womb, a soul which is subject to the norms of the society. Bharati Mukherjee proves the authenticity of the connection between this world and God—the Creator, the destroyer and the preserver: "Between incarnations, she said, the individual soul wanders in a dreamless state, like a seed between plantings, in the windy realm of Vayumandala, waiting for its allotted time to re-inhabit a living body." (4)

The novel's storyline or plot moves back and forth in time, as well as era and history and the Indian Diaspora in pre-Independence time is revealed through a series of letters that have been handed over to Tara by her American gynae, who is married to an Indian professor Yash Khanna. Victoria Khanna discovers the fact that she has Indian connections. Grand-daughter of Vertie Treadwell, she is of English origin. Looking for an Indian doctor in America, Tara hones on the name 'V. Khanna' and then realizes that "there are no coincidences in the universe." (7)

Vertie Treadwell, the uprooted English officer in India, is harsh, menacing and cold-blooded in his dealings. His expatriate status turns him into unleashing his bureaucratic rage on unsuspecting victims. Bharati Mukherjee attempts to equipoise and intermingle the love of past culture and heritage with her new identity of American immigrant in United States of America. Abbas Sattar Hai, the stalker from Tara's Indian past heritage, aggressively forces her to face her enemy and she does it like a warrior. Tara like her namesake does not back out from her destiny. The bombing of her house by Abbas Sattar Hai and her visit to India and Mishtigunj, and being presented with *Mist-Nama*, sets her on her journey of root-search, linking her present and future with her past heritage. She realizes that it was not the Muslims, who had lead to the relocation of her past, but it was the English British who were responsible for dislocation of identities, and this began not in 1947 but in 1833. The unrest was already there. Facing the atrocities in India Mishtigunj was left untouched due to John Mist and his cauldron of people around, who kept the English and British Raj at bay. John Mist, always a man of foresight, had deputed two levels of governance in his own personal empire. Old with new, Hindu and Muslim, were channelised together as he knew that these two had to be kept together to form a strong base.

> Hajji's Bengali translation simply states that Mist called together notables from as far away as Calcutta and Dhaka to create a utopian village. Jai Krishna had come from Dhaka, and the Calcuttan might have been Rafeek Hai. In what does utopia consist? Education, justice, health, food, a spirit of cooperation, and the uninhibited worship of one's god. It was agreed that "worship" was restricted to Hinduism and Islam. Christians were barred from Mishtigunj, on the orders of Mist himself. (149-50)

He never emphasised on the principle of "Divide and Rule" (as per British officers' rule) and gained popularity and respect among his people. It is ironical to say 'his' people but then, Mist's Kingdom denounced entrance of Christians in his empire. He severs his relations completely from his past culture to acclimatize in his new home and gains the status of immigrant, contrary to Vertie Treadwell's expatriate status. John Mist spreads like a mist over Mishtigunj, camouflaging his identity, and does his very best for the culture he enters. John Mist seems to emphatically point out the fact, which Bharati Mukherjee has kept on emphasizing throughout her life: a person has to embrace the new culture with open mind and there should be a sense of duty towards the culture that has welcomed one with open arms. Nigel Coughlin is another ICS Officer, who openly embraces his new country and becomes the first naturalized Indian in 1947. Contrary to this, Vertie Treadwell hates India and Indians for upsetting the Raj in India, uprooting him. He feels that the Indians could have been ruled for another 100 years and the servile nation would have been trained to become civil. It is evident in "Macaulay's Minutes," the famous lines declaring that the natives of the country should be educated in English so that they become well-versed in serving their masters, instead of being illiterate barbarians who do not know what is good for them.

Victoria Treadwell Khanna, a true American, refuses to baulk down under the pressure of her new identity, her connection to India gives her that extra weightage to her identity. She accepts her connection with Tara and Indian culture. She detests her grandfather but accepts his presence in her life. She takes everything in her stride.

She establishes a bond with Tara and following in her footsteps, she carouses through her own identity, digging out some more facts about her life and, in the process, gives more clues to Tara Bhattacharjee to work on. The stalker who is after Tara's life, bombs Victoria's house and instead of Tara, her friend dies. Even death does not make Victoria afraid. She is happy because she can face death after completing her Karma and is peaceful inside. "Of course, what did it matter in light of this exciting new discovery? I'm Indian." (242)

With the sheaf of papers handed to Tara by Victoria Khanna, things start falling in place, connecting the zig-saw puzzle. Victoria is related to Vertie Treadwell, whose path had crossed that of the Tree Bride, Tara's ancestor, and to add fuel to the fire, the psychopathic killer is related to Rafeek Hai, one of the allies of John Mist, a man who had been raised in Tara's ancestral home, the Mist Mansion. What is the reason behind Abbas Sattar Hai trying to kill Tara? While in Mishtigunj, Rafeek Hai offers to sell the Persian *Mist-Nama* to Tara and asks her to pay dollars, which could be used in the maintenance of a school. Was the denial to buy the *Mist-Nama* a reason for the stalker wanting to kill Tara or is there a deep-rooted resentment traced back to Sameena Hai, whose father was Jai Krishna Gangooly's cook but is reduced to the post of a guard, because the newly turned Hindu could not tolerate a Moslem in his kitchen? Sameena Hai was raised along with Tara Lata Gangooly and was married to a highly placed bridegroom. Nigel in his letters reveals this fact and wonders how Sameena is married to the person—was Mist Mahal promised as a dowry to the bridegroom? In the present day, Mist Mahal was infested by the Hais, so is it the fear of losing home or financial insecurity that leads to Abbas Sattar Hai joining the Dawood group and hounding Tara to San Francisco and trying to kill her twice. So many questions arise in the reader's mind as the story unravels slowly. Many sub-plots move along with the main plot. "In this vibrant novel, her best work to date, the author has fused history, mysticism, treachery, and enduring love in a suspenseful story about the lingering effects of past secrets."[4]

Bharati Mukherjee reconditions the story of Tara Lata, reconstructing the plot from snippets of family lore and the journals of three Englishmen—John Mist, a refashioned identity, who survives piracy on the high seas and a true disciple of Tom Crabbe, flaunting the inbred qualities of Col. Kurtz and Robinhood in the dense jungles of Shoonder Bon; Vertie Treadwell, a belligerent rebel who annoys with his pugnacity, a relic of the Raj with 125 tiger pelts, who feels that lions are ugly because they stalk their hunt in a pack, whereas tigers are the true predators who hunt alone, who feels that he is Indian, but is repulsed by the natives and feels cheated at the early demise of British Empire in India; Nigel Coughlin who declares himself to be a "White Hindu" and to whom Tara Lata gets attracted because he is totally immersed in the Indian soil, living a life like an Indian peasant, studies terra-cotta artefacts, advocating Indian Independence. Nigel inspires Tara to join the freedom-struggle.

> "In truth," said Coughlin, "We are monsters. Very few Britishers out here in India do not yield to some coveted fancy. Mine runs to terra-cotta, others to birds or Mughal paintings and there's a chap I've heard of in the United Provinces who parades around in tiger pelts." (266)

Marginalisation is evident in the society, and Nigel Coughlin moans the fact. This marginalisation exists on three levels: where the ladies are marginalized, there is division based on caste marginalising outcastes and then, marginalisation based on religion within the Hindu patriarchal socio-economic norms prevalent in the society, which divided the society into fragments. These very factors were used by the colonizers to divide the society very easily. But the marginalized existence of the Company officers in India is also a truth, which cannot be denied. Nigel Coughlin wishes that he could barter his pale skin and blue eyes so that he could be invisible in the country and be accepted as a Hindu and later on, he is. He is the "White Hindu" to be naturalized as an Indian. John Mist is the last "British Hindoo" who resorts to embrace Bengali as his language. Vertie Treadwell is the expatriate who refuses to acknowledge his British heritage, and is unable to assimilate in the new environment. Related to all these is Tara Lata, the Tree Bride, Tara Bhattacharjee's great grandmother, the Mother Courage of the Independence movement. A shy child-bride of five married to a Tree, she proves to be the rock support girding herself for the trials and tribulations to be faced in the struggle for freedom and gives invaluable support to the freedom fighters. The tree-bride learnt Sanskrit shlokas and educated herself by learning English, substantiating women empowerment. Her namesake, Tara Bhattacharjee evolves from a "society-page wife" to a divorcee, struggling to fabricate her own identity as an independent teacher, trying to be invisible in the white country. She refuses to be categorized in one slot. She wants to gain her identity, both as an Indian and American, trying to blend the two cultures to carve a new identity. In *The Tree Bride*, Tara nurtures and takes care of her crippled husband, besides nurturing a new life in her womb. In *Desirable Daughters*, Tara has divorced her husband. After the loneliness of a decade, she refuses to act like the Indian girl who believes or is rather taught to believe that a girl after entering the threshold of her husband's house, leaves it only on her death. She divorces Bish, has affairs, and lives in San Francisco with Andy (the live-in partner) and her son who is a gay. Tara leads her American life with flair but life changes. The Buddhist lover reciting Zen Koans could not tolerate Tara deciding her path to discover the truth in her life.

Tara Bhattacharjee in *The Tree Bride* is the bride who returns back to her crippled husband to cure him. Bish, though chained to the wheel-chair, soon recovers his senses and begins a new project with Yash Khanna. He also goes through the box of letters and documents that have been given to Tara by Vertie Treadwell's granddaughter. The biggest help that Tara gets as she scours her past to learn about her great-grandmother is the documents. Documentation of each detailed incident and maintaining records, helped the British officials. Documenting everything from the colonized natives to the season and flowers was an inculcated habit. Bharati Mukherjee has deftly used this obsession of documenting and tabulation as the basis of her protagonist's tool for her "root-search." Heavily pregnant, Tara is conformed to her condition but she enjoys it. She might detest it when she is not able to move fast but she is mobile enough to find out the intricacies involved in her search, helped by her gynecologist Victoria, Bish and Yash Khanna. Like an American, she bears the baby. She is not confined to the four walls of her house like Indian pregnant women. She is an independent woman, evolved and sure of her ambitions. The characters in the novel have been sketched with skill but they are elusive. Tara dreams in America and those dreams are about the past, while the future is embedded in her womb. In the present, she is pursued by the ghost of Tara Lata who wishes to be released, to leave for her heavenly abode. It is not a coincidence, but universe works through us to discover the buried truths about one's own. It can be pre-destined, but then universe answers and unfolds mysteries bringing solutions. One has to be watchful keeping one's eyes open. Tara Bhattacharjee wants to know about her past and she has visited Mishtigunj twice. She refuses to buy the Persian Mist-Nama and yet she meets Victoria who gives her the journals. Slowly, pieces start falling in place and Tara discovers the identity of her stalker. Histories and cultures, family tree and family secrets unfold, diverge and converge again, a drop of blood revealing the human history. The novel flaunts various references to historical figures, both from British and Indian history, which is authenticated by evidence from the history of the Indian past of the colonized. Convergence of British Empire, American Imperialism and the Mughal Culture in India before being colonized, form the colours on the great canvas of Bharati Mukherjee's novel *The Tree Bride*: "To be charged with sedition has absolutely nothing to do with anything you might have done," Coughlin tells Tara Lata. "To be charged means you have violated a new definition of what constitutes sedition, change the definition, and the government immediately expands the ring of suspects."

Tara smoothly assimilates into the culture of the new world, but she constantly looks back and retrospects over her family history in India. It is deeply rooted in her soul. Tara's family story unfolds in *Desirable Daughters*, unravels its riveting mysteries in *The Tree Bride*. The sequestered fabric has so many characters uncovering the story of nineteenth century, aligning the two cultures of India in the nineteenth century and San Francisco of the twenty-first century. Bharati Mukherjee deftly handles the plot, which moves back and forth between cultures and across continents, unfurling enchanting tales. Bharati Mukherjee quotes Yeats and Eliot to delve deep into the complex story of Indian freedom struggle. The basic notion that prevailed was to free the bonded souls from the British Raj. It is the intermingling culture of two nations—England and India, the conquerors and the conquered, the masters and the servile—that is projected in the novel. Simultaneously, Bharati Mukherjee analyses Tara's life and activities in the United States of America.

> The Brits chose India: we did not choose them, but the consequences are just the same. Information feels like the glue of the universe, one of those unimaginable calculations of time and distance, but one that restores a bit of human scale to the ungraspable proportions of space. . . . A drop of blood reveals all of human history. (234-35)

The Tree Bride exhibits a myriad of characters—contemporary or nearly contemporary to the Tree Bride. The readers are whisked into the medieval era of Indian history to London orphanage to seek John Mist alias B'tard Snow. He is made to dig and scavenge. One day while digging, he digs out his mentor Tom Crabbe. John survives in the orphanage by following a simple rule of opening his eyes and ears but being mute.

Tom Crabbe survives through sheer cleverness and art of speech. The basic fact is the survival of the fittest. A significant discovery of Darwinian theory, which coincidentally happened in the Victorian era. Science and progress was the basis of Victorian era, but there was hardly any effect on the colonies.

> Science and progress would be served and heroes would emerge, but the proud and vain Diligence Partridge would not be a pillar of the new establishment. In the next twenty-five years, the political ambitions of the British Empire and the commercial interests of the Honorable East India Company would be found incompatible. After the mutiny and the humiliation of British soldiers and civilians at the hands of sepoys in the Black Hole in the distant year of 1857, Viceroy Canning could dissolve the company and absorb it into the Raj. (107)

The freedom fighters were sent to face severe conditions in the Black Hole or "Kala Paani" in Andaman and Nicobar Islands, located far away from mainland India (roughly 1,200 km from Chennai). The Island was named after Hugh Rose. One of the Islands is the Havelock Island, named after a British General. Bharati Mukherjee's novel unravels its story through journals and documents, flaunts the names of the characters, which belong to the period—Canning, Havelock and many more. John Mist floats rootless through different situations in order to survive. He learns the ways of the world under the tutelage of Tom Crabbe and Capt. Partridge. John Mist is the male version of all the female protagonists of Bharati Mukherjee who re-invent and re-fashion their lives to adapt and reincarnate. Tom Crabbe is the new persona of Gabriel Legge of *The Holder of the World*. He knows how to deal with the sharks of the world and this one-eyed pirate leads John to his destiny:

> Crabbe had worked slavers, he'd survived the cannibalizing of his mates and delivered prisoners and orphan girls to Van Diemen's Land. He'd seen the Indies and travelled up the Amazon, he'd made four sailings on thousand-ton Indiamen around the Cape to Calcutta and China. He'd tapped sperm whales for casks of oil, and salted cod till all the juices in his body lay caked upon his shrivelled fingertips. He'd seen wild half-men, kangaroos, and thylacines. . . . And, he reckoned, Jack Snow had the makings of a mate. (79)

How a man can exist without speaking is a wonder. Mist sails through his life from being a bastard to becoming the Emperor of his Empire in Shoonder Bon. There is never a situation of conflict in Mist's mind. He seems to adapt to every situation, forging forward like Jasmine and Debbie di Martino. The only conflict that invades his peaceful world is his denial of identity to Olivia and he compensates by sending money to her. The ambition to drag Todd Nugent's name in dirt is not fulfilled as John snatches away his hand from Olivia's stretched arms calling for help. His guilt is with him throughout his life and he compensates it by giving financial support, liberating Olivia's soul from drudgery.

It is his silence, which saves him from the cataclysmic situations that confront him from time to time. It is his silence that saves his life and makes him learn the intricacies of being in genteel company and learn the secrets of sailing from the Captain on the Ship, Indiaman. He finds his 'voice' when he faces the trial, and that also to save his friends from death. He is sent to juvenile jail where he is given the task of making rope out of hemp. He bleeds handling hemp but it does not deter him from his task. This same occupation later on helps him. He exports hemp and things made out of it to London and earns money, which is used for the welfare of Mishtigunj and its people. Mist accompanies Olivia Todd on the ship. He listens to her but does not speak. Olivia plays harpsichord every now and then and he is enchanted by her beauty. Olivia is apprehensive about her visit to Calcutta and wants to know more about the place that she is going to reside in. She is like the ladies who were sent to India to marry the officers deputed on duty in India, as the officers did not marry the Indian girls. The Indian girls could be taken as Black bibis, the concubines, but the bride had to be imported from England. We get a similar picture of the company and its lifestyle in E.M. Forster's *A Passage to India.* Olivia, unfortunately, is carried away by the robbers to be dumped in some dirty, dingy bar where her beauty is displayed in front of the barbaric uncouth natives. She is beyond recognition and John Mist, who is assigned by Todd Nugent to identify his fiancée, denies her the identity that could have saved her. Mist's words impress the judge and the jury releases the ship crew. Instead of death sentence, they are sent to Hazaribagh to serve sentence. This is public humiliation for Todd, and Mist is informed by his lawyer that Todd might get him murdered. Rafeek Hai helps Mist to escape but before escaping he goes to Todd's residence slaughtering him and his assistant. Mist escapes to Shoonder Bon with his two accomplices, lays the foundation of Mishtigunj, building Mist Mahal. Mist Mahal, later on, is passed on to the Gangoolys where the Tree Bride resides with her husband's children—the "shoots" that her father had brought from the Shoonder Bon and planted in the courtyard had now grown into trees protecting their mother, giving her peace and solace. The Tree Bride was a young girl when her uncle John Mist and Rafeek Hai had been hanged to death by the British and their bodies were never handed over to the relatives. Obviously, the British felt that in this way they were preventing riots. The callous attitude of the colonizers has been projected through characters like Vertie Treadwell. The muck and treachery of English conventions deals a death blow to Jack Snow alias John o' the Mist alias John Mist, a persona who has much more to his character than he wishes to reveal. He has the grit, the passion to carve a niche for himself. He serves Mishtigunj selflessly, but he refuses to relent and make it easy for the English. He is the one whose sheer grit builds an empire and prevents the Empire to penetrate the impregnable walls of his Empire. Is it Mist who is the tiger or is it Vertie Treadwell, who professes to be a tiger and shows his strength by hunting and killing the tigers? It is the fear of being conquered that makes him kill and prove himself superior, whereas John Mist's acceptance of life, shows more character. His way of retaliation is severing all ties from his past culture. Both Mist and Treadwell are treated unfairly by their past culture. Ironically, Mist's transition is smooth whereas egoistic attitude of Treadwell leads to his downfall. Treadwell was born in

India and claims India to be his country but then, he is marginalized because he, like Mist, is illegitimate and is of British origin. He is not accepted by the nation where he is born and he refuses to have any concern with the Queen's Empire. Incidentally, an admirer of Winston Churchill, he also shares the date of birth with his idol.

> His parents and grandparents were born, or had died, in India. . . . Do not condemn me to a Second English death. Bury me beside my wife in Mysore. . . . And what did the future hold for him, unhoused by India, told he had no right to a plot of Indian soil? . . . He remembered draining a "tank" down in the United Provinces, watching the fish trapped in the diminishing water supply froth to the surface. Whoever guessed such big fish lived at the bottom of such a modest pool? He remembered their thick lips rising to the surface, gulping air. It is India, he'd thought, the surging population, diminished space and resources. Now, he realized, it is England, too. Elevation of the brutish bottom feeders, survival of the leeches and reptiles. Rapid death of the light-seeking, the surface skimming. (195)

Tara Lata's ghost haunts Tara Bhattacharjee in San Francisco. Is it a symptom of pregnancy and the trauma that she undergoes, or is it really the ghost of Tara Lata who sits on her kitchen table, requesting to be released from this mortal world? Is it because they share the same name or is it that Rabi is her great-great-grandson, or is it the fact that she is the one who is rummaging the closet to pull out dead souls? Mother, referred as Tara Ma, the perpetrator of freedom struggle was hanged in jail on orders of Mackenzie and her body thrown in the pit with thousand other bodies. After decades, she haunts Tara in San Francisco, and Tara switches on each and every light in her house in the evening to ward off evil, while Tara Lata's ghost floats above and around her. Her gluttonized body still makes the soul of Tara Lata hanker after her release. After lots of speculation and Bish's insistence, they plan to go to Kashi. Bish refuses to go to Kashi without marrying Tara and Tara gets married to Bish before going to Varanasi, the place which is mentioned in the Prologue. Kashi is situated on Lord Shiva's trident and when everything dies and the world comes to an end, Kashi survives. Bish's wish to get married before the visit to Varanasi emphatically points to the difference in culture. Varanasi, the centre of spirituality and the base of Hindu belief, is a place of confluence and convergence of so many creeds, the holy place where one has to be pure in mind, body and soul to visit. Bish's staunch belief, though he is not religious, in his culture makes him flounder and he refuses to visit Kashi while living in sin (by Indian standards). Tara herself believes that she is already a "mleccha," crossing the backwaters, pregnant out of wedlock, though the baby is of her ex-husband, a divorcee, having had affairs and a live-in partner, feels that she is not a deserving person who can take in responsibility of performing the Hindu rites. This is against the Hindu Dharma. In India "Dharma" means the right way of living and death which is a universal truth. This includes being honest and truthful and kind. The roots of Hinduism go back more than 5000 years. "Brahman" is the one supreme power. The Hindu law of Karma says that what a person does in one's life affects his or her future life. In Hinduism, the purpose of life is to do good things in order to free oneself from the cycle of rebirth. How does Tara's Karma relate her to Tara Lata? What ties connect Tara to her stalker? Abbas Sattar Hai is related to Rafeek Hai and his kin Sameena Hai. "Abbas Sattar Hai attached himself to our son as a way of burrowing into our family and destroying an Indian foothold in America." (235)

The letter of Nigel Coughlin reveals few more facts about Sameena's relation to the criminal who wants to kill Tara. Tara Lata lived all her life in Mist Mahal, which was transferred to Tara Lata after her Mist-Jethu was killed. The enmity in Sameena Hai's mind (her father being ejected from the kitchen to the post of guard and the Mist Mahal promised dowry to her affluent husband) must have carried down to generations making an impact on Abbas Sattar Hai. The three bloodlines intermingle and cross path—the Gangooly, Hai and Treadwell. The weapon used to bomb Tara and Victoria's house was a technological device, the medium of communication, something that refashioned her husband's life unmatched, making him the king of Silicon Valley—his discovery 'CHATTY.'

> The fairy-dust world of CHATTY, the billions of dollars that flowed from the application of that Sunday morning idea, the empire it built, the importance attached to every pronouncement from the Sage of Atherton, are gone. The Bay Area Bachelor to Die for came too close to death, as did the Rani of Rivoli. (165)

The novel is rich with characters, all intertwined into each other and their lives interlocked together. The author has ingeniously handled the criss-crossing. The writers are on a journey that rollicks from the 21st century of medieval colonial India and back. The atrocities of the colonial rulers changed hands with the modern colonial terrorists, which infest and hound the whole world. The marauders of yester-years who ruled all over the world, and it is believed that the sun never set for the Empire, the globalisation innervated terrorism in the world, the new colonial masters.

> Marx demonstrated that the colonial plunder of India—one of the principal sources of enrichment for the ruling oligarchy in Britain—caused the collapse of entire branches of the Indian economy and impoverishment of the people of the vast, wealthy and ancient country. The British, he noted, neglected public works and thus brought about the collapse of India's irrigated agriculture, which in turn doomed millions of Indians to starvation by breaking up local industries.[5]

Going to Kashi is the Karmic destiny that Tara Bhattacharjee is faced with. She is not so inclined with her pregnancy entering the last phase, but destiny cannot be discarded like a coat or identity. Performing the last rites after decades, would bring peace to Tara Lata's soul and to Tara Bhattacharjee who sticks to her "Dharma" of being a dutiful great-granddaughter and a responsible citizen.

Varanasi, known to the Britishers as Benaras, is the place of resurrection for both Taras. The river Ganga flows from south to north making it more holy. "It flows away from the Domain of Death toward the Realm of Rebirth." (269) Tara Lata who is described as handsome and not beautiful finally, meets her end as a married lady (she is married to immortal tree).

Bharati Mukherjee deals with the English Diaspora in India during the 16th century, about the officers who came to rule India. They are part of the Company, deferential to the Raj. Vertie Treadwell is the man who is not accepted in India and is estranged from his own country. A very interesting part of the novel is the conversation between Vertie Treadwell and Winston Churchill, Vertie being a Churchillian disciple. This conversation is to elevate his own position and flaunt his clever and cunning mind and the way he handles things. He reveals how he tried to entice the natives and was beaten by them, and how he tried to fool Tree Bride into submission and his ego is battered down instead, by Tree Bride and her men. Speculations of Vertie Treadwell about Tree Bride are typical like a male chauvinist. He wants to subjugate the spirit and body of Tara Lata, but Tara Lata is too quick on the uptake. Though she has never gone out in the real world but the men around her have taught her about the ways of men. The tiger hunter is unable to tame the tigress. Contrary to this, Nigel Coughlin instigates and inspires her to join the Indian freedom struggle. She who wanted reconciliation between the master and the servile, joins the freedom movement. She is not influenced by Gandhi as Bhadralok Bengalis hated the Gujarati, Nehru was true gentleman, it was Subhas Bose who stirred the emotions and blood because he is the lover who died for the nation.

> Coughlin understood her confusion, "Gandhiji is old and Nehru poses as a proper Englishman. I understand why they don't fire the blood. Netaji is a lover." She blushed. (269)

Marriage of a child at the age of 5 is an atrocious tradition, one followed from ages. Children still get married at that age in remote villages and towns. Getting the child married to a tree to prevent a lifelong widowhood was another prevalent shortcoming of the patriarchal society. The father, after getting his daughter married to a tree, proceeds to get married nine times to sire a son who would carry his name. The atrocities and treachery that exist in Hindu society—as well as other religions—can be traced to the original law-maker Manu, who believed that woman leads man to his downfall. Jai Krishna Gangooly could not get his daughter another match because society would accept it due to fear, but Jai Krishna Gangooly did not lack in his prowess to marry young girls so that he gets a son.

Sexual colonialism refers to the relationship between the sexes which is 'a relationship of dominance and subservience.' It refers to the relationship between sex and power and as Kate Millett puts it. "Through this system a most ingenious form of 'interior colonizaton' has been achieved. Men are the colonizers, the women colonized."[6]

Vertie Treadwell tries to analyse Tara Lata's physical anatomy with his sexual overtures and Tara Lata in turn, fixes her gaze on his middle portion. Naturally, his ego takes this signal as a "come on" sign. He does not feel for one moment that Tara Lata, a widow, might have felt degraded.

Tara Lata with her gesture ensnares him and one tends to applaud Tara Ma's empowerment. Jasmine in *Jasmine* had killed her rapist incarnating herself as Kali. Tara is another name for Kali.

> Why should he deprive himself of companionship just because the government had seen fit to isolate him in a corner of nowhere. She would be happy to see him. . . . During their first interview he had dropped his gaze to her bosom and she had not coloured or squirmed in discomfort. Indeed, she seemed to have dropped her gaze impudently onto his lap despite his steady crossing and uncrossing of his legs. . . . We can drop the pretence of her virginity, with her house and compound practically bristling with a small army of virile young men, her steady gaze and brazen confidence, even in the company of males and superiors. He was willing to overlook their unequal status. They were simply an unattached man and woman, finding themselves in a negotiable posture. (219)

Uprooted and displaced, Vertie Treadwell satisfied his ego by trying to subjugate the natives. His killing of the tigers enhances his male ego and the information given to Churchill is more or less biased. He points a finger at Nigel because he has the sense of betrayal from a fellow English officer who has deeply ingratiated himself in the Indian soil, which he himself craves for. He is an illegitimate orphaned child whose manhood cannot face the insult. He is caught between two worlds. Tara Ma is not a passive victim. She is a virgin, an individual who balances the old beliefs, is exposed to the new beliefs to attain the heights of empowerment. She has her own choices to make and no man can lure her to give up those beliefs. She does not need to reconcile to the old patterns of marital relationships with newer codes of sexual behaviour and expectations of intimacy. She does not delve in things that she never had. She does not have to lose what she never experienced. She did not go out of Mist Mahal to gain power and she never felt the urge to satiate her ego, but she entices the tiger to enter her world and beat him to submission like a true martyr.

> It appears at a distance that a meeting is taking place and he picks up his pace, curious to know the identity of her conspirators, but suddenly he sprawls and a primitive alarm of stone-filled can tied to a jute cord rattles in the yard like a ten-gun salute. From the bushes her private army rises up and circles him, kicking his head and face as he tries to rise. He curls his body and they descend upon him in a rain of boots

> and lathis. The pain in his head builds to a series of explosions. In the distance, a woman claps her hands and he hears the slapping of sandals in retreat. (221)

The Tree Bride is an attempt to assess the past history of one culture to sort out the present, living in another culture. The plot of the novel moves smoothly without any disjointed hiccups. The plot moves back and forth in time and one is reminded of Emily Bronte's ingenious style in *Wuthering Heights*. Bharati Mukherjee has used this technique of narrative and style in *The Holder of the World* also. A Time-Traveller has been used in the novel to move back and forth in time. The narrator of the novel had used the time-traveller to move from modern age to Mughal era in India and back to Massachusetts looking for "Kohinoor." This "Kohinoor" is a precious coveted stone which was carried by the colonizers. "Kohinoor" also signifies the inner knowledge, which helps to empower one's life. The plot of *The Tree Bride* moves back and forth from colonial India of pre-Independence times to San Francisco and back. Readers are confronted with the spangle of characters and their sequestered life in the new world and the old world co-instantaneously. The storyline does not seem simulated, creating an atmosphere of mysticism, moving to and fro, getting an insight into the ethos of the American Imperialism invaded by terrorism, and the British colonialism in India. The expatriate, exile and immigrants of colonial India are not much different from the expatriate exiles and exuberant immigrants in the new world. They are tossed salads in a bowl and that bowl is America, which was torn apart by the 9/11 explosions. Globalisation gives a different outlook in today's world but one thing that remains the same is the emotion of "fear" that has given birth to colonial rules. The emotional "fear" instigates man to curb the role of women and subjugate them. Their role is confined to the norms of family, their sexuality suppressed so that they are obeisant to the masters. The two novels, part of a trilogy, project a much balanced male protagonist, Bish, Tara's husband. The various characters in *The Tree Bride*—John Mist, Nigel Coughlin are men who do not feel the urge to suppress and achieve, but they are men who give space to the Other. Bish Chatterjee, contrary to Andy Karolyi, is a man who has the courage to let his wife have her space and he accepts her back without any qualms. He treats her like an equal, though he is also respectful to the traditions of Old World. He accepts Rabi, his son, as a gay and accepts life as it is. They do not need to change the world to suit their fabrications. "In *The Tree Bride*, entrepreneur Bish Chatterjee could have been one of those freshly returned engineers. Mukherjee is amazed at the confidence with which this new generation of Indo-Americans present themselves as having the best of both the worlds."[7]

The new ideas projected in the two novels show that the writer is at peace with herself. Bharati Mukherjee has created her space and is no more uprooted. She has rejected hyphenation and declares herself to be an American and not Asian American, challenging America to deliver the promises of its dreams to all its citizens equally. The style of the novel is handled with an equipoise, emphasizing the fact that what makes our world is creation of our own mind. The mind has to register the change and our lives change automatically. The novel is a "historiography metafiction" chronicling facts from colonial India and searching the links that bring the world together. Communication and globalisation have their advantages and drawbacks. The terrorism of this world has to be fought against, just like the Russian Revolution or the bloodless revolution of America or the Indian revolution of freedom.

"In *Desirable Daughters*, Tara concentrated on the very American pursuit of individual happiness," says Mukherjee. "Now she has to discover for herself how her identity has been shaped by social historical, political and colonial forces that are beyond the individual." (5)

The novel projects a dream, Tara Ma's dream of free India. She takes her roots in Mist Mahal and is like her husband. She does not leave Mist Mahal as her children are there, and this feeling extends to the whole of India. When Victorians dreamt they dreamt of future. Nothing could distract Tara from her dream of an independent nation. When Tara Bhattacharjee dreamt she dreamt of the past converging their destinies. Her "probashi" status had to be taken care of. The theme of spirituality adds the sustenance power. The rock-like confidence in Tara Ma comes from her faith in her dreams. The theme of spirituality is an eternal part of Bharati Mukherjee's novels. Tara Ma follows her "Dharma" of a married woman, her life-long alliance to the Sundari tree and moves on the path of Karma. Her namesake, Tara Bhattacharjee wants that connectedness, to seek her own Kashi. "When the cosmos chars into total blackness, Kashi glows because Shiva created it as a sacred space where to die is to be saved." (5)

NOTES

1. Bharati Mukherjee, *The Tree Bride* (Hyperion, 2004).
2. Sandip Roy, "Bharati's Visible Ghosts," http//www.Indiatimes. com
3. A. Bimol Akoijam, "Colonial Seduction," *The Times of India.*
4. Publishers Weekly (Starred review)
5. *The Times of India*, May 16, 2007, p. 16.
6. *Women's Writing: Text and Context*, ed. Jasbir Jain, p. 223.
7. Sandip Roy, "Bharati's Visible Ghosts."

Chapter VIII

Conclusion: Cultural Differences

> This is a tale of two sisters from Calcutta, Mira and Bharati, who have lived in the United States for some 35 years, but who find themselves on different sides in the current debate over the status of immigrants.[1]

Married to a Canadian-North American Clark Blaise, Bharati Mukherjee faces demeaning conditions in Canada (in spite of having the citizenship of Canada). Degraded and victim to dissection in the literary world, her works were not accepted in Canada. Categorized as a writer of 'minority,' her writer instincts dissipated. Facing the trauma of her house burnt to ashes, bruised and battered, Bharati Mukherjee returned to India to find solace. Clark Blaise points out significantly in *Days and Nights in Calcutta*: "West mount fires were swift and deadly, but always discreet." (6)

The memories of the house and identity as a writer dashed to pieces (Clark Blaise's manuscripts were destroyed in the fire), and the officials taking the incident casually irked the couple to go to India, so that they could retrospect on the past events and decide their future. As Clark Blaise says in his writing, the journey to India was more of a quest in understanding Bharati Mukherjee and their marriage. Understanding each other in the environs of Indian culture gave a new perspective to their marriage and strengthened their conjugal life. Clark Blaise gives a vivid description of the Indian culture in their journal (*Days and Nights in Calcutta*). All events are minutely observed and noted down to be developed into a book. The description chronicles life in the cosmopolitan suburban areas in Bombay. Facing the bureaucracy of Indian customs on the airport harasses him with paperwork. Not used to this type of delay, Clark Blaise's first impression of the Indian culture is of bureaucracy which induces witty remarks from him and he, like a foreigner, describes India in a nutshell. 'Patience' taught by Indian culture is something which he acquires very easily melting into the Calcutta environment.

> Everything that is a subtle analysis of Indian might reveals present in this first encounter: contrasts, hierarchies, discomfort, and small abuses; dignity, abasement, protocol, theatre, humor, affection. The uniforms; white that cannot be crushed or questioned; blue that guards, distributes, and collects; Khaki that serves and carries. Fascinating but in 105 with Wurst, Bier and Gebratenes Huhn and a sleepless night to churn it up, best contemplated under a fan, behind dark curtains. (*DNC*, 12)

In comparison, Bharati Mukherjee with her sarcastic cynicism seems harsher, though her anger and attitude can be justified. With the traumas of Canada fresh in mind, she lashes out at the traditional patriarchal dominance of male-oriented environment of India. Women, in spite of being highly educated, succumb to their passive roles in their in-laws' house. The existence in servility of women even in affluent families, disgusts Bharati Mukherjee and she finds the freedom of the West more affable to the restrictive frustrating existence in India. Blending of modernity with the perversity of backwardness in the suburban areas, co-existent in modern Indian subcontinent, is more like a veneer camouflaging the poverty-stricken countryside. The colonial attitude of upper class towards the labour class is unable to subterfuge the dual existence of Indians.

Bharati Mukherjee's education in a convent school and her background, her ignorance of realities of the outside world are reflected in Tara in *The Tiger's Daughter*. Her nostalgic memories come to a halt as soon as she comes face to face with the realities of Calcutta. Uprooted in Montreal, the racist attitude of the Western world seems less dreadful, as she undergoes a drastic change, with violent attack on her sensibilities. Worried about muggings in Montreal and being attacked in the subways seems a lesser evil than the evil prowling free in India.

The spiritual awakening to realize her self is infused into the structure of her novels with a subtlety, religion being an integral part of India. The philosophies of Hinduism and Buddhism also reflect the doctrine of 'Karma' being the primeval factor in an individual's life. The philosophies drive the characters to their self-realization, but the self-emancipation of female protagonists comes through in the form of self-purgation of old traditions.

The individualistic attitude forms the basis for Devi in *Leave it to Me*, which reflects the doctrines of the *Gita* (the Hindu Scripture). Devi is more American in her attitude, an heir to her serial-killer Bio-Dad, who is an Indian. A blend of her bio-parents, promiscuity comes easily to her. The socially-sanctioned freedom of sexual relationships in America reflects her origins in the hippie culture.

The freedom of expression and release from the traditional attitude of regarding one's own body as a banal topic, the protagonists of Bharati Mukherjee surge forward, exuberant in their Americanness. The initial hesitant moves, either through self-inflected violence, as in Dimple's case in *Wife*, or violence from outside, as in *The Tiger's Daughter* and *Jasmine*, pushes these individuals towards renunciation. Themes of transnational transformations into self-mutating heroines permeate the novels. It consequently authenticates the theory of re-inventing selves by re-birth. The heroines undergo pangs of re-birth to immerse into the imperialistic America which believes in colonizing the immigrants and aliens.

The transformation is mutual as America adjusts and adapts amicably to the strangers infiltrating the peripheries of the First World. "In the twentieth century, however, new international or paranational formations occur, and they have tended to be avant-garde in the metropolitan centre. To some extent, these formations—Paris 1890-1930, New York 1940-70—are a result of newly effective market forces that internationalize culture. For instance, 'Western Music,' twentieth century art, European literature. But more interestingly, contributors to avant-garde movements were immigrants to such a metropolis, not only from outlying national regions but from other and smaller national cultures, now seen as culturally provincial in relation to the metropolis."[2]

Negating the notion of existing in the state of hyphenation and hybridization, Bharati Mukherjee establishes herself as an American writer. *Leave it to Me* is an effervescent declaration of her American rootedness. Her style reflects the involving of the 'Other,' as her writing diction gets Americanized with each published work.

Back in Calcutta, Bharati Mukherjee's diction is colloquial. The ingenious quality of observing the colloquial languages, each of her novels flaunts a varied backdrop. Reference to mythological aspect of Hinduism and ideologies of America, retained in her mind, find a way in her writings. The sophisticated drawing room talk and sympathy with the poor are finely etched on the canvas of her non-fiction *Days and Nights in Calcutta*. "She told me that her anger against Manu (ca. 500 B.C) bore resemblance to the intensity of the anger of some American feminists against Freud." (236)

Bharati Mukherjee's mind, fashioned by her silent but strong-willed mother, her resilience to traumatic experiences in Indian traditional families is reflected in her themes of rebirth. Freedom and power of the self are the in-built traits of Hinduism, but the suppression of female counterparts is due to the fear of their becoming more powerful. The idols of 'Sita' and 'Kali,' the juxtaposed forces embodying suffering and self-empowerment and power to destroy respectively, are revered by the patriarchal society, but ironically the women in the society are suppressed, in case they assert their superiority. The powerful individual female figures such as Draupadi of the *Mahabharata* as an embodiment of intellectual genius, and Radha as pure sensual being, exist on the fringes of the Indian society to be looked upon with reverence but, acceptance of their individuality is played down in the Hindu imagination. Counterpoised to this are the ideals of 'Sita' and 'Savitri,' paradigms of 'Pativrata' (who consider their husband next to God), is highlighted in the conventional patriarchal set up of Indian culture. Women resisting the role model are castigated on the pretext of them being harlots. Contravention of norms set by the men has innervated the women to protest against the age-old atrocities. The revolt is poignantly mirrored in the character of Dimple in *Wife*. The projection of 'Kali' is women re-inventing themselves to release their power to self-emancipation. Goddess 'Parvati' reincarnating herself into 'kaushiki' to kill 'Raktabija,' and again, she re-invents herself into the revered form of 'Kali' to slay the demon (who supposedly, with each drop of blood falling on the ground, multiplied into several forms), to save humanity. Each of the characters of Bharati Mukherjee re-incarnates itself into new 'self' with a new name to pave a path to a future, which provides freedom of expression, be it in their sensuality or be it the voicing of their suppressed selves. "Can wanting be fatal." (*J*, 142) Unsurreptitiously, Jasmine savours the freedom of new world, renouncing the old tradition which is not difficult, though the self-recrimination haunts her, before the shelving of old self.

Devi's journey is more like sauntering through the realms of her Asian-Indian origins to discover her inherent psyche. The two protagonists, emblematic of 'Kali,' are a terrible form of Goddess Parvati (who devours the demon single-handedly with her own self-empowerment), to avenge the wrong doers. "The idea of the powerful woman is very much part of the culture that has devised ways to channel this superior energy."[3]

The manifestation of self-empowerment is in the hands of the women. Another motif from Hinduism, an integral part of the female protagonists, is the self-realization of their 'Power,' either forced through violence like rape as in *Jasmine* and *The Tiger's Daughter* or the internalized conflicts leading to murdering the symbol of oppression in *Wife*, the infidelities of a husband leading to the release of the bonded self in Hannah Easton in *The Holder of the World*, or the fury of Devi venting her frustration on unsuspecting individuals in *Leave it to Me*.

The women of first generation who believed in attaining renunciation and power through suffering and their complete surrender in their God, is exemplified in Taramoni's mother. Tara's name is itself significant of another form of Goddess Parvati. Her self-realization is brutally forced on her, but her intellect does not innervate her to question Tuntunwala's treacherous act unlike Draupadi, whose self-endurance is beyond anyone's imagination, an intellectual beautiful lady who is emboldened by her spiritual strength and will power, to question her husband Yudhisthira.

Compared to this manifestation of female power, the women of West lament the status of passivity and powerlessness. In spite of the freedom of expression and liberation of sexual liaisons, their position is that of a second citizen. "Now, woman has always been man's dependent, if not his slave, the sexes have never shared the world in equality."[4]

The motif of sexuality, i.e. the freedom in senses, is an acknowledged way to establish oneself in the new world. It has two different connotations to the term. The dominant role of Jasmine in bedroom pleasuring Bud Ripplemeyer (and she is aware of all the methods that can give him pleasure) marks her complete rootedness in the new world. An illegal immigrant helped by the white, forges forward nimble-footed, towards a future unknown to herself also. Ready to be adventurous, risks in life give her pleasure. Jasmine embraces the new world ebulliently.

The adventurous spirit of Hannah leads into an effete conjugal life, finds her sensual pleasures in the arms of Hindu Raja Jadav Singh, whereas Devi in *Leave it to Me*, a modern paradigm of Freudian philosophy, sleeps with Ham (who is supposedly her mother's lover also). The ambience and the amicability that is found, as Jess Dupree discusses with Devi her sensual pleasures with her Indian lover, might ruffle the delicate sensibilities of many readers, but the significant aspect is that the American mother-daughter relationship is established emphatically. The pleasures sought by Nafeesa Hafez are more like seeking endorsement of the whites on her inculcated Americanness.

The era of the *Mahabharata* also saw a very strong self-empowered mother in Kunti who for the sake of her progeny established relationship with the demi-gods. Her younger sister in-law's procreating through relation with two men simultaneously, however shocks her. The mother-figure in Kunti is revered, as the traditional Indian conventions shower respect on a woman as a mother.

Somehow the ambitions of Gandhari (the elder daughter-in-law of the Kuru Vansh) for her sons are not realized. The familial bonding of India repulses Bharati Mukherjee, her own experiences in joint family being bitter. In *Days and Nights in Calcutta*, her cynical viewing of the rituals and showering of love and criticism at one go sometimes make the readers smile. The genius in Bharati Mukherjee's style and use of words lies in the way that her narration of the air crash of Indian Airlines plane, resulting in hundreds of Indian deaths moves the readers to tears, whereas angst at the plight of Tara and Jasmine, and Dimple's schizophrenia are emblematic of young girls, who go through mental traumas. The marginalization in the new world is not that great, the husband rebuking her, and his condescending tone making her more reticent and angry. Ina Mullick with her rib-cage-showing tops, lures her into another world and guilelessly Dimple moves back and forth crossing and reverting on the borderline, never merging with either side. Her act of butchering her husband symbolizes her self-assertion towards freedom from life of servility and doomed life of banality. The exotic 'other' Milt and an Americanised Indian housewife lure her to step out of the white circle, just like Sita to be captured by the demon.

> "The tricky part, sweetheart, is to beat the yolks while you dribble the hot syrup in this gook here." And because she seemed to stiffen at the word *sweetheart*, he said with a soft laugh, "I was doing a weak Humphrey Bogart-via-Woody Allen imitation. Okay, sweetheart." (*W*, 170-71)

The affair with Milt Glasser is more of a romance with Americanism. Role is reversed in *The Holder of the World*, with Hannah having a blissful relationship with Hindu Raja, and on a larger canvas, her affair is with the exotic environs of the mythological history of India.

> "I am neither wife nor queen," Hannah retorted. A bibi had the right, the duty, to live for love. Gabriel's black bibi had seized happiness for Gabriel and for herself; a bibi had the power to laugh in the face of a *firangi* wife. (*HW*, 254)

Quoting the *Gita* along with Keats is Bharati Mukherjee's blending of the east and west. Raja Jadav Singh's recital from the *Gita* and crediting it as the Hindu Bible, is a warrior who was born to lead men. Her ex-husband who was also a warrior seems to jade in comparison to Raja Jadav Singh in a similar way that Renata finds her ex-boy-friend a weaker version of her new-found love, an Afghan.

The emancipation of Sita in the new version of feminism is emphasized in this novel. Hannah Easton wonders at the plight of Sita being captivated and her inner thoughts are focused on the women who have lived their life suppressed. "If during her first exile, the forest had disclosed to her only its dangerous blandishments, then during her second exile the forest had disclosed to her its wise secrets about eternity and redemption." (*HW*, 254)

The two different aspects of exile exemplify the duality of existence and the duality that is the very basis of human existence. The exile of Sita is thrust on her forcefully by her own attraction to the exotic (a golden deer symbolizing the materialistic gratification) whereas the second exile is forced by her husband and she lives in the house of a hermit. The self-emancipation or the renunciation is internalised. Patience and reverence for her husband is her strength, but the doubts of Rama innervate the self-effacing Sita to mutate into an independent, detached person, who lets herself be swallowed in the earth than to agree to go through the undulation of proving her chastity to her husband. She stands against Ayodhya, self-asserting her individuality. "Did the Hindu Sita like the puritan Mary Ronaldson question the rules that her husband had pledged to uphold."

The white male protagonists, Milt Glasser in *Wife* and Taylor in *Jasmine*, represent the informal America, which the female protagonists are attracted to and with whom they realize themselves. The expression of sexuality is released from age-old bondings to let go their servile selves. They are allured to the attractions finally, being treated as individuals.

Mr. Bhowmick is representative of male egoism who accepts inter-social marriage but detests the very idea of his modern daughter seeking American definition of motherhood, the renouncing of male dominance in impregnating women.

The duality of male egoism with exceptions has the same definition all over the world in every culture. Indian male is reverent to motherhood, worships Goddess 'Shakti' in all forms, revels in the age-old traditions of the Sati. The seclusion of widows in home where they are subjected to atrocities of the male members exemplifies the male egoism defining the status of women on two different planes. The hypocrisy is prevalent in the First World except that the feminist point of view is voiced in a loud and clear resonant voice. The European and American countries witness the feminist movement with alacrity, and are forced to give importance to them. Akin to this is the fact that women are assaulted in India and the continents to suppress them into submission. "If we are to gain understanding, we must get out of these ruts, we must discard the vague notions of superiority, inferiority, equality which have hitherto corrupted every discussion of the subject and start afresh."[5]

Apart from sexuality and religion, a major ambivalent issue of racism figures on the horizon of Canada. The racism drives Bharati Mukherjee to her tether's end and consequently pushes her towards her future as an immigrant in America. Being marginalized and existing on the periphery exhausts her very being. The short stories in Bharati Mukherjee's *Darkness* exemplify the problems of immigration and yet the immigrants wish to stay back instead of moving forward by changing track. It is self-annihilation but when considered from their point of view, the validity of their action is established. Returning to the former culture seems equally hazardous to changing job and risking the security of their present life.

Bharati Mukherjee's decision to immigrate to U.S.A is her refusal to settle down for the obscurities and dual existence in India and the extremities of Canada. Balance in her life—the balance of freedom of expression and recognition as a writer and responsibilities as an American citizen—is achieved.

> In terms of psychic violence and female sexuality, I grew up at a time and in a class in Calcutta when you couldn't say the word 'sex.' I'd never said the word 'sex' and we certainly were not allowed to think it; I didn't even know how the male anatomy was constructed, so for me and my characters who are coming not from villages but upper-class, urban Indian settings, sexuality becomes the mode of resistance or a way to rebel. After all, if you're coming out of society where sex is unspeakable, the unutterable, then doing it or acknowledging your sexuality results not only in individual rebellion but actually constitutes an attack on a whole patriarchal, Victorian, hypocritical society.[6]

As she vehemently points out, the groups were the most helpful to the South Asians in Canada in fighting the racial discrimination. South Asians were at the bottom in Canada's racially based society. Bharati Mukherjee's revulsion for feminist extremism seems to generate from the unfairness of the feminist activists in Canada.

Bharati Mukherjee's statement that one changes every moment has an essence of self-realized person, who looks at the world from both sides, blends the myth with reality to make a whole individual. The idea permeates each of her characters, with all their negativities and positivities, somehow making them real and tangible. Diasporic culture is authenticated in her writing as her characters raise themselves above the surface of ghettos and diasporic existence. Her characters are varied, some are still undecided in their stride, beset by stagnant existence in the past, but most of the characters of Bharati Mukherjee decide their own future. They are adventurous in seeking the future—the real people, who know that their past will reflect on their present and their present would shape their future. They are open to transformations and new experiences (violent in nature), changing themselves every nano-second. "Several of my characters fail to move from expatriate to immigrant in the diasporality spectrum, some of the characters don't try, don't want to. In my narratives, I want to represent a varied set of responses to the experience of un-housement."[7]

The 'hamburger' and 'pizza' culture of America torments Dimple in *Wife*. The tin culture of America somehow bewilders her. She rates herself as a novice in the culture and thinks that she could have been a better wife if she could produce more "glamorous leftovers." (*W*, 119)

Trying out Marsha's bath robe (wrap around) is an act of being Americanized. Every action becomes an endurance. Perfecting the American style and continuously watching T.V. wear her out. Time and again, she is nostalgic about Calcutta which did not demand much, except being a dutiful wife and a good daughter-in-law. Amit asks her to try sauna because American women love saunas. Amit's rebuking her continuously makes her more fidgety. Amit's frame of mind ignores his wife's depression on the pretext that she is becoming more and more American with each passing day. American women seem to have frequent nervous breakdowns. The patriarchal conditioning of the Indian culture hesitates and vehemently refuses to acknowledge the turmoils undergone on daily basis by the individuals. Female/male in India visiting a psychologist is categorized as 'mad' people. Unable to understand the pressure on a housewife's mind going through her daily chores, it is taken for granted that she is unofficially a sophisticated domestic servant.

Jasmine, termed as 'day mummy' when she is appointed as a caregiver in Taylor's house, somehow astonishes her. What might have been a menial job in India is somehow glorified in the new culture. Bud Ripplemeyer is not only confined into the wheelchair but he is also symbolic of American colonial attitude—refusing to blend with his environment. Set in his ideas, he hates to change: "I wonder if Bud even sees the America I do." (*J*, 109)

Expression of solidarity by hugging each other is a form of salutation in America which gives a feeling of equality. However, the touching of feet as a way of salutation in India is more like a person (who is younger) letting go his ego in bending down at another's feet.

The countryside, which is no different from the Indian scenario, somehow gives a sense of dissipation and sighting a beggar on the street makes Jasmine feel that she is too late in arriving in America. The changing face of America conflicts with the impression that is conjured up in her mind through Prakash's chronicling the wonders of America, the first world economically and financially so strong as to dictate the third world countries.

The immigrant women in the new world try to get out of the oppression of enclosed atmosphere of the past culture, try to balance the values and traditions of past culture with the present one. Their continuous strife to acculturate into the culture of the United States changes them which is not recognized by the male spouses, who are interested in realizing their American dream.

Even in *Jasmine*, Bud refuses to accept the past of Jasmine for the fear of losing his present. The existence of metaphysics theoretically and practically is evident in Mary Webb's stating her out-of-body experiences. The fact is that neurosis not only exists in the mind of the citizen of the third world, but the western world awakening to its spirituality and seeking their own identities they travel to India, to find peace from the chaos of commercialization. The role-reversal is evinced in the character of Devi. Debbie's search could have taken her into some other realm but co-incidentally, her origin lies in the Asian backdrop: "'Theoretically, I believe in reincarnation,' I say. I am astounded by all this, the American need to make intuition so tangible, to *possess* a vision so privately." (*J*, 125)

The killing of Amit Basu by Dimple is to release herself from a difficult marriage. The difficulties are internalized in Dimple herself, with Amit playing a part in aggravating the situation. The ultimate catastrophe that befalls Amit would have been the other way round in India. In the Indian culture, women, instead of retaliating, succumb to their distress. In America, Dimple tries to question her emotional break-down, takes steps to restore her emotions. Her strife to establish herself in the American culture is her quest of identity as an individual. She refuses to be a daughter to her father and a wife to Amit Basu. Her own gender limitations are a hurdle in her path to submersion in the New World. "While 'inventing their roles,' the two worlds, until they have to choose between them in order to find a space to inhabit."[8]

Manifestation of unhappiness, evidently due to the acceptance of the doctrine of detachment in American society, is a common notion. Lack of emotional attachment leads to hazardous consequences, whereas in Indian culture, excess of love smothers the natural growth. The thin line that exists between assimilation and hesitancy in embracing the new culture and its ideologies tends towards marginalization of 'self' and 'others.' The "mestiza consciousness" that works through Bharati Mukherjee's mind and her works, reverberates the ideologies of Hinduism, proving the dual existence. The creation of vacuum inside Tara, after being victimized by a wily politician, reflects the Buddhist ideologies of complete "sunyata," an absolute emptiness which transcends a human being.

The American culture imbibes a different facet to the infiltration of the peripheries. Due to the fear or rather an imperialistic attitude, they have always tried to prevent their culture from getting impure, which naturally led to revolutionary movements in America. Being a country of ethnic groups, America can hardly deny the freedom of expression to the culture which they themselves instigated to form. Yet arrogantly America's self-assertion of being the most powerful is evident from the various wars that have been waged against the cultures all over the world. A new breed of black Americans (a cross between slaves and Americans) came into existence. A black character appears in *The Tiger's Daughter*, who is introduced as a guest in the social circle of Taramoni, instigates lots of speculative furore about his origins, and who finally, supports the riots in Calcutta, shocking the delicate sensibilities of the women of upper-class society. For the selfish interests in the development of America, the First World invested in its future by importing nationals from different parts of the continents, who tend to change the very essence of America. The myth of 'melting pot' and 'American Dream' has lured many generations to leave their home and merge in the new world.

In the short span of the settlement of the Indian immigrants in the United States, only few have gained an important position. One such exception is the election of Dalip Singh Saund from California to the House of Representatives in 1956. Recent years have marked recognition of Indians in America for their support in raising funds for the American government. The notable Indians like Zubin Mehta, Dr. Hargobind Khorana, Dr. S. Chandra Shekhar, Ravi Shankar and

Bharati Mukherjee herself have excelled in their field to gain appreciation and awards from both the cultures.

American born Asians are still considered exotic, an alien who has to be complimented on being able to speak English fluently. Dimple and Amit in *Wife* keep trying to speak English fluently and keep an itinerary of words which can improve their vocabulary.

The second generation of the South East Asians in America tends to innervate hostility into the immigrants of first generation. Born and bred in American environs, their views clash with the older generation. Mr. Bhowmick of "A Father" is unable to appreciate his daughter. The belligerent and much Americanized daughter of Kusum in "The Management of Grief" is not able to console her mother, rather her help is rejected with vehemence. "Western culture and our own culture, about differences in lifestyles, about different situations to adapt to, when one is in a different environment."[9]

NOTES

1. Bharati Mukherjee, Two ways to belong in America, p. 1 http://www.ncl.ac.uk/~5311095/main1.html.
2. Edward W. Said, *Culture and Imperialism* (Vintage, 1994), p. 294.
3. S. Emmanuel Nelson, *Bharati Mukherjee: Critical Perspectives*, p. 37.
4. Simone de Beauvoir, *The Second Sex*, p. xxvi.
5. *Ibid.*, p. 33.
6. "The Holder of the World," An Interview with Bharati Mukherjee by Tina Chen and S.X. Goudie, p. 17.
7. *Ibid.*, p. 16.
8. The Effects of Acculturation and Assimilation on Traditional Gender Roles, p. 2. Paula Womack, http://www.1/tc.unl.edu/ prwomack/pwomack_resarch.html13.0KB.
9. Renuka Singh, *Women reborn: An Exploration of the Spirituality of Urban Indian Women*, p. 7.

Bibliography

Primary Sources

Mukherjee, Bharati. *The Tiger's Daughter.* New Delhi: Penguin, 1971

_____. *Wife.* New Delhi: Penguin, 1975.

_____. *Darkness.* New Delhi: Penguin, 1985.

Clark, Blaise and Mukherjee Bharati. *The Sorrow and the Terror: The Haunting Legacy of the Air India Tragedy.* Canada: Penguin, 1987.

Mukherjee, Bharati. *Immigrant Writing: Give Us Your Maximalists.* New York Times Book review, 1988

_____. *The Middleman and Other Stories.* New York: Grove Press, 1988.

_____. *Jasmine.* New Delhi: Penguin, 1990.

_____. *The Holder of the World,* Viking India, 1993.

Clark, Blaise and Bharati Mukherjee, *Days and Nights in Calcutta* (Hungry Mind find) Paperback, October 1995.

Mukherjee Bharati. *Leave it to Me.* London: Chatto and Windus, 1997.

_____. *Political Culture and Leadership in India* (A Study of West Bengal), 1991

_____. "American Dreamer." http://www.mojones.com/mother_jones/JF97/mukherjee.html

_____. "Two Ways to Belong to America." *New York Times,* 22 September 1996

_____. Bless This Day. Writers Workshop Miscellany (Twenty)

Interviews with Bharati Mukherjee

Basbanes, Nicholas. Bharati Mukherjee, George Jr. Internet monthly, Oct-Nov, 1997 http://www.georgejr.com/oct97/ mukherjee.html.

Carb, Alison B. Bharati Mukherjee: The Immigrant Sensibility, 1987.

Chen, Tina and Goudie, S.X. "Holders of the world: An Interview with Bharati Mukherjee," 1997.

Hogan, Ron (Beatrice Interview). "Bharati Mukherjee, Outsider Looking in, Insider Looking beyond," Http://www.beatrice.com/interviews/ mukherjee.

Vignisson, Runar. "Bharati Mukherjee: An Interview," *Span,* No. 34-35 (1993) Http://www.ds.murdoch.edu.au/~cntimum/litserv/SPAN/ 34 Vignisson.html.

Mosaic. 'An Interview with Bharati Mukherjee." http://www/~mosaic/spring94/page/html.

Secondary Sources

Agnivesh, Swami. 'Mirror Image,' *The Times of India*, 15 August 1999, p. 11.

Alam, Fakhrul. *Bharati Mukherjee: Criticism and Interpretation.* Twayne's United States Author's series, 1996.

Badrinath, Chaturvedi. 'Sex and the Sage: The Wisdom of *Kamasutra*,' *Life Positive*, Nov. 2001www.lifepositive.com

Banerjee Divakaruni, Chitra. *The Mistress of Spices*, Black Swan, 1997.

_____. *Arranged Marriage*, Black Swan, 1997.

Bhatnagar, Manmohan K. *Feminist English Literature*, Atlantic, 1999.

Bhongle, Rang Rao, ed. *Contemporary American Literature: Poetry, Fiction, Drama and Criticism*, New Delhi: Atlantic, 2000.

Blume, Mary. 'Homely Pleasures,' *The Asian Age*, 17 October, 1997.

Chua, C.L. "Passage from India: Migrating to America in the Fiction of V.S. Naipaul and Bharati Mukherjee." *Rewording: The Literature of the Indian Diaspora*, 1992.

Councils of Economic Advisers for the Presidents Initiative on Race, Changing America, Indicators of social and economic well being by Race and Hispanic origin, Sept. 1998, U.S. Govt. Printing Office, Washington D.C.

Dave, Shilpa. 'The Doors to Home and History: Past Colonial Identities in Meena Alexander and Bharati Mukherjee,' *Amerasia Journal*, Vol. 19, No. 3, 1993, pp.103-13.

Chakranarayan, Mohini. *Style Studies in Anita Desai*, Atlantic, 2000.

Chopra, Deepak. *How to Know God.* Harmony Books, U.S.A., 2000.

Cixous, Helene. 'Pure Woman does not exist,' *The Times of India*, Review, Feb. 16, 1997.

De Beauvoir, Simone. *The Second Sex.* Vintage, 1989.

Desai, Anita. *Voices in the City.* Orient Paperback, 1992.

_____. *Cry, the Peacock.* Orient Paperback, 1995.

Dingwaney, Anuradha and Carol Maeir, ed. *Between Languages and Cultures, Translation and Cross Culture Texts.* New Delhi: Oxford University Press, 1996.

Dirlik, Arif. *The Postcolonial Aura, Third World Criticism in the age of Global Capitalism.* Westview Press.

Dhawan, R.K. *The Fiction of Bharati Mukherjee, A Critical Symposium.* New Delhi: Prestige, 1996.

_____. *Indian Women Novelists*. 18 Vols. New Delhi: Prestige, 1991, 1993, 1995.

Fernandes, Naresh. 'Choti to Maearena' *The Times of India*, Review, Feb. 16, 1997.

Forster, E.M., ed. *A Passage to India*. Penguin, Abinger. 1979.

Gandhi, M.K. *Hindu Dharma*, Orient Paperback, 1997.

Ghadially, Rehana, ed. *Women in Indian Society*. New Delhi: Sage.

Gokhale, Veena. 'Till divorce do us part." Newsmakers, *The Times of India*, Review Feb. 16, 1997.

Hope Franklin, John. *From Slavery to freedom, A History of Negro*. American Third Edition.

"Idols of Otherness, The Rhetoric and Reality of Multiculturalism," *Mosaic*, September 1996, Vol. 29, No. 3.

IJAS, Special issue on Critical Literary and Social Theory, Vol. 23, No. 1, Winter 1993.

IJAS, Special issue on Toni Morrison, Vol. 23, No. 2, Summer 1993.

IJAS, Special issue on Indo-American Transaction, Vol. 24, No.1 Winter 1994.

IJAS, Special issue on Ethnic Voices in American Literature, Vol. 24, No. 2, Summer 1994.

Jhabvala, Ruth Prawer. *Heat and Dust*. Penguin, 1994.

Kishwar, Madhu. 'How the West is run. *The Times of India*, 15 August 1999, p. 11.

Koshy, Susan. A Review of *The Holder of the World*, *Amerasia Journal*, Vol. 20, No. 1, 1994, pp. 188-90.

Kristeva, Julia, *Desire in Language, A Semiotic Approach to Literature and Art*. Oxford: Basil Blackwell.

Kumar, Mina. *"Buying out Assimilation," India Currents*, Sept. 1994, Vol. 8, No. 6.

Kumar, Poonam V. 'Brand New Kids.' *The Sunday Review* December 3, 2000.

Kumar, Seema. "Staying On, India Calling." *Hindustan Times*, Feb. 9, 2003.

Lahiri, Jhumpa. *Interpreter of Maladies*. U.S.A.: Houghton Mifflin, 1999.

Louis Gates Jr., Henry, ed. *Black Literature and Literary Theory*. New York: Methuen, 1984.

Mani, Lakshmi. "Search for Identity, The Myth and Reality of the Diasporic woman," *India Currents*, Dec. 98-Jan. 99, Vol. 12, No. 9.

Mishra, Vijay. "A Critique of Bharati Mukherjee's Neo-Nationalism. Diasporas," *Span*, 34-35 (1993).

Morrison, Toni. *Sula*, Vintage, 1998.

Nabar, Vrinda 'The way I write has changed dramatically.' Newsmakers, *The Sunday Review* Dec.' 31, 1995.

Nair, Premnath, 'Writing four Times,' *Gentleman*, Jan. 1999, pp. 42-48.

Naipaul, V.S. *A House for Mr. Biswas*. Penguin, 1981.

Nelson, Emmanuel, S. *Writers of the Indian Diaspora: A Bio-Bibliographical Critical Source Book.*

_____. *Reworlding: The Literature of the Indian Diaspora*. 1992.

_____. *Bharati Mukherjee: Critical Perspectives*. Garland, New York, 1993.

Panjwani, Narendra. 'Encounter with an Immigrant Newsmakers. *Times of India*. Review, April 9, 1995.

Patil, Z.N. *Style in Indian English Fiction*. New Delhi: Prestige, 1994.

Pathak, R.S., ed. *Quest for Identity in Indian English Writing*. New Delhi: Bahri, 1992.

Pinto, Jerry. 'Bharati but American,' *The Sunday Review*, Jan. 5, 1997.

Prakash, Anjana and Seema Prasad. 'Goddess worship harms gender equality.' *The Times of India*, Patna, Oct. 24, 1999.

Raimundo, Panikkar. *The Vedic Experience Mantramanjari: An Anthology of the Vedas for Modern Man and Contemporary Celebration*. All India Books, 1983.

Raj Rao, R. "Indian Writing in English: 'East meets West,'" *Gentleman*, pp. 72-77, Jan. 1999.

_____. 'And one last thing, Mr. Rushdie,' Limelight. *The Times of India*, p. 97. Aug. 24, 1997.

Rao, A.S. *Myth and History in Contemporary Indian Novel in English*. New Delhi: Atlantic, 2000.

Roy-Chowdhury, Sandip 'Bright Brash and Hard Boiled,' *India Currents*, March 1998, Vol. 11, No. 11.

Said, Edward W. *Reflections on Exile and Other Literary and Cultural Essays*. New Delhi: Penguin, 2001.

_____. *Culture and Imperialism*. Vintage, 1994.

Sant-Wade Arvindra and Marguerite Radell, Karem,'Refashioning the Self: Immigrant Women in Bharati Mukherjee's New World,' *Studies in Short Fiction*, Vol. 29, No. 1, Winter 1992, pp. 11-17.

Sen, K.M. *Hinduism*. Penguin, 1987.

'Sex a taboo subject in Egypt' *Statesman*, September 1, 1994.

"Shakti." *Hindustan Times*, Patna, October 14, 2002.

Sengupta, Jayashree. 'Spakung Heritage' *Sunday*, IV, 9 September 2001.

Sinha, Vimmy. "The Great Indian Diaspora." *Hindustan Times*, Jan. 15, 2003.

Singh, Renuka. *Women Reborn: An Exploration of the Spirituality of Urban Indian Women*. Penguin, 1997.

Smith, D. Nichol Shakespeare Criticism: A Selection, 1623-1840. The World's Classic, 1968.

Suraiya, Jug. 'It and the Autumn of the Political Patriarch,' *The Times of India*, Jan. 26, 2000, p. 16.

Swami Prabhupada, A.C. Bhaktivedata, *Bhagavad Gita As It Is*. Bhaktivedanta Books, 1989.

Swapan, Ashfaq. "Passage to America." *The Week*, Aug. 31, 1997.

"The Asian Way." *The Times of India*, Aug. 29, 1994.

Trivedi, Harish and Meenakshi Mukherjee, ed. *Interrogating Post Colonialism, Theory, Text and Context*. Shimla: Indian Institute of Advanced Study, 1996.

Tucker, Sterling. For Blacks only: Black Strategies for Change in America. Wm. B. Eerdmans, 1971; Indian print 1972.

Vaidyanathan, T.G. "Naipaul on Indian Narcissism," p. VII, *The Hindu*, Sunday, Oct. 21, 2001.

Varghese, Suma. 'Wanting vs. Intention,' *Life Positive*, June 2002, www. lifepositive.com

Vedic Studies Programme. An Insight into our ancient heritage. *United New of India*, New Delhi, July.

Vyas, Ravi. "His Third World," *The Hindu*, Sunday, Oct. 21, 2001.

Warner, Alan. A Short Guide to English Style. Oxford University Press, 1960.

Wright, Mills, C. *The Power Elite*. New York: Oxford University Press, 1956.

Review Material on Slides

Appiah, Anthony. 'Giving up the perfect demand,' *The New York Times Book Review*, Sec.7 (*Holder of the World*).

Cincotti, Joseph. 'Same Trip, Opposite direction,' *The New York Times Book Review* (*Holder of the World*).

Gorra, Michael "Call it Exile, Cal it Immigration," *The New York Times Book Review* (*Jasmine*)

Healey, Barth. 'Mosaic vs. Melting pot' *The New York Times Book Review*, June 19, 1988, Sec 7, p. 22.

The Tiger's Daughter, *The New York Times*, June 2, Sec. VII, p. 16, 1972.

Kakutani, Michiko. "Third World Refugees Rootless in the U.S." World and Image (*Jasmine*). *New York Times*, September 19, 1989

_____. "Into the unknown to find Herself" (*The Holder of the World*) *The New York Times*, Friday, November 12, 1993.

_____. 'A Map Cap Search for Bio-Mom' (*Leave it to Me*). *The New York Times*.

Raban, Jonathan 'Savage Boulevards, Easy Streets' (*The Middleman and Other Stories*) *The New York Times Book Review*, June 19, 1988, Sec. 7.

Sage, Lorna. 'Wrath of the Goddess' (*Leave it to Me*), *The New York Times Book Review*, Sec. 7

Ward, Elizabeth 'Notes from a New America' (*The Middleman and Other Stories*), Book World/ July 3, 1988